Your Painting Questions Answered from A to Z

HELEN VAN WYK

Books by Helen Van Wyk

CASSELWYK BOOK ON OIL PAINTING

ACRYLIC PORTRAIT PAINTING
(OUT OF PRINT)

SUCCESSFUL COLOR MIXTURES

PAINTING FLOWERS THE VAN WYK WAY

PORTRAITS IN OIL THE VAN WYK WAY

BASIC OIL PAINTING THE VAN WYK WAY
(REVISED EDITION OF "CASSELWYK BOOK ON OIL PAINTING")

YOUR PAINTING QUESTIONS ANSWERED FROM A TO Z

WELCOME TO MY STUDIO

COLOR MIXING IN ACTION

WELCOME TO MY STUDIO
(NEW REVISED EDITION)

MY 13 COLORS AND HOW I USE THEM

COLOR MIXING THE VAN WYK WAY
(REVISED EDITION OF "MY 13 COLORS" AND "COLOR MIXING IN ACTION")

HELEN VAN WYK'S FAVORITE COLOR RECIPES
(REVISED EDITION OF "SUCCESSFUL COLOR MIXTURES")

Your Painting Questions Answered from A to Z

HELEN VAN WYK

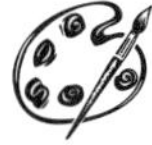

Edited by
HERB ROGOFF

Published by
ART INSTRUCTION ASSOCIATES
Rockport, Massachusetts

Distributed by
NORTH LIGHT BOOKS
Cincinnati, Ohio

YOUR PAINTING QUESTIONS ANSWERED FROM A TO Z

Published by Art Instruction Associates
2 Briarstone Road, Rockport, MA 01966

First Published in 1988

ISBN: 0-929552-04-0

20 99 98 97 96 5 4 3 2 1

Distributed to the book trade and art trade in the U.S. by
North Light, an imprint of F&W Publications
1507 Dana Avenue, Cincinnati, OH 45207
Telephone: (513) 531-2222 (800) 289-0963

Edited by Herb Rogoff
Design and Production by Stephen Bridges
Project Coordinated by Design Books International
5562 Golf Pointe Drive, Sarasota, FL 34243

On the Cover: *Lunch in Cannes* by Helen Van Wyk, 1978, 12 x 16, Oil on Masonite
Back Cover: *Self Portrait* by Helen Van Wyk, 1982, 20 x 28, Oil on Canvas

PRINTED AND BOUND IN THE UNITED STATES OF AMERICA

Paintings by Helen Van Wyk

Paintings by M.A. Rasko

Introduction

My mother-in-law, Anna Rogoff, was a little person (only four-eleven) but every inch a lady. She was extremely intelligent and a talented "one-liner," prompting me to label her many wise sayings "Annaisms." The one that's appropriate to this introduction is *"The world is at the tip of your tongue."*

Mother Anna was never lost, physically or intellectually, because she was never afraid to ask anyone anything. And the answers to her many questions always excited her own intellect; she either used the information practically or to add to a more complete understanding of a subject. Her philosophy, *"The world is at the tip of your tongue,"* is responsible, in a way, for this book.

The *world* of painting is *yours* now through the many questions and answers I've dealt with during my many years of teaching painting to a wide variety of students. The 320 entries are organized alphabetically for easy reference and reading. The cross-references will help you to orchestrate the profound complexity and inter-relations of painting: The craft of it and the art of it. And there is also an index to direct you to ready answers.

Had Mother Anna been interested in painting, her questions about it would have opened a world for her to use to the best of her ability. I hope the knowledge you will gain from the Q's and A's in this book will guide you, the painter, to better, more satisfying results at the easel; and to you, the audience of painting, to knowing more about the world of paint and painters.

Helen Van Wyk
Rockport, Massachusetts

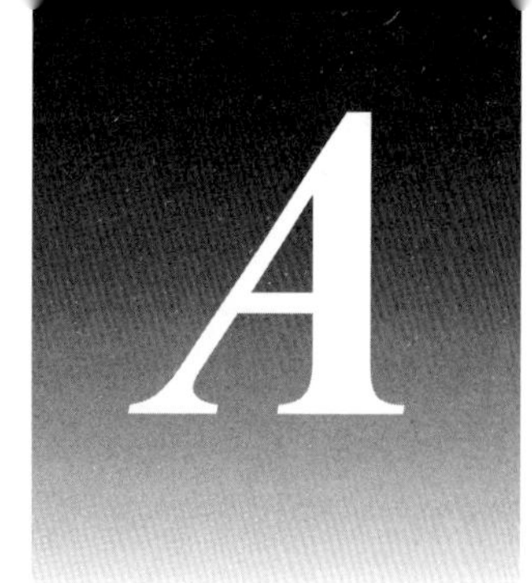

ABSTRACT

Should I look for an inner meaning in an abstract painting?

No. An abstraction does not recollect any natural form that most can recognize. An abstract painting has shape, tone and color that only defines a design. It's my opinion that we respond emotionally to an abstraction without any intellectual communication. Don't discount the beauty and value of an abstract painting in the two-dimensional surface expression. Realism without good design isn't as worthy of admiration as a well-designed abstraction. Very often in my analysis of a realistic painting, I will say, "I like its abstract pattern." I always mean this as a compliment to the artist's wise use of his design elements.

It is simplification on a continuum. Impressionism abstracts.
Photo Realism ⟶ Total Non Representationalism

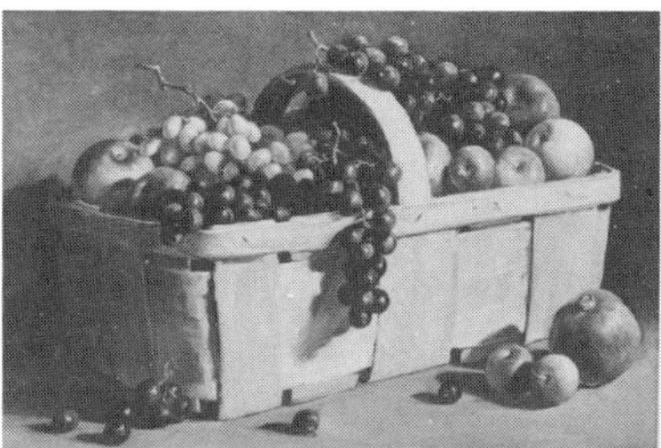

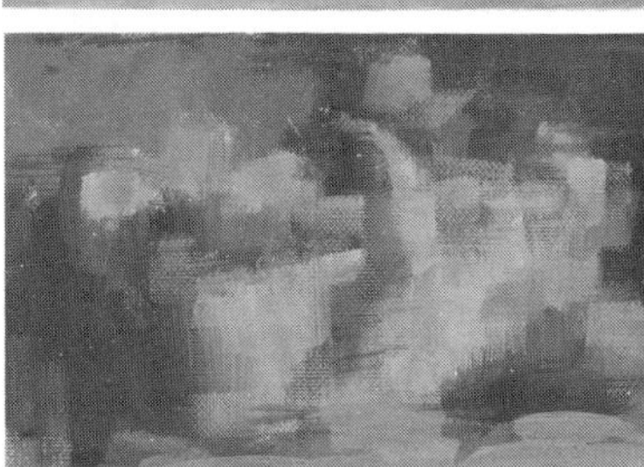

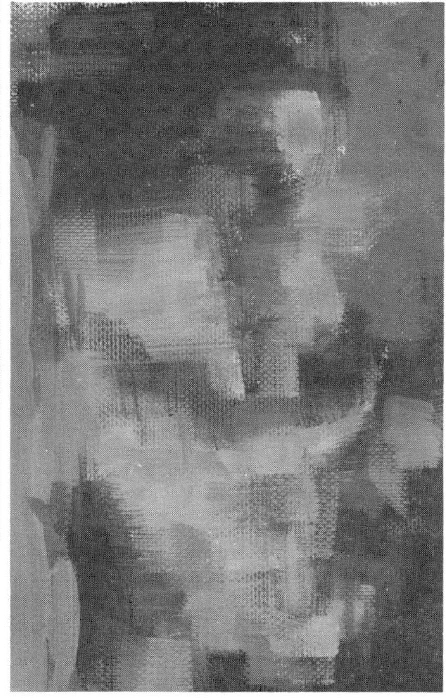

The abstraction of my painting, "Summer Fruit," is pictured both horizontally (below) and vertically (at right) to show that good design doesn't have a top or bottom.

ACRYLIC COLORS (see Painting Media)

ACRYLIC GESSO (see Gesso)

ADHESIVE (see Painting Mediums)

AERIAL PERSPECTIVE

My landscape painting was criticized and said to look flat, not having a feeling of aerial perspective. Can you tell me what is meant by that?

The tones and colors of things in the distance cannot be the same tones and colors as those same things in the foreground. Aerial perspective is an effect that is obtained on a flat surface by lightening the tone and diminishing the color of things that are farther away from your point of view.

To help you recognize how different the tones and colors of foreground things and distant things are, look at a plane of a subject in the foreground, which means an up-and-down plane of a barn or a tree, and actually paint a spot of that tone in the foreground of your canvas. Now, look at something in the distance that is also up-and-down, such as a mountain, and paint a spot of *that* tone in the upper part of the canvas. These two tones will act as your tonal control for all the colors from far to near and improve the appearance of aerial perspective.

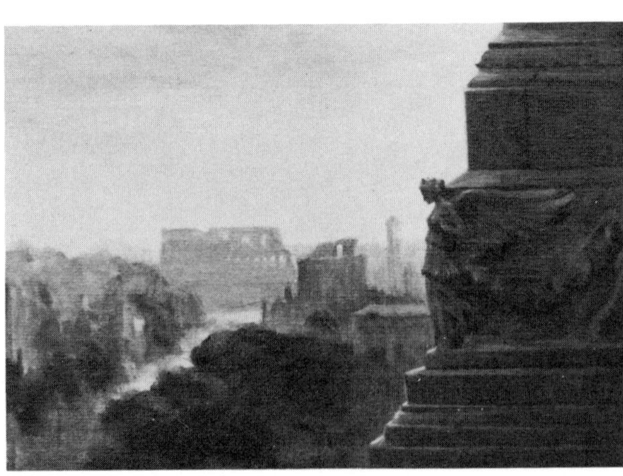

Compare the lighter tone of the Colosseum in the distance with the darker tone of the building in the foreground.

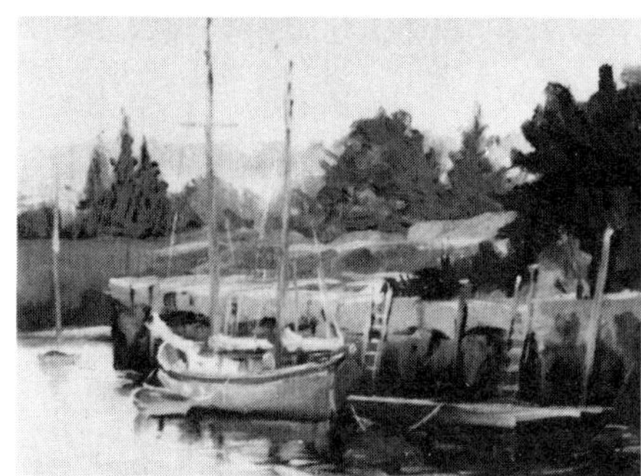

Basically, most landscapes have a background, middle ground and foreground. The degrees of contrast sharpen as they are seen closer to you.

ALIZARIN CRIMSON

How come some teachers say that Alizarin Crimson is primary red when in your books your primary red seems to be a redder red than Alizarin Crimson?

The three primary colors in light are actually yellow-green, turquoise and magenta. The paint primaries are slightly different. Even though paints record the *effect* of light, they can not be the same as the *colors* in light.

The colors I consider to be primaries are not any tubed colors in particular; they are mixtures that I feel represent the primaries for painting.

Some artists claim that the primaries are Cadmium Yellow Light, Ultramarine Blue and Alizarin Crimson. If the use of violet red (Alizarin Crimson) as primary red were valid, how then could one ever hope to mix the red of the American flag with only these three colors on the palette?

To me, Alizarin Crimson can only be thought of as a source of violets. The true hue of a tubed color is exposed in its tint-out with white. Alizarin Crimson, as everyone who has ever used this color knows, becomes very violet when tinted with white, and makes lovely violets when mixed with various tones of gray (black and white).

If Alizarin Crimson is to be used as a red, it should be in a mixture with another red: Cadmium Red Light, Grumbacher Red, etc. The successful appearance of a color is solely dependent upon its juxtaposition with its complement. So, when using Alizarin Crimson in your mixture and the resultant color is red violet, the complement has to be greenish yellow. When the mixture is termed a red, its complement has to be green. And when the mixture appears orangey red, its complement has to be greenish blue.

I use Alizarin Crimson to paint red things, but my results look terrible. What is Alizarin Crimson used for?

Alizarin Crimson is a dark, transparent reddish violet which can easily be recognized when it's mixed with white. Alizarin Crimson is indispensable on your palette as a source of violet when it has any degree of white in admixture and a source of a darkening agent for all the reds on a palette. Alizarin Crimson with a red is a red. Alizarin Crimson with white or a gray is a violet.

Here are some examples of uses for Alizarin Crimson:

To make dark rich brown — Burnt Umber and Alizarin Crimson.

To mix a rich black — Alizarin Crimson and Thalo Green.

To mix apple red — Alizarin Crimson and Grumbacher Red.

To make a variety of violets — Alizarin Crimson with white; Alizarin Crimson with light gray; Alizarin Crimson with dark gray.

Whenever I use Alizarin Crimson, I get a "poisonous purple" instead of the bright red that I was led to believe this color would give me. How come?

Alizarin Crimson is highly versatile. Its true character has to be understood in order to control it. First of all, you must accept Alizarin Crimson as a violet rather than a red, especially if it's mixed with even the barest amount of white. This color is only red in hue when it is mixed with another red, such as Grumbacher Red, the cadmium reds, Light Red, Venetian Red and Indian Red. When Alizarin Crimson is mixed with an orange or a yellow, it acts like red but will also mute the resulting orange mixture because of its violet nature. You will also find that Alizarin Crimson, when mixed with tones of gray made of white and black, is an excellent source of a wide variety of violet tones.

ALLA PRIMA

What does alla prima *mean?*

Alla prima is an Italian term that means "at the outset." This describes a direct approach of painting in contrast to painting in stages of development utilizing glazes, scumbles and other techniques. An *alla prima* painting is always a record of paint that's been applied opaquely. Generally, any loosely painted picture is usually categorized as an *alla prima* painting.

There are three distinct ways to apply oil paint:

1. A glaze — an application of transparent color.
2. A scumble — an application of semi-transparent color.
3. *Alla prima* — an opaque application of paint, in itself an independent tone and color.

All three applications can be used to develop an oil painting: Start with a glaze over a monochrome, then scumble to slightly change color and tone and, finally, *alla prima* to define the passages of the lighter lights and the passages of the darker darks and, lastly, the details.

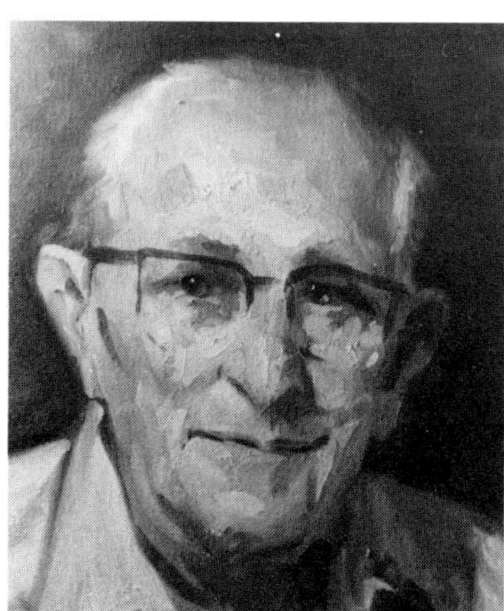

This detail of a portrait is a good example of ***alla prima*** *painting with its opaque, thicker, lighter passages that define the skin and expression.*

How can I make corrections and still maintain an alla prima *look?*

Constant corrections as you work is part of the painting process. It's been said that a painting is a record of a series of corrections. After you are finished and the painting has some obvious flaws but the overall effect is well established, you can make the necessary corrections with *alla prima* applications.

A WORD OF CAUTION: Control yourself and don't start overworking, thereby losing the spontaneous, overall look.

Alla Prima is the crowning achievement of pictorial expression and the ultimate of craftsmanship. It is the fruit of practice, knowledge of painting principles and the confidence that these two give you.

AMATEUR (see Professional)

ANALOGOUS COLORS

Why should I know the colors that are analogous to others?

It will help you to get a variety of color in your color design without making drastic color changes in the overall composition. Analogous colors are ones that lie next to each other in the spectrum. If we think of the color wheel as the diagram of the spectrum, analogous colors are the ones that are next to a color on the color wheel.

An example of using analogous colors in painting is to add some dull orange touches to a generally dull yellow-colored background. Analogous colors can excite an area without imposing a change, especially if the analogous color is the same tone as the tone it is added to.

The analogous colors to the basic colors are:

Blue is analogous to green and violet

Red is analogous to orange and violet

Yellow is analogous to orange and green

Orange is analogous to red and yellow

Green is analogous to blue and yellow

Violet is analogous to red and blue

ANATOMY

Do I have to study anatomy to be a painter?

I like to use the word *structure* rather than anatomy because the latter suggests a medical study instead of a careful inspection of the makeup of a form. Anatomy also suggests that the study of form is limited to those painting the figure or face and not to those painting flowers, fruits, trees, buildings and all other inanimate objects. It's important to inspect the makeup of the object you want to paint so your understanding of your subject can direct your accurate interpretation of it.

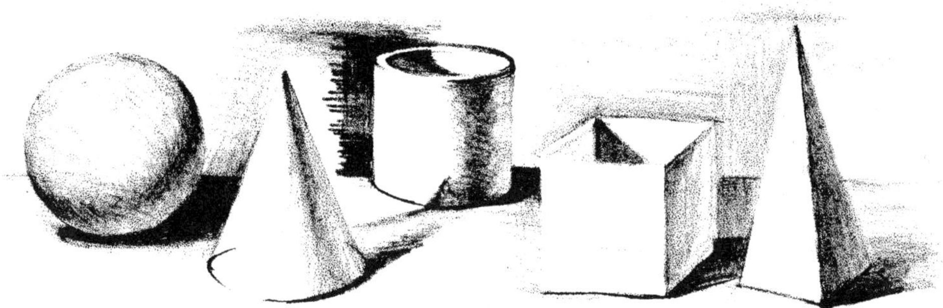

The Five Basic Shapes: Sphere, cone, cylinder, cube, trihedron (solid triangle). If you can classify all things you see as one or a part of these shapes, you will be able to better paint a dimensional appearance of the subject, especially if you understand how one source of light affects these forms. Understanding the cylindrical shape of the milk can served as great direction for painting it realistically and accurately.

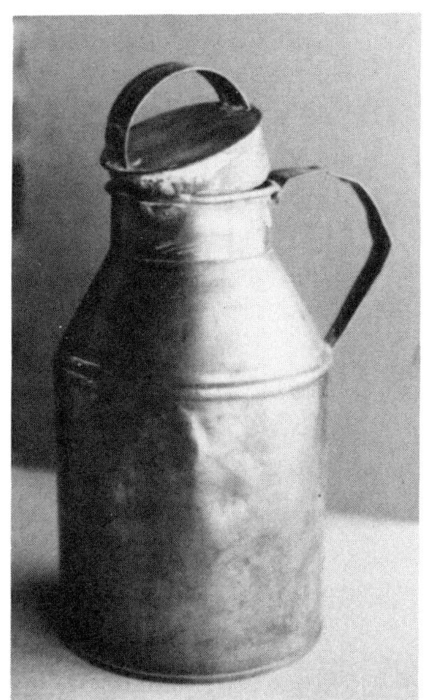

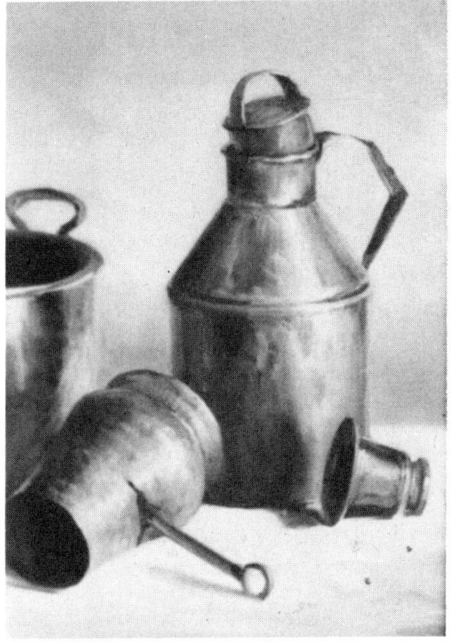

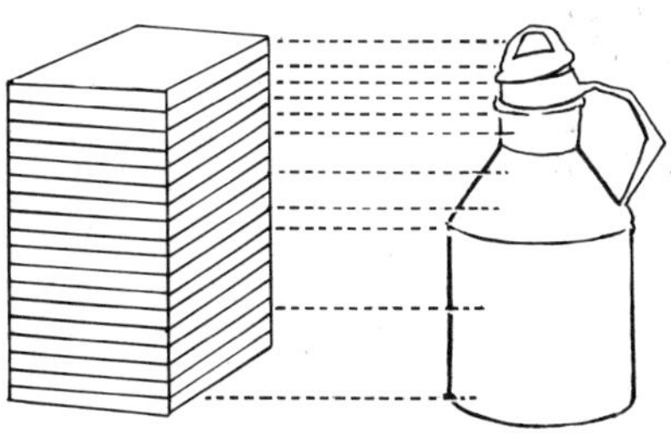

Make believe the subject you are looking at is a loaf of bread standing on end and each of the subject's components are slices of different shapes. Seeing them and realizing their importance makes your observation more analytical and your painting becomes more realistic or plausible looking.

AQUARELLE (see Painting Media)

ARTIFICIAL LIGHT

What is the best artificial light to paint by?

Lighting on the subject is the whole clue to painting. It determines the tonal composition because of light and shade and shows off the colors. The lighting on the subject is as important as the lighting on your easel.

The best way to emulate natural lighting is to set up a combination of fluorescent and incandescent lighting. There are lighting fixtures that are combinations of both with a circular fluorescent and an incandescent bulb in the center. This lamp can be adjusted to many positions and is ideal to mount close to the subject to impose a strong light on it. The light on your subject should be stronger than the light on your canvas. And your canvas or painting area can be in general illumination that is also a combination of incandescent and fluorescent lighting.

Another way is to just use a spotlight of a 150 Watt bulb on the subject and paint in a room that is generally illuminated with fluorescent and incandescent. The worst lighting you can paint by is fluorescent lighting alone.

Greatly illuminating your canvas will make your painting only look right under a strong light but it will be drab under the general light condition of most rooms. It may seem strange to you but the truth is that you will paint a darker picture under strong light and a lighter picture on a canvas that is partially shaded.

The luminosity and beautiful contrasts we admire so much in the paintings of the past could very well be attributed as much to the absence of electricity as it is to the ability of the artists.

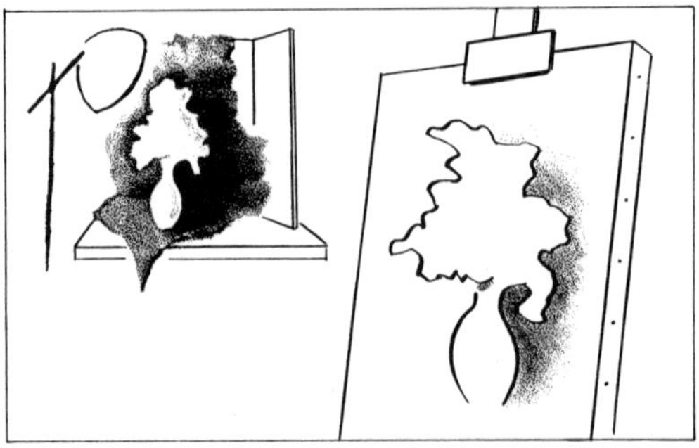

To record dimension, you must see the shadow side. Do so by setting up as illustrated — the light, the subject and your easel.

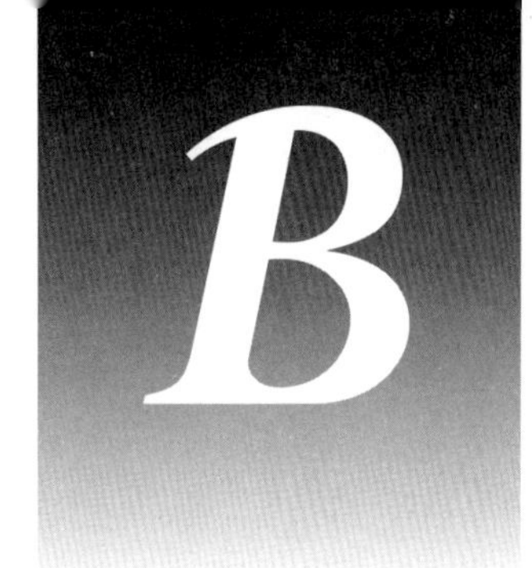

BACKGROUNDS

Backgrounds are my problem. How do I decide what color to paint the background? Do I use the subject's complementary color — or colors — or would I use the complement of the main subject and also use some of the other colors of the subject in the background? I have this problem whether the painting's a floral or a still life.

All the questions you have raised can be answered with the word "sometimes":

1. Approach your choice of background from a standpoint of tone, forgetting what color you want that tone. Your choices are: Light in relation to the subject; dark in relation to the subject; a gradation from light to dark; or one of medium tone.

2. Next, decide on the color of that tonal choice: Dull subjects, intense colored background; colorful subjects, less colorful background; a warm coloration of subject needs a warmed version of a cool color (one that is grayed); a cool-colored subject, or a cool-colored interpretation, needs a warm version of a cool color.

3. A general rule for painting backgrounds is that they should be grayed colors. The best way to start to paint a grayed color is to mix black and white to establish the tone and then add to it the color you're choosing. Then, add that color's complement.

4. You must paint a version of the tone that you actually see your subject up against, meaning you can't *look* at flowers against a light background and decide to *paint* a dark background. Always have on hand three drapes — one light, one medium, one dark — to put behind your subject to see which one shows off the subject best.

5. Good general rule: Light subject, dark background; dark subject, light background,

6. The color of the background should look like a natural setting for the

subject and extend the mood of the subject. For instance, silver can stand an elegant color but a picture of vegetables can't.

7. Use the process of elimination to choose. Ask yourself these questions: What tone would not show off the subject? What colors would not look right? What colors would look right — yellow, orange, red, violet, blue or green? What intensity version of that color (bright or dull) would look best? What would look natural?

8. The background sets the mood of the painting and, thus, its appearance is dictated by how you want to interpret the subject. Light suggests airiness and crispness; dark is more brooding and mysterious. Try to put into words the effect you want and associate words that describe color and tone to match that effect. For instance, an earthy look could be recorded with earth colors, warm greens and tans and of medium tone. Dramatic looking backgrounds could be recorded with strong contrast of tone of background to subject and of a definite color contrast also.

9. To sum up, the choice of tone is initial, then its color is a grayed complementary one or an analogous one.

The choice of a suitable background is much a matter of personal taste. One way to develop artistic taste is to study paintings of the past. Your eye will become so accustomed and trained by them that when you lay in an unfortunate background choice, you will recognize it as such. Studying and viewing great paintings don't teach you what to do as much as teaching you what not to do.

I spend a lot of time modeling my backgrounds, but they always look flat. How can I paint a large area smoothly?

Many students try for the final effect too soon in that they try to paint the background color and get it smooth at the same time. Paint must be applied, and then worked in for the desired effect. Follow this basic instruction:

Paint in all the tones of the large area in small strokes, one-half-inch long, so you can see a subtle fusion or gradation of tone. Then, with a large, soft brush, dust or feather all those strokes. This dusting will blend them together.

If a smooth effect is tried for in the initial lay-in of color, the result can be boring because there isn't the faintest degree of juxtaposition of color. Any large area of tone, be it one tone, a gradation from light to dark or dark to light, should be done in strokes no longer than one-and-a-half inches, in a rhythm of similar strokes. This unifies the area. Then, smooth these strokes out in strokes that are opposite to those in the initial direction. You can leave some of the slight variations of tone remain or, if you desire, you can smooth the paint completely.

BALANCE (see Composition)

BARIUM (see Cadmium Barium)

BINDER

What is meant by binder? What is meant by the statement, "turpentine destroyed the binding quality of the paint"?

First, a binder, or a vehicle, is a liquid medium; it is the substance that's mixed with particles of pigment to make paint. A binder has to have the capacity to film. A binder should also allow an optimum effect of color such as depth and brilliance. Linseed oil is the basic binder or vehicle for oil paint.

Now, here's where turpentine comes in: Oil paint can be thinned with turpentine to a degree but if it's thinned too much, the binding quality of the linseed oil is reduced by the dispersal. Greatly thinned oil paint can be applied in the very beginning stages of a procedure but not in the subsequent layers. With the continuous flow of color foremost in the artist's mind, the thinning of oil paint at this stage can be done with any of the following: more linseed oil; stand oil thinned with turpentine; or a medium that's made of an oil, a varnish and turpentine.

Many types of oils are used as binders or vehicles. Some are:

STAND OIL: Heated linseed oil

SUN-BLEACHED OIL: Linseed oil that's been left to stand in the sun

BOILED OIL: Oxidized linseed oil

The three types of processing are to make the linseed oil faster drying and to reduce its yellowness. Stand oil is excellent to use as an added medium; sun-bleaching is an old process used many years ago; boiled oil nowadays is inferior because it has drier added to it rather than being naturally and purely oxidized.

WALNUT OIL AND POPPYSEED OIL are also used as binders for oil paints. Many experts regard these oils as inferior to linseed oil, and I agree with them.

BLACK PAINT

Why am I taught not to use black?

Disparagers of black say, "Don't use black because it is not a color!" While this can't be denied, it's not a sound reason for rejecting black. White isn't a color either, but you must use it in opaque rendering as a lightening agent for colors. Black, by the same token, can be utilized as a darkening agent for colors, as long as this darkening isn't done to make a color shaded. Black should only be used to help establish the tone of a color. Since color is ever-present, colorless white and colorless black should never be used without mixing them with color.

Don't paint with black? Sure it can be done. You can make a dark tone to simulate black by mixing a dark color with its dark complement, such as Alizarin Crimson and Thalo Green, or Thalo Blue with Burnt Umber. Then you can mix this with degrees of white for lighter tones of gray, adjusting it to be a warm gray by adding more of the warm color, or a cool gray by adding more of the cool color. Here's an example — mix Alizarin Crimson, Burnt Umber and Thalo Green together. The mixture of Alizarin Crimson and Burnt Umber makes a dark red. Thalo Green, therefore, would be its complement. If, when this is mixed with white, the mixture looks cool, add more Burnt Umber and Alizarin Crimson; if it looks too warm, add more Thalo Green. Finally, you end up with the neutral gray tone that's so necessary in color mixing to adjust the tone of shadows on colors. But you have done one heck of a lot of mixing, which always tends to deaden color.

Using black is an easier way to get the tone of shadows on colors. Mix the tone of the shadow with black and white, then add the complement of the color you want to shadow, and add this mixture to the color.

Tones of gray made of black and white are invaluable in admixture with cool colors to vary their tone and intensity. Here are the ways to make various tones and intensities with the use of black in the mixtures:

> A little black and a lot of white added to Thalo Blue make a dull, light-gray blue.
>
> A lot of black and a little white added to Thalo Blue make a dull, dark gray blue.

Degrees of black and white added to Thalo Green or another green make gray greens.

To appreciate and justify the use of black, it's important to stress the role that tones play in painting any picture. I have found that I can clarify the tones of color by following, as an example, the procedure of four-color printing: In order to produce faithful color reproduction, the printer uses four plates — red, yellow, blue and, to add the depth value to the colors, black.

I've found the use of black is very helpful in painting backgrounds. For warm, dull-colored backgrounds, I use black, white and warm colors; for cool, dull-colored backgrounds, I use black, white and cool colors. Of course, these types of backgrounds are varied in tone by employing the complementary color theory: The cool ones are grayed by warm colors and the warm ones by cool colors. This produces a juxtaposition of warm and cool grays that simulates the ever-presence of warm and cool color.

BLACK SUBJECT MATTER

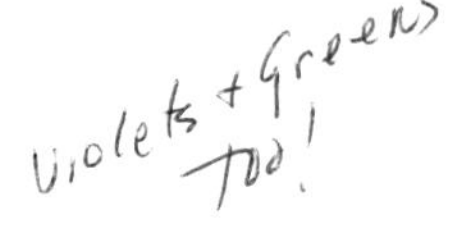

What flesh mixture can I use for black skin?

Flesh tones are made of yellow, orange and red mixed into white where illumination strikes the planes of the face. The flesh tone of black people is a darker, duller version of these colors and is darkened and dulled with the warm colors' complements in the planes that are in shadow. Remember that light is warm and it lightens any color. Black flesh, therefore, is warm color lightened. These colors can be umbers, siennas and earth reds. The highlights are cool colors much more in contrast to the flesh color than on so-called white skin.

How can I paint black subjects such as wrought iron without using black paint?

You can use black in your mixture to record black subjects but you can't use it alone. Mixed with white it can aid you in getting the tone value of a black cooking pot or wrought iron, but you must add color into that tone: Either a warm color for warm-looking black or a cool color for cool-looking black. Light shining on any black thing must be a lightened black. When you want to record the darkest value you see on a black object, you can use Alizarin Crimson and Thalo Green; or Thalo Blue, Alizarin Crimson and Burnt Umber.

BLACK (Tubed Color)

What's the difference among Ivory Black, Lamp Black and Mars Black?

Each of the blacks has distinctive characteristics:

IVORY BLACK is very transparent, is permanent and is made of carbon, a result of burning bone. Because of its transparency, in admixture with color it's not overpowering. When mixed with white, Ivory Black makes a cool gray.

LAMP BLACK is as opaque as Ivory Black is transparent. It is made of carbon collected from the soot from burning oils and fats. It is not a good black to use in *alla prima* painting unless with great care to adjust the hue and tone of warm colors when an extremely cool hue of the color is desired.

MARS BLACK is an opaque black with a warm hue. It is a better opaque black to use in admixture with warm colors than is Lamp Black.

I personally only use Ivory Black and feel very comfortable with it on my palette for the help that it gives me to mix tones of gray to add color into. Surely, I never use Ivory Black alone and mostly use it in the mixtures when painting large muted areas such as backgrounds. Don't keep black off your palette because someone told you to do so. Your experimentation should always be part of your personal development.

BLENDING

Can you give me some pointers on blending? What brushes to use and how to use them?

The blending of colors is a constant manipulation that the artist has to do in painting. It is necessary to effect a gradual gradation of one tone to another. It is a vast area of the painting process; you will find some added information in questions under *Brushes*. Here are some basics about blending:

1. Don't try to apply color and blend it in one action.

2. Cross hatching is the term used to describe how to fuse one tone into another without disturbing the shape of the contrast. These contrasting tones are laid in next to each other, then with a clean, small brush pull one tone into the other with "teethlike" strokes: to the left, to the right, to the left, to the right, and so on. Using a large dry brush, smooth out these

"teethmarks" by stroking lightly over them in a direction that's opposite to the way they've been put in. If you have a small blend to do, use short teethlike strokes; for a larger blend, use the same procedure except with larger strokes and larger brushes. This type of blending action is often referred to as modeling color.

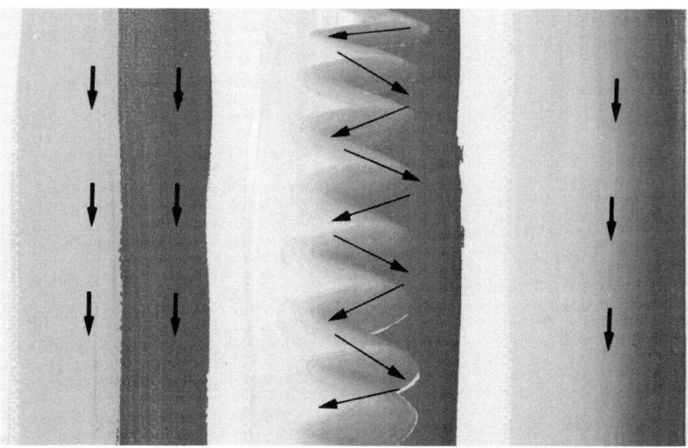

3. I would like to stress that blending color means to effect and move color that has already been applied.

4. Subtle blending per stroke is mostly a matter of pressure that you exert on the brushstrokes.

5. Remember, your brushwork records your picture and your interpretation of its subject matter. No blending can be effectively manipulated with stiff, poorly cared-for brushes. I have a special drawer for my blender brushes and save their softness and precious ends for that purpose only. Painting with them (that is, applying color) will wear down their fragile ends. These brushes are mostly large sables; I also use *Hake* (pronounced *hockey*) brushes, available at most art material stores. You can make your own blenders by flattening the ferrule of a large, round sable brush. The hairs flair out and make an ideal blender for smaller areas

6. For blending large areas, see *Backgrounds*.

BLUES

Could you tell me the differences among the many blues that are available to the artist?

All of these blues are reliable, permanent colors:

CERULEAN BLUE: Light and opaque

COBALT BLUE: Darker and more transparent

MANGANESE BLUE: Darker and very transparent

THALO BLUE: The darkest. Extremely transparent

ULTRAMARINE BLUE: Violetish in hue and transparent

PRUSSIAN BLUE: Very dark, transparent, slightly reduced in intensity

Of all the blues which ones do you use and why?

I use Thalo Blue and am avid about its properties in comparison to other blues.

1. It is very transparent, thus clean in admixture.

2. It is neither too fast nor too slow drying.

3. It is extremely potent; a little goes a long way.

4. It is the darkest of the blues so its range of tints is vast. If I had Cobalt Blue on my palette I would have to supplement it with a darker blue. Thalo Blue can be made to simulate all the other blues through admixture.

5. It is not only the darkest blue it is the most intense. As a result, bright blues can be made by mixing Thalo Blue with white. If I had Cerulean Blue on my palette, I would have to supplement it with more intense blue since Cerulean Blue is a grayed, light blue.

6. In admixture with grays made of black and white and blue's complement, orange (Burnt Sienna or Burnt Umber), I can make many tones of grayed blue.

7. Mixed with Burnt Umber and Alizarin Crimson, Thalo Blue makes a rich, very dark tone that is far more luminous than any dark tone that has black in its admixture.

Thalo Blue is Grumbacher's proprietary name for blue that's made from phthalocyanine pigment. Other manufacturers have given this blue *their* distinctive trade names.

Do you ever use any of the other blues that are on the market?

Yes, but only for special instances. Blue is mostly a decorative color in still life and portrait painting. Decorative coloration is best applied as a glaze which is most successful if the color used is not an intermix. In this case, I use any of the blues that are closest to the type of blue that I want to impart to an area. Two of my favorites are Manganese Blue and Payne's Gray (actually a dark, dull blue) because of their transparency. Even though Cerulean Blue is somewhat opaque, I will at times use it to impart a breath of blue.

My blues are always criticized for being too blue. What does this mean?

The best way to overcome the difficulty of recording the color blue is to understand and appreciate how our natural lighting effects this extremely cool color. All lighting presents a feeling of warmth, so even cool colors have to be warmed when they are in light. The color blue, if not warmed, looks raw and flat. Most of the tubed blues are not grayed, so a graying effect or a warming effect has to be imparted to them by admixture with gray and/or blue's complement, orange.

A very simplified practical solution to being in more control of blue is to first mix the tone of the blue you want to record by mixing Ivory Black and white together and then adding the blue color into that gray tone. It's better to start out with a *too gray blue* and then brighten it than to lay in a *too bright blue* and try to tone it down. Brighter versions of colors should always be added into grayed color for accents. Big areas of any bright color always look flat.

BODY SHADOW (see Tone Value)

BODY TONE (see Tone Value)

> THERE IS NO ABSTRACT ART.
> YOU MUST ALWAYS START WITH SOMETHING.
> — PABLO PICASSO (1881–1973)

BROKEN COLOR

I have heard the terms "broken color" and "juxtapostion of color." What are they?

Both terms mean the same thing: Colors set down next to each other rather than mixed together. Georges Seurat (1859 – 1891), a founder of neo-impressionism, was the most prominent practitioner of broken color, which he called *pointillism*. A prime example of this technique is his painting *Un Dimanche a la Grande Jatte* (Sunday Afternoon in the Park). When you look at colors in juxtaposition, your eye mixes them for a color effect of the subject. The many strokes of different colors of the same tone value record the general color effect of the area or subject. This use of color creates a color vibration that is very exciting. It tends to give to a painting a bright feeling of color. *(See Pointillism)*

a dry brush lets the underlying colors break thru this is broken color to.

BROWN

If there are only three primary colors — yellow, red and blue — and three secondary colors — orange, green and violet — what color is brown?

Brown is a form of yellowish orange. It is not yellow as we think of yellow: The color of a lemon. But it is a yellow nonetheless. Brown is a dark, low intensity yellow and is almost ever-present in nature: The tans of winter fields, the light gray browns of rocks, the trunks of trees, and so on, are all tones of brown. The artist has Burnt Umber, Burnt Sienna and Raw Umber as a source of these natural colors. Since all these tubed colors are yellows, or yellowish orange, the complementary blue or violet must be used in conjunction with them to make them look natural. For instance, the light on a tree trunk could be a mixture of Burnt Umber and white. The shadow on that tree trunk has to be made by adding violet (black and Alizarin Crimson or blue and Alizarin Crimson) into that color.

green + red
yellow + violet
yellowgreen + red violet

Don't think of brown as a shadowing color. This is a very common mistake of the beginner painter. He thinks of umbers as dark tones instead of realizing that they are color. The caution to "not use black" has contributed to the use of umbers for shadows, which is the culprit in making muddy-looking shadows. Shadows should always be made by graying a color, never by "browning" it.

BROWN MADDER (see Madder Colors)

BRUSHES

How many brushes do I need to start with?

Because there are many types of application in the development of paint effects, it's better to invest in many brushes than trying to make just a few do the job. Using a brush that's not suited for the purpose can ruin it for what it is really meant for. In the end, a lot of brushes will be more economical than starting with a few. Here is a list of the brushes you'll need for each phase of your painting:

For general massing in of color — White bristle filberts, sizes 6, 8, 10

For large areas — White bristle Brights, sizes 10, 12

For furthur developing paint on paint — Red sable Brights, sizes 8, 10, 12

For refining — White bristle filberts, sizes 2, 4. Red sable Brights, sizes 4, 6

For signature — Red sable round, size 4

I am very confused by all the different types of brushes that are stocked in art supply stores. How does one ever hope to know which brushes are the right ones to use?

As confusing as it may seem to you there are only three types of brushes on the market today: 1. Natural white bristle; 2. natural soft hair; 3. synthetic. Where the confusion comes in are the many different styles within the framework of these three types.

WHITE BRISTLE. Aside from the differences in quality, which dictates how much or how little you are going to spend, are the degrees in softness and hardness of white bristle, the best of which comes from the backs of Chinese hogs.

SOFT HAIR. We are all familiar with red sable, the Rolls Royce of brushes, and almost priced as much. Red sable quailities are identified as Finest Pure Red Sable, Fine Pure Red Sable, Pure Red Sable and Red Sable. These designations are determined by the amount of male red sable in each brush (male being the best for brushes). A mixture of male and female is next and female alone comes last. Of course, there is also a mixture of red sable and sabeline (ox hair) which makes up the lowest quality and least expensive of the red sable brushes. Ox hair, which comes from the ears of oxen, is surprisingly soft, and when it's dyed the color of red sable it's called *sabeline.*

SYNTHETIC. The advances that have been made in the manufacture of synthetic fibers has made it possible to produce brushes of great stamina that hold a lot of paint and are inexpensively priced. These brushes are available in bristle types and sable types in all shapes and styles.

I've listed below more information about brushes that should help clear up your confusion:

1. Each bristle in a bristle brush has a multiple-tip flag at its end. This flag is much like a ruling pen, which makes it possible for it to hold a lot of paint. Take good care of your brush by cleaning it well and when painting, make sure that it's well lubricated with paint instead of trying to make a little paint go a long way.

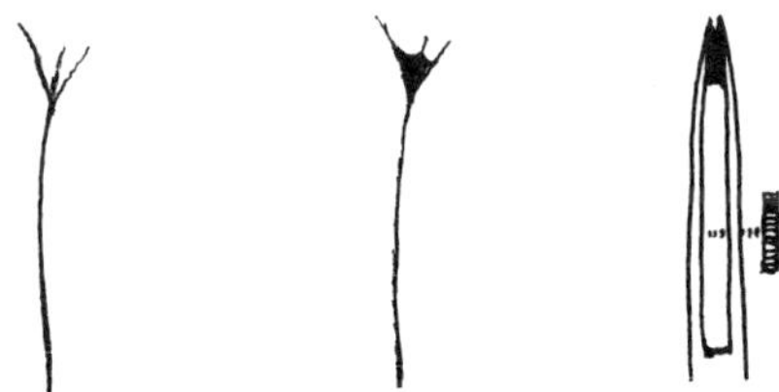

2. Each hair of a red sable brush has a tip, a belly and a root. This is what differentiates red sable from any other soft hair: ox hair, squirrel, etc., which are straight hairs just like human hair is. You can feel the difference between a red sable brush (any shape) and other soft hair brushes by running your thumb and index finger along the brush, starting at the ferrule and moving up. In red sable brushes, you will feel an actual bump, or belly, while in other brushes there is none; the shape is absolutely the same from ferrule to tip. By locking the belly into the ferrule at the right spot, the brushmaker creates a brush that has maximum "snap," or springiness, qualities not as prevalent in the other soft hair brushes. The main feature of a red sable brush is its tender tip that can chisel in the various shapes that you encounter in painting. When using a sable brush, you don't exert the pressure to "mash" the brush against the surface; you load the brush and paint with its end.

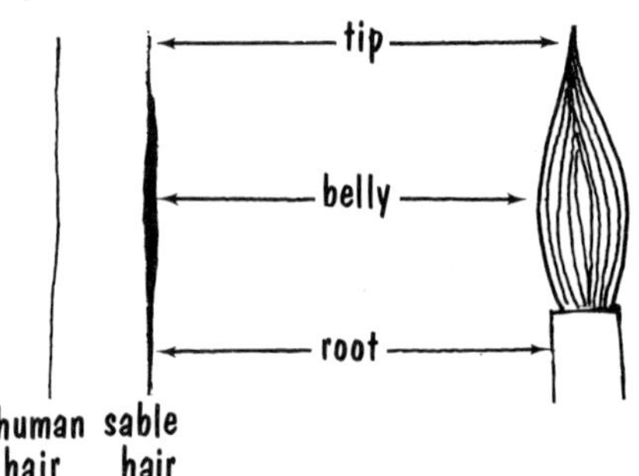

3. Synthetics today can be produced to have the flag that is present in natural bristle and also simulate the softness of ox hair; never, though, of red sable. Nor can it ever have the belly that is so distinctive about the red sable hair.

4. The three types of brushes all come in these basic shapes: Round, flat, Bright, filbert.

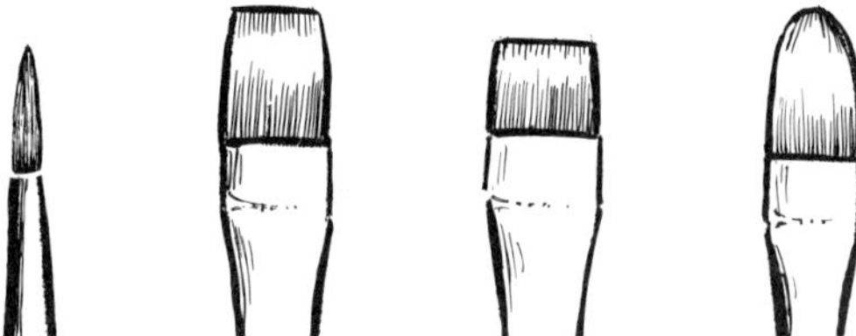

Four basic brush shapes from left to right): Red Sable Round: For finishing and details. White Bristle Flat: For massing in. White Bristle Bright: For heavier applications; Red Sable Bright: For painting into paint. White Bristle Filbert. For fitting tones together; for blending.

All brushes vary in size, from small size 1 to large size 20 and even larger in some manufacturers' brands.

What brushes do you recommend for beginners?

I always make beginners use medium-size brushes: 6 to 10, white bristle flat. Beginning painters tend to want to pick around with little brushes instead of translating the subject into broad applications of color, leaving the finishing touches for the end.

Finally, your technique, as is everyone's, is very much the result of practice and trial and error. Books can guide you, but you have to put this guidance into your own way of painting.

BRUSHES (Blenders)

How can I get that smooth look to my subjects and large areas?

Two things will give you this effect. The first is to have a variety of brushes to use as blenders. These can be a variety of large rounds, wide soft flats or any brush that feels soft and has a limp "flip-flop."

The second is a procedure that's made up of two distinct parts: 1. The actual painting of the tones of the shapes of the subject. This can be done quite boldly. 2. With a blender smooth out and blend in what you've recorded. This should diffuse the original application so much that it could then be redefined.

Many students try to paint and blend at the same time which doesn't work as well as my two-part approach.

A smooth look can also be a complete overlay over the tones. Do this when your painting is dry. These overlays are greatly thinned paint that are slightly lighter tones than the tones they are painted on.

To get a blended effect, you can't be afraid of ruining what you have done. Oil painting is so much a matter of painting in an area and then adjusting that area. It's much like building it, tearing it down a little, and then rebuilding it.

Here are some blender brushes that you can work with:

1. THE FAN BLENDER. This is the most popular one in use. For general blending, however, it is the most ineffectual. It's only used successfully to make extremely subtle fusions in small areas.
2. HAKE BRUSH. These bunny-haired Japanese brushes make excellent blenders because of their irregular endhairs. *Caution:* Keep the brush clean.
3. CAMEL HAIR WATER COLOR BRUSHES. One of my favorites.
4. EXTRA LARGE SIZED SOFT BRISTLE. Either those very large sizes made by art material manufacturers or those you can find in a hardware or paint store.
5. MY OWN INVENTION. Large round, soft brushes, either soft bristle or synthetic, which have little use in general painting, can be made into a good blender. With a hammer, gradually flatten its round ferrule. You will see the hairs flay out making a somewhat filbert-like shape.

What brush will best give me a smooth effect?

A smooth effect is obtained by massing in the tones and shapes and blending them with a large, soft, dry brush. The progression follows: Develop more contrast and color and blend; add more detail and then blend again. it's a matter of do it, blend it, do it, blend it. A large soft brush such as Grumbacher's 1″ camel hair wash, a flat, oval watercolor brush, is ideal. Since blending does little to wear your brush down you will have it and use it for years as long as you clean it well after every use.

> A PRIMITIVE ARTIST IS AN AMATEUR
> WHOSE WORK SELLS.
> — GRANDMA (ANNA MARIE) MOSES (1865–1961)

BRUSHES (Brights)

Why are short-haired flat brushes called Brights?

They are named Brights for a very logical reason: They were designed by a man named Bright. They have nothing to do with getting bright pictures.

Do you use Bright brushes in your painting?

Yes, but in red sable only. I find that I can't make a Bright white bristle flip-flop as well as I can a flat white bristle brush. This flip-flop action makes for easy, adequate coverage. It also is one that makes a brush last longer.

The tendency among many painters is to want to scrub with a bristle brush. Scrubbing, as you know, wears down the brush's tender tips and once the end of the brush is worn down you can consider it useless. White bristle ends have natural flags, which means that the ends are split, making it easier to spread paint. Once those flags are destroyed, the brush's capacity to hold paint and to spread it easily has been destroyed with them.

Most red sables are in the Bright shape, except for some by a few manufacturers. These longer red sables, I find, can only be used as blenders because the length of the soft hair brushes is too weak to withstand the pressure of application. For feathering out small strokes or harshness of tonal changes, these longer red sables are ideal.

If you buy one of these brushes for blending, take good care of it by cleaning it well after blending with it. It may seem as though it isn't dirty because you have just dusted with it but that little bit of paint on its end, when dry, can kill it as a blender.

BRUSHES (Camel Hair)

Are camel hair brushes made from the hair of camels?

No. Camel hair is a general term to describe any soft-haired brush that has been manufactured by using hair from animals, such as donkey, horse, goat, and other inexpensive natural material. Sable, oxhair, squirrel are never classified as camel hair.

BRUSHES (Care of)

What is the best way to clean my brushes?

Before I tell you how to clean your brushes I want to alert you to the way that most brushes are ruined. The painting process does cause a certain degree of wear on brushes, but the greatest reason for the deterioration of brushes is the artist trying to make a little amount of paint go too far. If you don't use enough paint the brush isn't lubricated enough, somewhat like trying to run an automobile with no oil in the crankcase. The bristles wear down under the friction of the applications.

Another improper use of brushes is a matter of trying to make do with not enough brushes. You need large brushes to cover large areas and small ones for working in confined little areas or little touches here and there. Bristle brushes can do the hard work; red sables can be used to apply paint on paint or to paint more paint into paint.

A typical oil painting's development really requires using about ten brushes. From large to small bristles for strong application and about five sables from size 14 to size 4. Then you will need a large blender and a few rounds. This many brushes will last longer than trying to make a few of your brushes serve as jacks-of-all-trades.

All other projects of craftsmanship required the proper tools: A carpenter wouldn't think of using a jigsaw to cut a two-by-four. Why do art students think that talent can be the salvation of all their problems when the right brush for the right job would be a better and easy solution?

Now for the proper way to clean brushes:

First, never let paint dry in your brush; it can never be reconstituted well. So when you are finished painting and don't want to clean brushes, or don't have the time at that particular moment, lay them in a tilted tray that is partially filled with turpentine. Their ends will not be bent by the pressure that would be imposed on them were they stood upright in a container of turpentine.

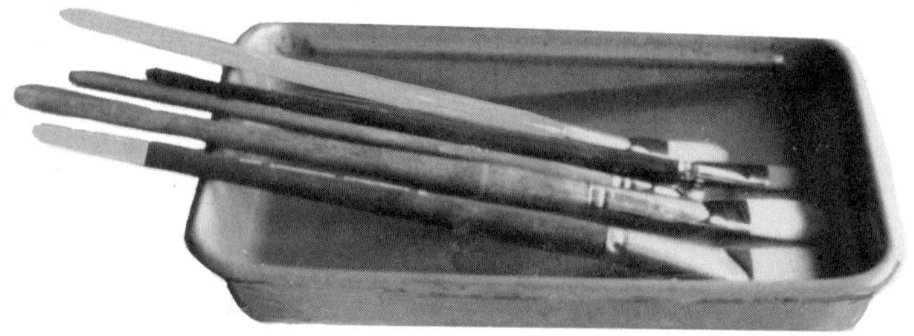

The best way to take care of your brushes is to immediately swish them around in a generous amount of turpentine to clean out the paint, and then wash them with soap and water. Do so by pouring liquid detergent (Wisk is a good one) in a container (a one-pound coffee tin is ideal) and add a cup of warm water. Slosh the brushes in the solution, trying not to beat the brush tips on the bottom of the container. Then, with your fingers, starting at the ferrule up toward the ends of the bristles, work the dirty turpentine out of the brush. This way you are flushing the dirt out of the brush. If you rub a brush on a bar of soap, as done in every art class in the country, you actually push the paint up into the ferrule; this tends to make the hairs and bristles of the brush spread, making them look more like a shaving brush than the chisel-like shape that helps the brush to function so well. After the wash in the liquid detergent, rinse the brush under warm (never hot) water and shape the hairs or bristle back to chisel edges and set aside to dry.

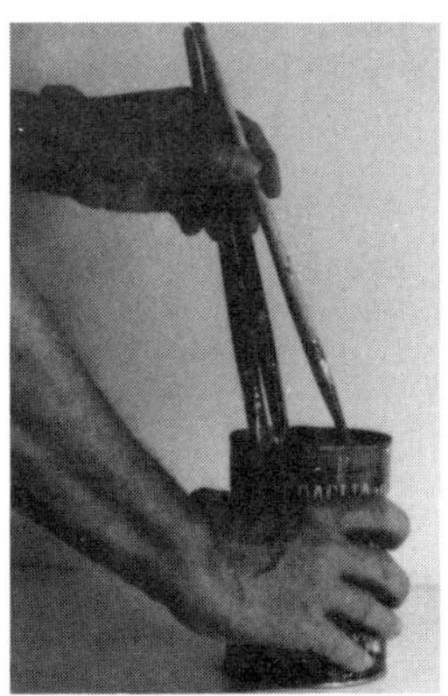

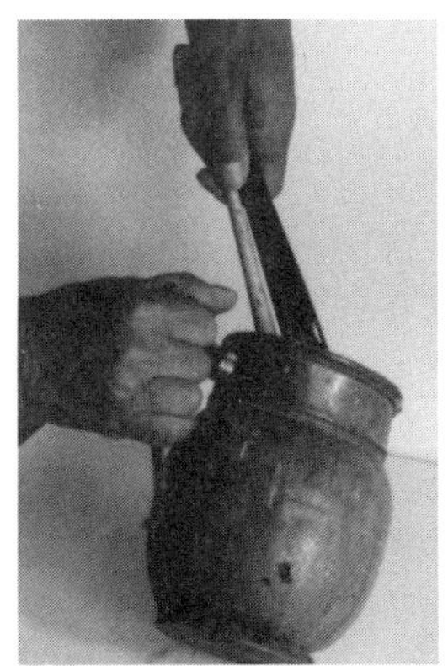

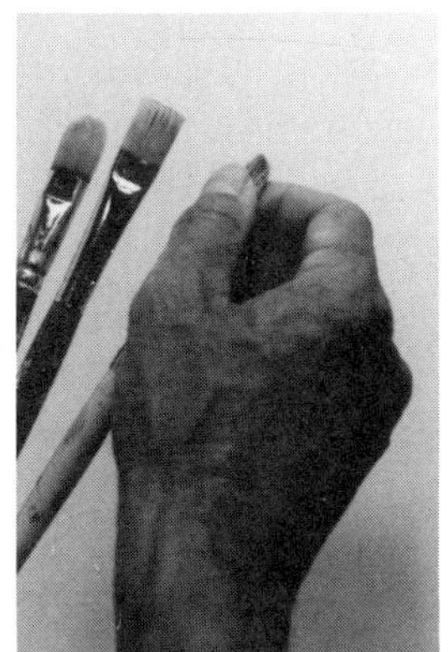

If a brush's shape is stubborn, or if you find that it's taking some time to get your brush back into its normal shape, you'll have to put it into what I call a brush splint. It always manages to get the job done. Refer to the illustration.

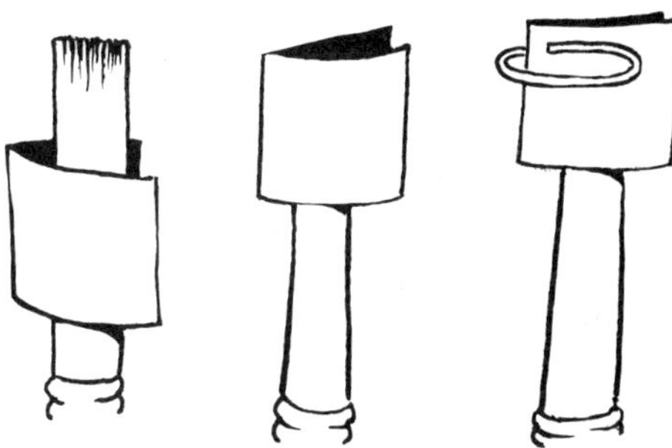

How can I remove paint that is lodged up near the ferrule of my brushes?

Prevent this from happening by cleaning your brushes properly after each painting session. A corrective measure is tedious work but if the brush still has a good tip, it's worthwhile. With a large needle, comb through the bristles from the ferrule out. As you work, swish the brush in turpentine. It takes time, but with patience and perseverance you will be able to rejuvenate your brush in this manner.

BRUSHES (Filberts)

Do you use filbert brushes?

Yes, in both red sable and white bristle. I love the easing effect of color next to color that the tapered hairs on the two edges of the filbert make. I have recently found filbert brushes in Italy that are made of synthetic material and have added them to my supply of favorite brushes. This is not to say that American made synthetic filberts aren't good. I've heard the complaint that filberts are hard to get. The reason is that dealers have little demand for them. However, your dealer will be glad to order them for you specially. There are three lengths of white bristle filberts available to choose from: Short, long, extra long. As avid as I am about the long, that's how negative I am about the short and extra-long filbert brushes.

BRUSHES (Flag)

I've heard the term "flag" used in conjunction with a brush. What is it?

The flag refers to the split ends of the bristles in a natural bristle brush. The flag is where the paint lodges so the stroke can pull the paint out of it and thus have a free flow of paint onto the surface. When these flags are worn down the brush will have lost its efficiency. Don't ever cut down a bristle brush to try to improve its end; in the process you will cut off these all-important flags and without them, your brush is virtually useless. The early synthetic brushes had no flags. For this reason, the paint would just slip off the tip. Now, with modern technological advances, most synthetic artists' brushes that simulate natural bristles have split ends that approximate the flags in natural bristle.

BRUSHWORK (Broken Color)

What brushes are best to use to get a broken color effect?

White bristle filberts, sizes 2 to 6, I find, are the best for this kind of application. I've also used white bristle rounds, sizes 4 to 8.

The larger size brush can be used to lay in the initial strokes of color and the smaller one is for adding smaller strokes of color onto the bigger masses. Be sure to clean your brush well from one color to another because the cleanness of the strokes is very important in this technique. Furthermore, it would be advantageous to use a fast-drying medium so the many strokes can lay independent on and next to each other. A good, fast-drying medium is:

4 parts damar varnish
2 parts stand oil
3 parts turpentine

BRUSHWORK (Glare)

The light seems to hit many of my brushstrokes causing an annoying glare. I don't want to smooth out my brushstrokes, but how can I eliminate the condition that causes the glare?

A large area of canvas is best painted with a rhythm of opposing strokes. When light hits a variety of brushstrokes, those opposite to the light's direction will show. This can be annoying but can be eliminated. You do so by lightly feathering out the strokes after they have been applied, by using a large, soft, dry brush. Just hold the brush parallel to the canvas and lightly drag its hairs in to the paint, not hard enough to blend the colors but just enough to generalize the strokes of the brushwork in one direction. This is more important to do to thickly painted areas where brushstrokes will usually show up. Thinly painted areas are generally unified by the texture of the canvas that is still visible.

BRUSHWORK (Thin Lines)

What brush do you suggest to paint thin little lines with oil color?

Dark lines are not much of a problem. A small brush, either a red sable round or a filbert held in such a way that you can twirl it as you stroke the surface, can make a nice fine line as long as the paint has been thinned enough to flow.

Oddly enough, a fine line of light tone is done with a large red sable Bright brush. You load the end of the brush with paint and pat it onto the surface, moving the brush along as you pat. This is illustrated in the bottom photo.

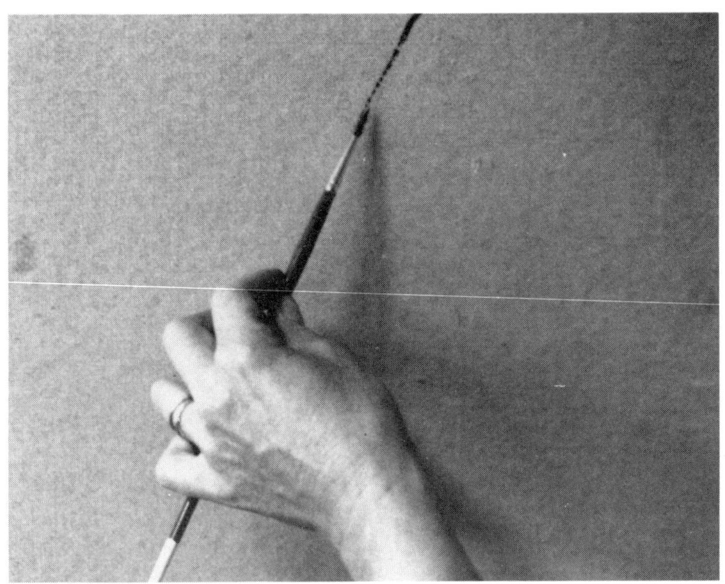

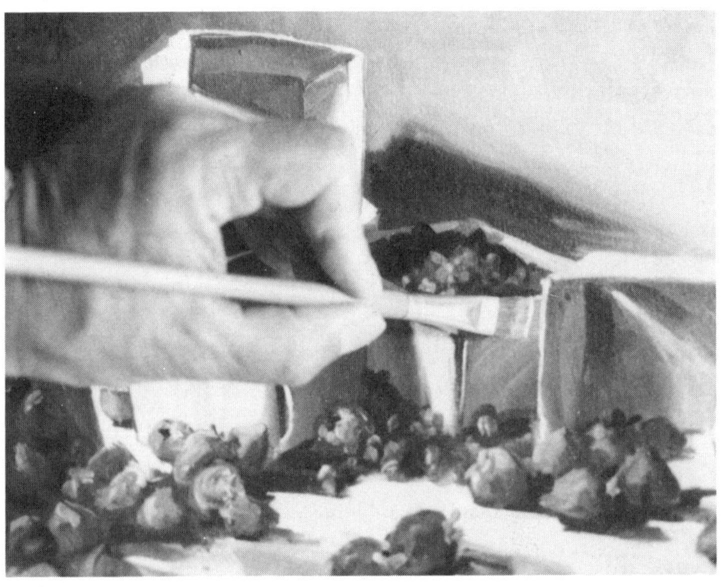

BRUSHWORK (Wet-on-Wet)

When painting wet-on-wet, how can I stop my brush from smearing into the paint that I've already applied?

Since a brush is used to mix a color and then subsequently to apply a color, the way it is loaded with paint has to be adjusted. You do this by wiping the brush on a cloth between the mixing and the painting stages. The painting rag now must be regarded as more than just a cleanup tool. It is an important assistant to the function of a brush. I use, exclusively, turkish toweling cut into small squares of 5" x 5". The roughness and absorbency of this type of cloth serves the brush well.

For accuracy, a brush has to be loaded with paint not *filled* with paint. The painting rag enables you to clear the brush of paint and then you can return to the mixing area and, with the brush, scoop up the mixture on the brush's end. A brush that's loaded with paint this way is how to paint wet-on-wet successfully. *(See Painting Rags)*

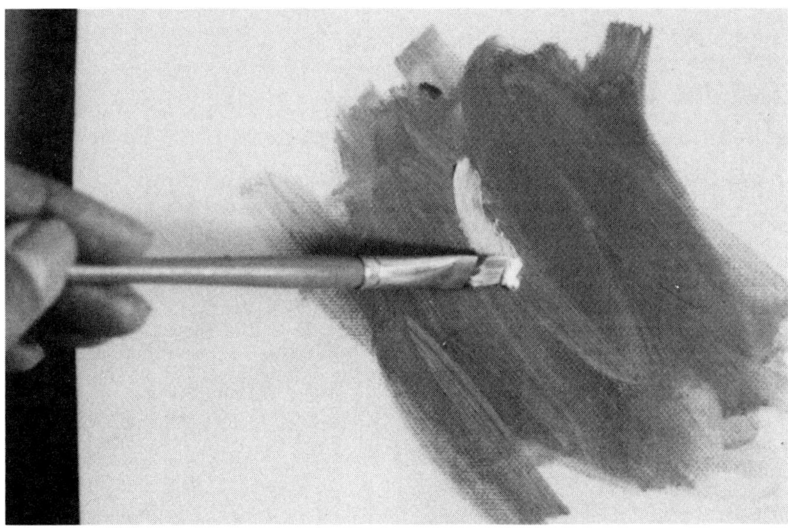

A wet-on-wet application has to be a progression of thicker paint applied to a thinner layer of paint. The pressure that you apply to your brushstrokes will affect the degree of blending.

BURNT SIENNA (see Earth Colors)

BURNT UMBER (see Earth Colors)

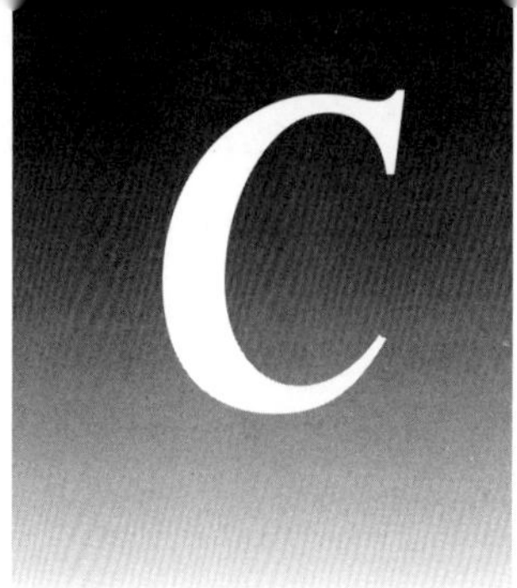

CADMIUM BARIUM

What is the difference between cadmium colors and cadmium barium colors?

Cadmium barium is cadmium sulphide plus barium whereas pure grade cadmiums are only cadmium sulphides. Ralph Mayer, author of *The Artist's Handbook,* writes that the cadmium barium colors are as permanent as the more expensive pure cadmium sulphides, but less powerful in tinting strength.

I feel that all of our colors today are superior to the ones used in the past. I sure wish I could get the results with our materials that the Old Masters got with theirs. I'm confident that I'm not alone in this wish.

CADMIUM COLORS

What caution should I exercise when using cadmium colors? I've heard that they're not permanent.

The cadmium colors have been around a long time and are the artist's source of bright yellows, oranges and reds. They are permanent, opaque and slow drying. These properties make their use more a matter of subsequent layers and additions to the duller, faster drying initial layers of the oil painting procedure.

The hues of the cadmium colors vary from manufacturer to manufacturer, who all have these basic colors:

CADMIUM YELLOW LIGHT. The lightest, brightest yellow. Cool in relation to Cadmium Yellow Medium, which, because of its darker tone, is not as versatile on a palette as Cadmium Yellow Light.

CADMIUM YELLOW DEEP, CADMIUM YELLOW ORANGE AND CADMIUM ORANGE are joys to have on a palette, especially Cadmium Orange, but are not really necessary since versions of them can be made by mixing Cadmium Yellows with a tone of Cadmium Red Light. But for the landscapist who wants sparkling, warm passages and a chance to vary his greens, and for the portrait painter who wants subtle variations of orangey flesh, these cadmiums go beyond being a joy and become necessities.

CADMIUM RED LIGHT is the most versatile of the cadmium reds in admixture. It is the closest in hue to Vermilion.

CADMIUM RED MEDIUM AND CADMIUM RED DEEP in admixture with white are really quite purple in hue and dull in intensity. As these colors come out of the tubes they are deceiving. You may think they will produce the pretty reds seen in roses and sunlit barns only to find them to be drab reds when they are mixed with white.

I have found that switching from one manufacturer's brand of cadmium to another has been a very difficult adjustment. They not only vary in hue but also in tinting strength. Since tints of bright colors are so much a part of the final stages, their unexpected reaction to white causes overmixing, which deadens a color.

CANVAS

Why is canvas the traditional surface to paint on?

In the past, canvas, or woven material, was the most practical surface available. It was light in weight, could be spanned on stretchers to make a flat surface, then removed from the stretchers to be secured to a wall.

Today, the word canvas seems to be used as a generic term for a painting surface. It is also used as a synonym for a painting, as in "I like that canvas." I personally don't like a work of art referred to as a canvas. I'd rather have someone refer to my painting as a picture. Incidentally, this designation is frowned upon by the very people who would insist on calling it a "canvas." *Pictures* are paintings on the canvas; it's the *picture* that we view, like or criticize.

Is it important to use only linen canvas?

Linen is the best fabric we have; it will last the longest and its appearance (the texture of its weave) is quite lovely in relation to the even, mechanical look of cotton canvas. But cotton is an adequate surface to paint on. Your choice of cotton is largely dictated by the effect you have in mind. I hate to be repetitious, but a painter is always thinking about the paint effect he wants, and chooses his materials accordingly. Since he is the only one who has an inkling about the effect, he can't rely on what someone else tells him to use but has to decide to do this or that because the materials' properties seem to him to bear the possibility of success.

The slight irregularities in the weave of linen canvas work to the advantage of the artist's brushwork, more so than the regular weave of cotton.

What is the tooth of a canvas?

It is a word that refers to a surface's texture. Smooth surfaces have little or no tooth; rough surfaces have strong, pronounced "tooths."

The term is used because paint is pulled off the brush by the surface's texture (tooth) which bites or grabs the paint. The kind of tooth on the canvas regulates the way the paint comes off the brush. Oddly enough, it's easier to blend paint on a rough-toothed canvas than on a smooth one. The brushwork that's so important to the *alla prima* look is best done on a smooth canvas. The roughness of your canvas will mute the brushwork; a smoother surface will make every brushstroke show. Incidentally, the plural is not teeth.

What is the difference between single-primed and double-primed canvas?

First of all, single-primed canvas has one coat of prime; double-primed canvas has two coats of prime. A single-primed canvas is more pliable than double-primed and is less likely to crack.

The double-primed canvas is a harder type of surface to work on, more rigid and, as you can imagine, more expensive. The double coat of prime that's applied to this canvas tends to fill in the tooth more so than the coat of prime on single-primed canvas, making it smoother. This smoother surface is advantageous to certain applications.

A single-primed canvas is best for larger pictures since large spans are more apt to give and be affected by expansion and contraction. These reactions to atmospheric conditions are what cause double-primed canvas to crack. In this day and age we needn't worry about the durability of a single prime on a good fabric. The atmospheric conditions of our homes and museums are far better than they were years ago.

I only use single-primed canvas, and have done so for forty-some-odd-years. I have never had a problem of any cracking.

Will a painting on cotton canvas last?

I think so. The cotton canvas of today is quite strong and when properly sized, makes a good painting surface. Purists worry about its flexibility. But it's this flexibility that makes it easy to stretch tightly. This is what makes it hold its stretch better, very often, than linen can.

Good cotton is stronger than cheap linen, so it stands to reason that you have to use only the very best quality of cotton which, if cost is the factor that determines permanency, can be every bit as expensive as linen. The strong cotton canvas has a somewhat coarse weave. The tooth of a painting surface is an important consideration that's dictated by personal preference.

CANVAS BOARD

Is a canvas board durable?

In my opinion, it is. I have a painting that my teacher, M.A. Rasko, painted in 1939. It's on canvas board and has been hanging for sixteen years in my teaching studio which, when not heated, has temperatures as low as thirty degrees. I obtained the painting in 1962, and have no idea what kind of care it had up until that time. Being a quick demonstration sketch, about twenty minutes, I suspect that the picture received no more special care than I had given it for all of these years. It is in perfect shape, which has to contradict the many people who claim that canvas boards are inferior painting supports.

The mystique that a painting is more valuable if it has been painted on stretched canvas may be romantic, but it is inconsequential.

History has proven that paintings on rigid supports fare better than those on spanned canvas. In fact, many masterpieces in the world's best museums have been taken off their stretchers and laminated to rigid supports. Check for yourself the next time you visit your local museum: The paintings that are in better condition, you'll find, are those that have been painted on panels.

There's no denying that the resilience of a stretched canvas under the pressure of a brushstroke is very pleasant and contributes to a nice brush technique. This is mostly experienced when painting on sizes larger than 16" x 20"; it is not as noticeable when working on smaller sizes.

Today, permanence seems to obsess many painters. But with the many materials that we have available, superior to those with which Rembrandt and other painters of his and other periods had to work, durability should not be a deep concern. If your pictures are well painted and sincerely inspired, posterity will be very kind to them and care for them well.

CANVAS (Repair)

How can I mend a small tear in a canvas? It's located in the background of a portrait.

A home remedy for a tear in a canvas is to first put a piece of adhesive tape on the back of the canvas to cover the tear. Now, using the back end of a large needle, fit the torn weave together. Make sure you back this torn and patched area with a rigid support (a thick magazine, book or anything else that's the same thickness as the canvas's stretchers) to form a base for the pressure you'll have to exert on the front of your canvas. Then, using a palette knife, spread a matching color over the tear and scrape away the excess, leaving the paint to only fill in the tear.

How can I repair a dent in a canvas?

The small dents that so often are caused by screw eyes can easily be repaired by smearing a little acrylic modeling paste on the back of the canvas. This will make the canvas shrink. In time, this area may crack but it is the lesser of the two types of defects.

A larger dented area can be remedied by influencing the back of the canvas with steam from a steam iron that is held eight inches away from the back of the canvas. Be careful to not let the steam influence the canvas too much or the ground coat may loosen.

Can I paint over a used canvas?

Yes, in some instances you can. If the paint layer on the canvas is thin there is little danger of it interfering with the new painting. But if the paint is thick or slick, I wouldn't advise this type of economy. Paint adheres to a canvas not because it has any adhesive quality — it hasn't — but because the roughness of the surface holds the initial application on, due to the paint being embedded into the interstices of the canvas's weave.

If you insist on re-using an already painted canvas, here is a tip: Before starting to paint, rub the canvas down with turpentine. If the paint of the painting is somewhat smooth, you'll have to sand it before washing it with turpentine.

Working on a used canvas is an interesting psychological practice. Perhaps people who do this feel they have nothing to lose the second time around. Also, the anxiety to cover up the old may make for a freer more practical approach. Often, a spanking, brand new canvas is very inhibiting, imposing a fear of mistakes or reluctance to ruin the canvas's white purity. I think everyone who paints — professionals as well as those who paint for a hobby — has the same apprehensions upon beginning a picture: "Am I going to be able to get the look that I have in my mind's eye?"

CANVAS (Stretching)

How do I go about stretching a canvas?

First, you need a good canvas pliers; I prefer the kind that has a three-inch head. You will also need a medium-weight staple gun. Gone are the copper tacks that painters of the past used. Here's the procedure:

1. Cut the canvas four inches wider and longer than the dimensions of the squared stretcher strips.
2. You can make sure that the assembled stretchers have been squared by fitting the "frame" into one of the doorways in your home. Then, to make sure that the stretchers maintain their square during stretching, staple a cardboard to one of the corners, aligning the right angle of the cardboard with the right angle of the stretchers.
3. Now, begin by attaching the canvas to the stretchers, starting with one staple in the center of the width. Then, on the opposite side, place one staple in the center of that stretcher bar. The tension will cause a dimple in the canvas.
4. This step is very important. Pull one-half of the dimple out by stretching the canvas and placing a staple in the center of the stretcher bar on the length. Then, go to the opposite side and stretch out the other half of the dimple by pulling the canvas and attaching it in the center with a staple. A good beginning is all important to a successful job of stretching a canvas.

- You will get ripples along the edges if you don't pull toward the corners as you stretch.
- Also, try to make the degree of your stretch consistent during the entire process.
- Don't rely on the keys to improve the span when you first stretch canvas. Keys should only be used to fix the span if atmospheric conditions should cause the canvas to loosen.
- And don't cut the excess canvas away. You may need to re-stretch in the future and it is impossible to do so if there's no canvas for your pliers to grab.

Continued on Page 38

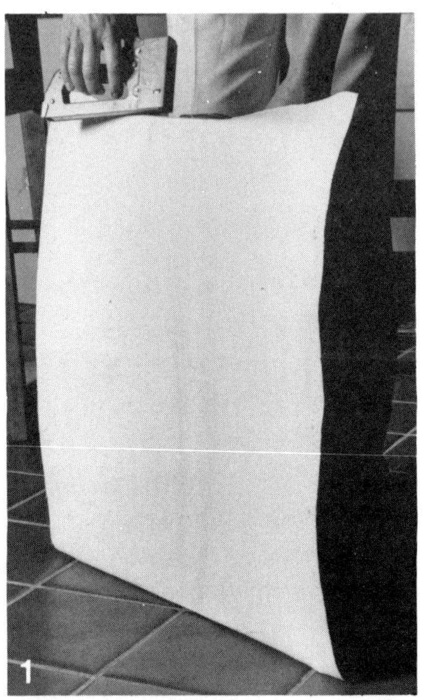

1. After positioning the canvas against the stretchers, start attaching it at the middle of the rollersized stretcher. The tautness of the stretch will cause the canvas to have a bubble all down the length.

2. Next, along the larger-sized stretcher, place a staple right in the middle. Pull the canvas so that half of the bubble is flattened.

3. Do the same on the opposite stretcher. The canvas will be taut right in the middle. Beginning this way is the most important part of the canvas-stretching process.

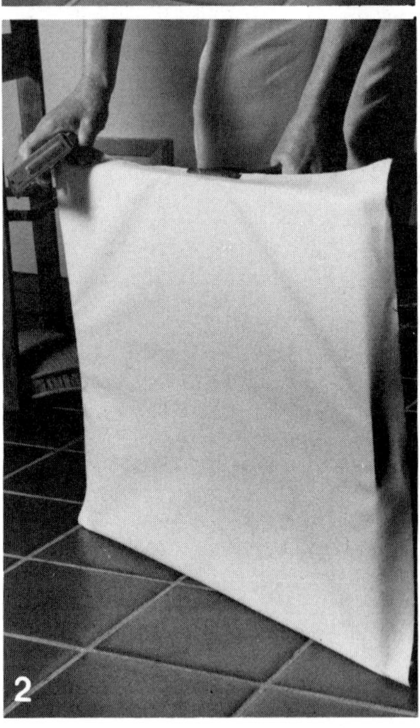

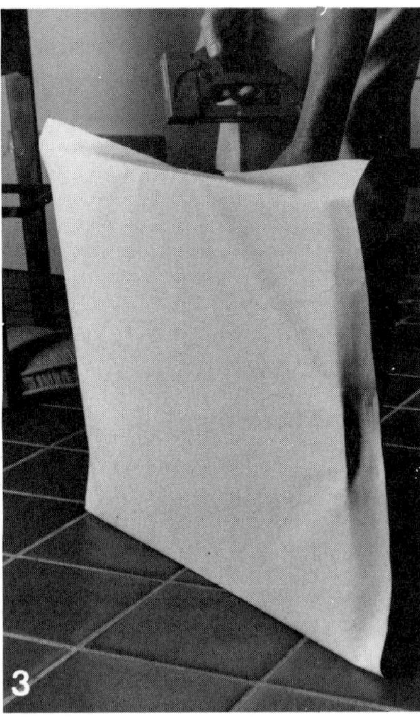

4. Now work out toward the corners. Do not do a corner at a time, but alternate opposite sides, stretching and attaching as you go along.

5. Finally, fold over the excess canvas at each corner and attach.

6. This closeup shows how the canvas pliers are held to stretch the canvas to prepare it for the staple gun.

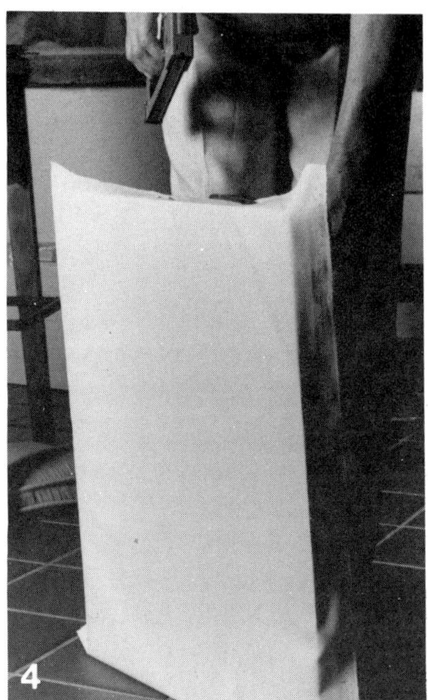

4

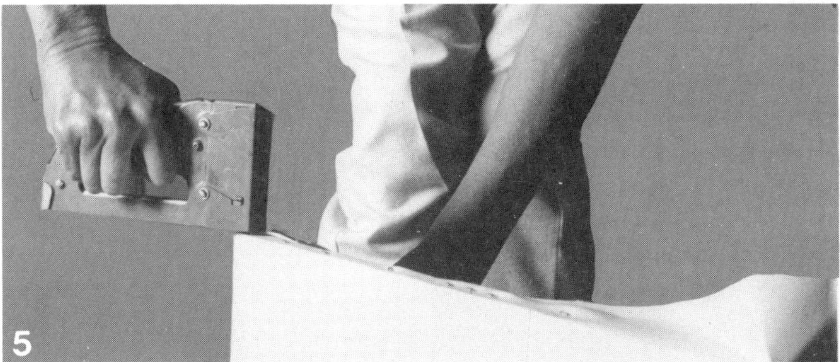

5

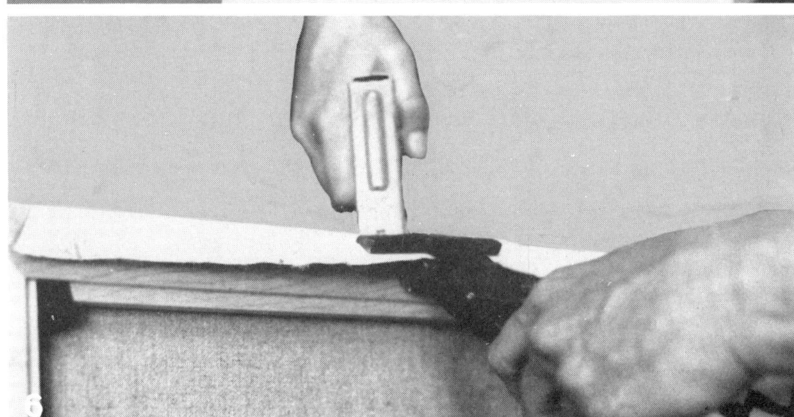

6

There is a practice that seems to be common among artists: Wetting the back of the canvas with a damp cloth after stretching to tighten the stretch through shrinking. I don't recommend this. It's far better to wash the face of the canvas — the primed side. The shrinking won't be as effective because the sizing isn't as porous as on the back of the canvas, but it's certainly safer; I feel that dampening the back may loosen the prime coat.

CASEIN (see Painting Media)

CAST SHADOW (see Tone Value)

CENTER OF INTEREST (see Composition)

CERULEAN BLUE (see Blues)

CHALKY COLOR

What is meant by chalky color?

A chalky color can be:

1. A color that is too light in relation to its surrounding area.
2. A light-toned color that is too thinly applied and looks weak because it doesn't adequately cover the area.
3. A very light color, or gray, that doesn't have enough color in it.

How can I stop my colors from looking chalky?

Here are the major ways to deal with color without getting a chalky look:

1. Never use white alone. Always add a bit of color into it even when painting snow, white flowers, clouds, white eggs and white hair.
2. Never thin out very light tones with medium. Very light areas have to be applied thickly enough to adequately cover the surface.
3. Often a chalky area is one that is too light in tone value in relation to the other values in the picture.

I think a good procedure in painting anything that is quite light in tone value is to initiate the color and tone value of the subject a bit darker and more colorful than it actually is so lighter, brighter versions of the color can be added into the first tone. It not only helps to model the form but it adds depth to the color and avoids a chalky look.

CHARCOAL

Can I start my painting by drawing with charcoal and then paint over the charcoal?

My "yes" to this question is with extreme reservation. If you dust away a lot of charcoal and then fix it with a spray of damar varnish, it is all right, then, for you to start with a charcoal drawing. A better way to initiate the drawing and placement of the subject is to use a wash of a dark color, such as Raw Umber or Burnt Umber and turpentine. Mistakes in drawing and placement can be easily corrected by wiping them away with a rag soaked in turpentine. This procedure is a much better surface for subsequent oil applications.

CHIAROSCURO

Since all realistic paintings are done with patterns of light and dark, why are only some of them referred to as chiaroscuro?

Chiaroscuro is a lovely Italian word (pronounced keearoscuro) that means a respectful rendering and observance of light and shade caused by one source of light. This term is usually used to describe *extreme* contrast of light and dark, the type of tonal evaluation of the effect of light that was first done by Caravaggio (1569 – 1609) and that was later eloquently utilized by the great Dutch painter Rembrandt.

CHROMA (see Intensity)

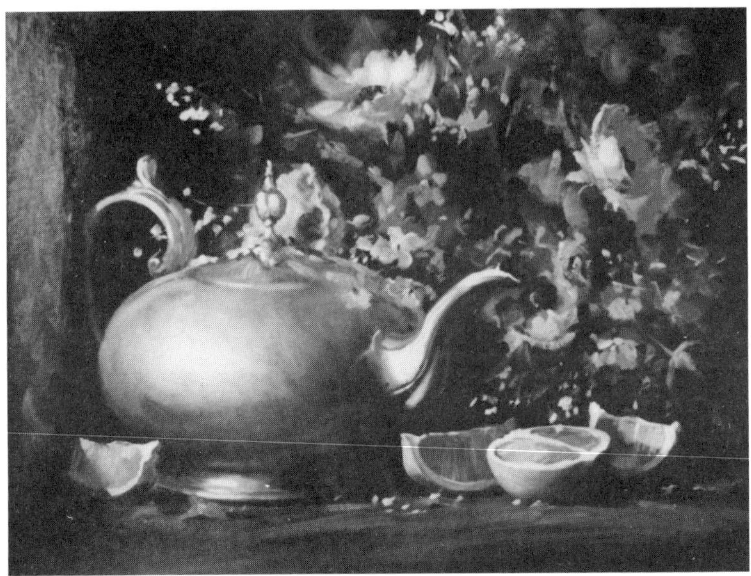

The extreme contrast in the still life, "Old Pewter Teapot," is an example of chiaroscuro. *It dramatizes the simple subject matter. "It's not what you paint but how you paint it."*

CHROME COLORS

What are the characteristics of chrome colors?

I remember my first paint set, when I was a youngster, having some chrome colors in it. This was a long time ago; chrome colors are no longer in use today. Chrome colors are lead chromates that range from light yellow to deep reddish orange. They are opaque and are not permanent. They have been used mostly to make cheap paint. The cadmium colors are far better and extremely reliable. Many artists confuse today's Chromium Oxide Green with being a chrome color; this is not so. Chromium Oxide Green is not a lead chromate, and it is a permanent color.

CHROMIUM OXIDE GREEN (see Greens)

CLEANING BRUSHES (see Brushes)

CLEANING PAINTINGS (see Canvas)

COBALT BLUE (see Blues)

COLOR MIXING

How can I learn more about color mixing?

Most of the questions about color are asked in the form of "What do I mix to get this or that?" Here is a simple, yet complete, way to come to a correct conclusion about mixtures:

1. There are only six colors — yellow, orange, red (the warm ones), violet, blue, green (the cool ones). Every color in question should be described as one of these six. Don't use terms such as tan, beige, brown, rust, etc. You must always identify what you see as a color that is one of the six.
2. These six colors vary in three ways:
   - In intensity (or chroma): How bright or dull these look.
   - In tone value: How dark or light they appear to be in their particular situations.
   - In hue: How they seem to deviate from their normal look, such as a yellow can be a greenish one or an orange one.
3. Four questions answered can help you mix a workable color:
   - What color do I see?
   - What intensity is that color?
   - What tone is that color?
   - What is that color's hue tendency?

Let's put these four questions into action and see how they draw you to a correct color mixture: A BRASS TRAY.

What color is it? YELLOW.

What intensity is it? BRIGHT.

What tone is it? MEDIUM, because it's only the highlight that's light.

What hue is it? A GREENISH YELLOW.

The answers to these questions will direct you to mix a bright yellow — Cadmium Yellow Light — with a darker yellow to darken it to a medium tone — Burnt Umber — and a touch of Thalo Yellow Green to add the hue of green.

Another example: A TOMATO.

What color is it? RED.

What intensity is it? BRIGHT.

What tone is it? MEDIUM LIGHT.

What hue is it? ORANGE-RED.

Color mixtures as a result of the answers to these questions:

Grumbacher Red, white and Cadmium Orange. This is a red, lightened and "oranged."

A deeper red tomato color would be Grumbacher Red with a touch of Alizarin Crimson.

How can I accent certain colors? I use bright colors but they don't look right.

The nature of color is such a relative condition. A color only appears to be what it is because of its surrounding colors. A less intense color is only seen as such in comparison with a more intense one. The importance of neutral colors in composition is to show off the more intense ones. Neutral colors are also grayed colors. Never be afraid to mix color into a tone of black and white to make the muted colors that so well accent the brighter color of your composition.

What is the most common color mixing problem?

Many students think they have trouble with *color.* The real problem, however, is not realizing how important the *tone* of the color is. Actually, tone values are hiding out in the many colors that are squeezed out on the palette. Before the tone of a color can be mixed, it has to be recognized in the observation of the subject. Sometimes this is obscured because of pre-conceived notions about color. You must look at the color in question in its particular situation. Here's an example: A red can be dark if it's surrounded by light tones, but the same red could be light when it is surrounded by dark tones. The question you must ask, then, is: *What is the tone of the color as I see it against its surroundings?* Here are some color mixing procedures that will help you get the correct tone of the color:

1. If you have determined a color to be light, move a gob of white into the mixing area and then mix the color into it.
2. If you see a color that doesn't look light, dip into that color and adjust its tone with lighter colors and/or white, or darken it with a darker version of it.
3. Basically, colors in light have white in their mixtures. Colors in shadow are grayed and darkened with the colors' complements. Unsuccessful color in a painting is often the result of the coverage not being adequate. Good advice: Mix more than you need since you really don't know how much you'll need.

COLOR WHEEL

I have always been told to refer to my color wheel to understand color and color mixing better. But I have to say that I don't understand color any better by having a color wheel and looking at it.

A color wheel shows just the spectrum, starting with its optimum light bright color yellow and gradually getting darker and changing to orange, then red, then violet, then blue, then green because it is returning to yellow. Colors directly opposite each other are complements to each and if mixed in equal proportions will make a tone of gray. Knowing this does not explain the complementary color theory. Color wheels aren't helpful for color mixing. My students have bought color wheels for that purpose and end up being more confused trying to use the wheel rather than relying on their color intuition and color observation.

COMMISSIONED WORK

Do you think commissioned work is less original or less creative than work that is self motivated?

Absolutely not! The challenge to create within a given assignment taxes an artist's imagination, ability and originality just as much as one that is personally commissioned or, as you put it, self motivated.

We must appreciate the artistic quality of commissioned work when we realize that most of the great masterpieces of the past were commissioned works: Rembrandt's great portraits, Van Dyck's portraits as well as those of Velasquez and most of Rubens' paintings were done on commission, as well as Michelangelo's masterpiece, *The Sistine Chapel.* Painters of the past rarely worked on speculation. There are, of course, quite a number of pictures that they painted just for themselves, but can you say that they are any more important than their commissions?

May I caution you to only accept commissions if you think you can freely express yourself as well as satisfy the demands. A good way to do this is to have a good understanding with your client. Make it clear that you want free rein and that he can only view the picture upon its completion. I always work under the condition of: Like it, buy it; don't like it, don't buy it. This gives me the freedom to do as I please. Financial pressure inhibits my artistic point of view. After all, you can't do what the client wants because he can't pictorialize his desires. You, as an artist, can.

COMPASS (see Drawing Instruments)

COMPLEMENTARY COLOR

What is a complementary color?

All colors seen in nature are influenced by light, which is made of red, yellow and blue — the primary colors. When painting red, for instance, yellow and blue (which make green, red's complement) have to be incorporated to insure the effect of nature's lighting. Yellow's complement is violet — the mixture of red and blue. Blue's complement is orange — the mixture of red and yellow. A color plus its complement adds up to the three primary colors. A cool color's complement is a warm color. Using a color in conjunction with its complement strikes a balance of color that is so characteristic of color in nature. The very word *complement* means that which fills in a deficiency. If a color's complement is not used in conjunction with it, the color looks flat or unnatural.
(See Luminosity; Tone Value)

> EVERY TIME I PAINT A PORTRAIT I LOSE A FRIEND.
> — JOHN SINGER SARGENT (1856–1925)

COMPOSITION

I've never been given a definition of composition. I've only heard the comments: "It's a good composition" or "It's a bad composition." Can you explain composition to me?

Actually, any spot on a canvas is a composition, even if it's just a dot. Since a mere dot isn't an artist's motivation for a picture (although, today, who knows?) compositions are more than a dot. Composition can become, in fact, quite involved. In objective pictorial expression, composition presents persons, places and things in arrangement in accordance with the artist's preferences. No matter what the subject is, a composition has to have a *focal point*, which is a place, in the overall composition, where the artist forces the viewer to look at first. The focal point is the place where the pictorial story begins and is the placement of what the artist's eye has focused on. These can be a simple subject, a pattern of light and dark, or an idea that has taken on a pictorial form.

A composition is a recollection of an experience, thought or feeling that seeks to find expression and form on a flat surface. A composition can have only *one focal point* and it cannot be in the middle of the canvas, because it would then be equally distant from all the edges of the canvas. Equal spacing is not only monotonous but does not allow for any other element to be added to the picture without throwing it off balance. The focal point has to be substantiated by auxiliary areas that are treated with unity, variety and balance. An artist's interpretation of the qualities of these three factors is so much a matter of his taste that there isn't a definite way to define them to guarantee a good composition. Here are definitions to guide you to your own interpretations of them:

1. UNITY means that there is an order of all the elements that will contribute to one cause. This can be done by making all things sensibly fitting and suitable to each other.
2. VARIETY means that there isn't an obvious feeling of monotonous repetition of shapes, spaces, tones and colors.
3. BALANCE means that a stable state has been caused by the elements of the composition. All the elements must serve to keep the focal point level.

No one intentionally makes an unbalanced, un-unified, monotonous composition with no focal point. These mistakes just happen because of neglect or lack of judgment about:

1. The placement of the focal point from side to side and top to bottom.
2. The size of the focal point in relation to the size of the canvas.

Better compositions are a result of some careful considerations in the very initial stage of the painting. You must limit your thinking to only compositional factors and not be distracted by other thoughts. Before you proceed to be involved in the complexity of the development of a painting, ask yourself these questions about your composition:

1. Does the subject look too low or too high? Too much to the left or to the right? Or just where I like it?
2. Does the subject seem to be the right size in relation to the size of the canvas? Does it look overgrown or too puny?
3. Would anything in my composition look questionable or indistinguishable to an onlooker?
4. Do I have only one focal point or are there many points of interest fighting for the spotlight?
5. Are there any spacings or objects that are so much the same looking that there is repetition?
6. Is it a design I like and close to what I had in mind?

Never begin to start the painting process until you have judged the composition.

Is a focal point an object?

No, it is an area where there usually is an object: A barn in a landscape, a vase in a still life or a part of the face in portraiture. The best way to describe a focal point is to compare it to the place where a pebble falls in the water. The concentric circles that result can be likened to the rest of the composition. This spot is classically never in the middle of a canvas nor in any of the corners. The four areas that are somewhat in the third portion of the canvas are where a focal point can be placed. The focal point should never be left to accidental selection; a painter stages it much like a director designs where he wants the starring actor and the rest of the company to stand on the stage.

Robert Henri said, "A good composition is a clever feat of organization. The eye should not be led to where there is nothing to see."

> THE HUMAN FACE IS MY LANDSCAPE.
>
> — SIR JOSHUA REYNOLDS (1723–1792)

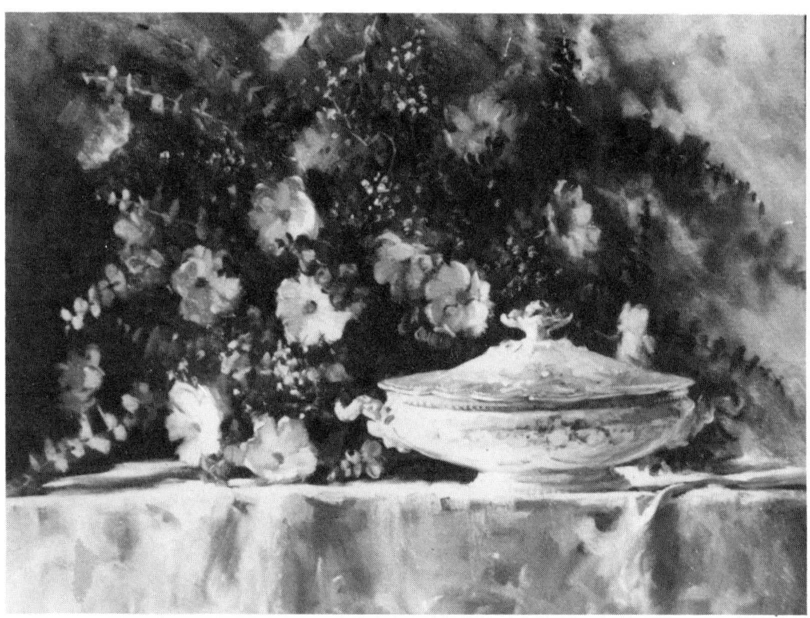

The objects in this composition are flowers and a vegetable bowl, but the focal point is neither of these objects. It is the place where the light on the bowl is in strong contrast to its dark surroundings. Focal points often are places of strong contrast.

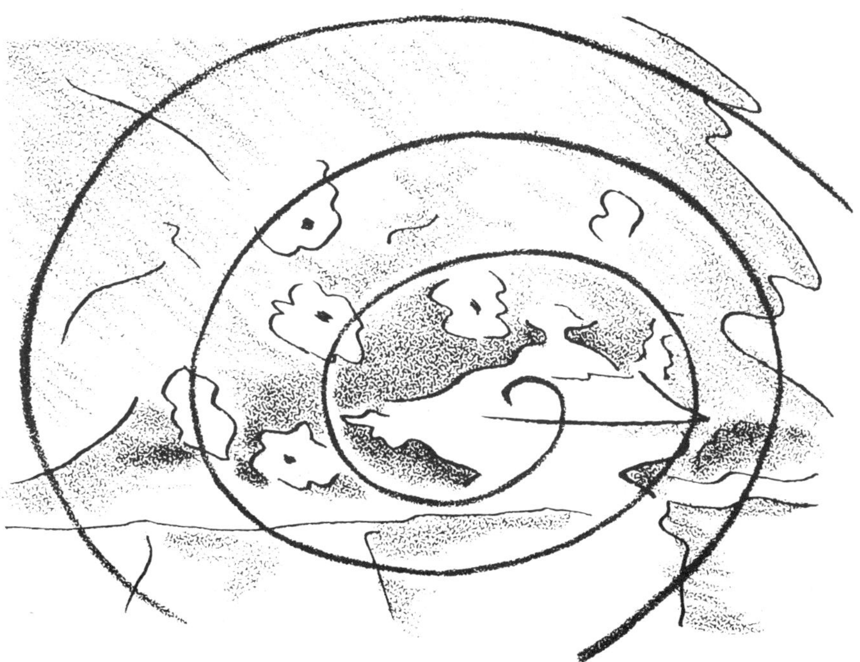

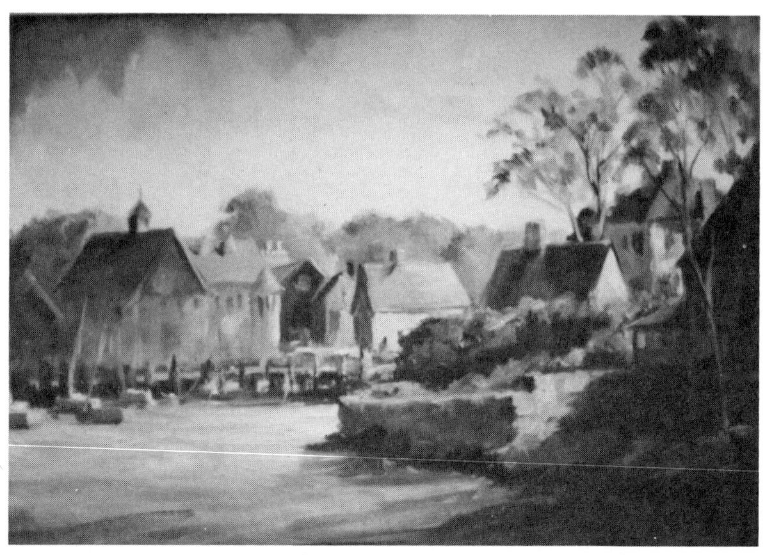

In the landscape, "Gloucester Houses," the focal point is where the foreground granite wall meets the distant elements. Again, we see strong contrast. A focal point in your picture records the seed of your inspiration.

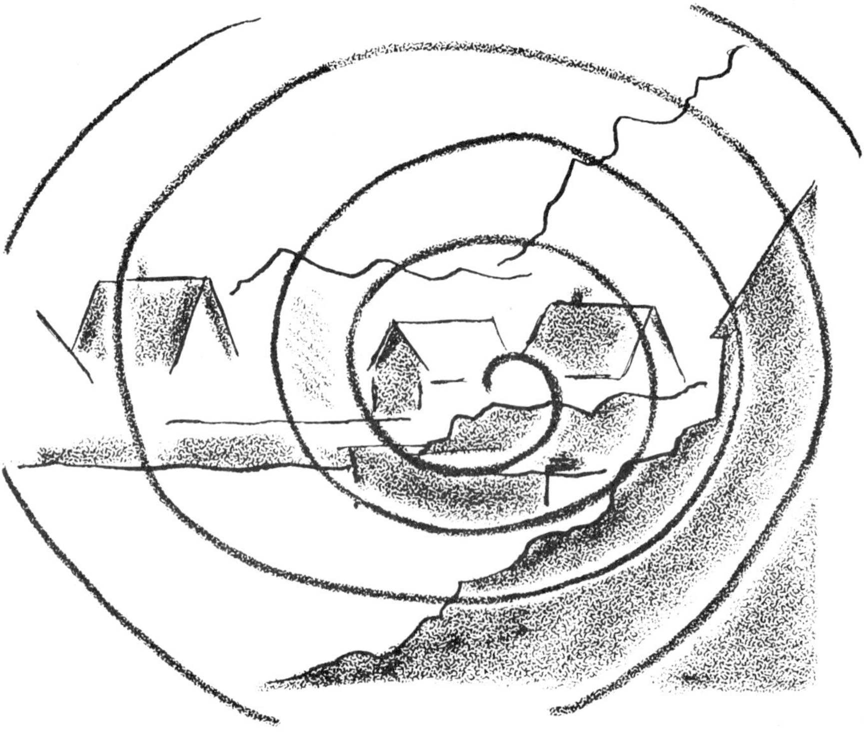

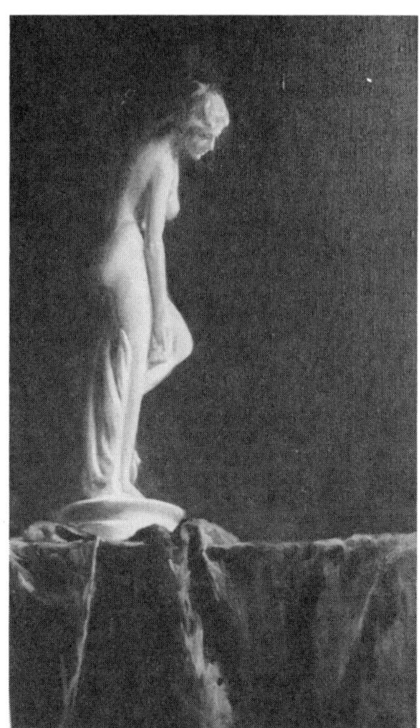

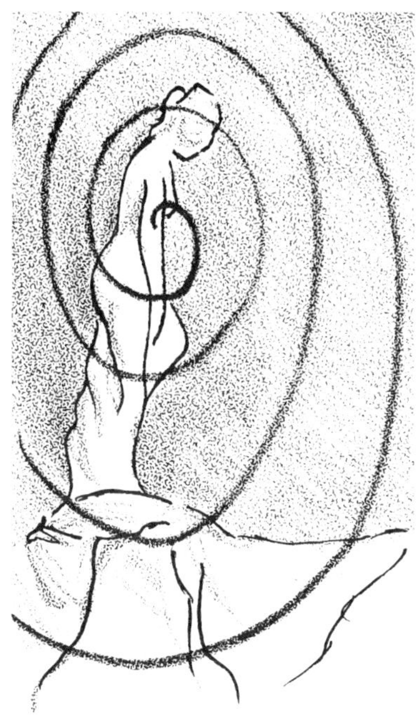

A subject matter's action can suggest a focal point. The statue looking down from the left makes the upper one-third portion of the canvas the focal point. How odd the subject would look if there was a lot of background to the right of the figure.

I don't understand the difference between a focal point and a center of interest.

Art terms can be confusing. This is understandable because art teachers have to put into words explanations of their interpretations of painting techniques and principles. These confusions can usually be cleared up by students asking more questions so the term is dissected and, thus, more carefully understood. Some art teachers use these two terms interchangeably but there is a difference that can prove helpful in dealing with the intricacies of composition.

A focal point is an actual area in a composition. It is deliberately determined in shape, placement and size. Center of interest is the theme of a picture; it is the crystallization of the painter's motivation and inspiration.

You might say that a center of interest makes an artist zero in on a focal point.

Usually the Same

What is balance in composition?

Balance means an even distribution of weight. Since a composition of an idea has a focal point, the location of the focal point imparts a weight of interest on the surface. That place has to be supported not interfered with by the other elements of the composition. Compositional factors are only guidelines for an artist's taste. An unbalanced composition has areas that seem to pull the viewer's interest away from the focal point. This can be done with uninteresting empty space or, conversely, a crowded confusing area that detracts from the focal point.

Balance is a state of distribution in which all action has come to a standstill. M.A. Rasko said, "The exception makes the rule for a composition." A picture of a personal vision can't be done by rules, but by knowing all the general rules of composition, you will be guided away from what you should not do.

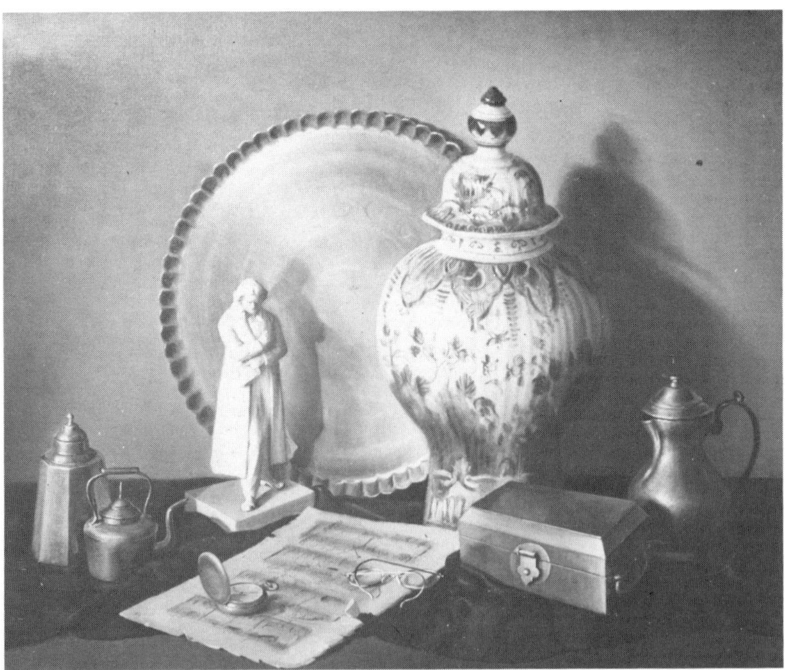

This still life was commissioned by a person who was interested in music. It is an arrangement of things that he owned. I arranged them hoping that I had interlocked and placed them to impose a focal point as well as to impose some importance on each subject.

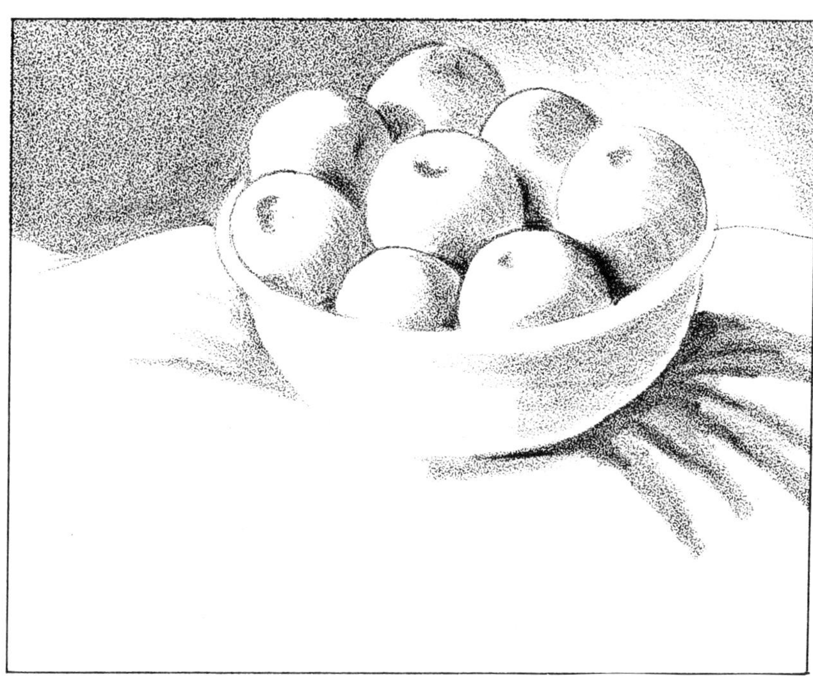

See how the space to the left of the bowl of apples in the illustration above makes the bowl of apples tip the canvas's weight over to the right. The picture is more balanced in the illustration below.

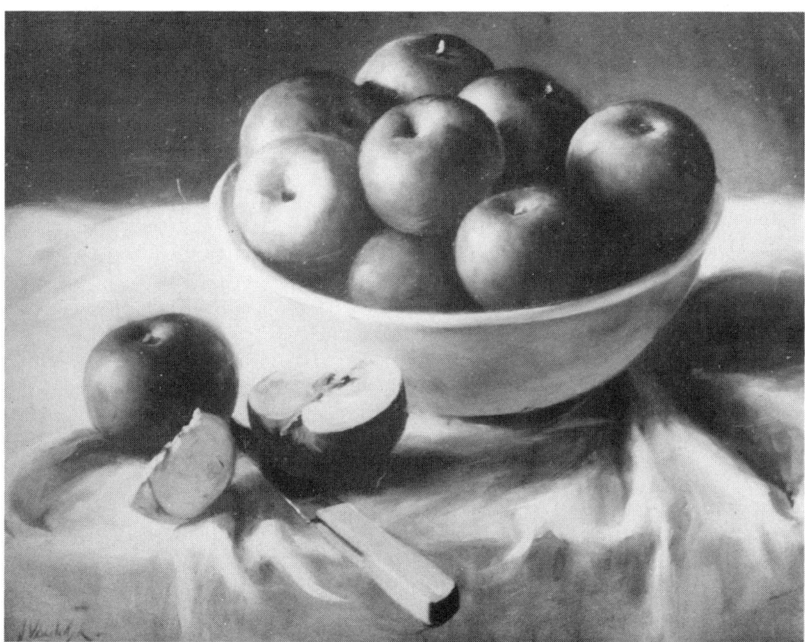

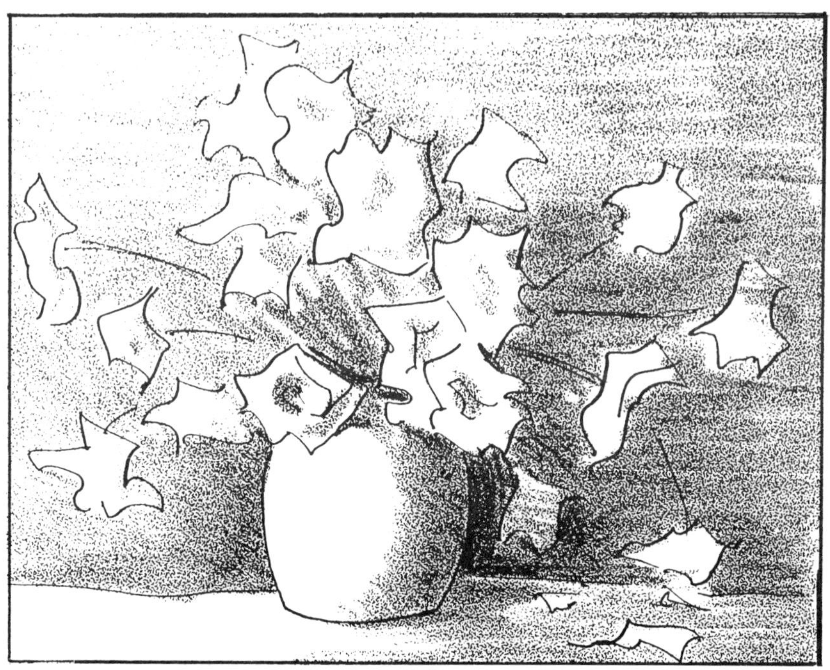

Compare the painting with the rabbit in it with the illustration that excludes the rabbit. Notice how the rabbit stops your interest from draining off the canvas on the right.

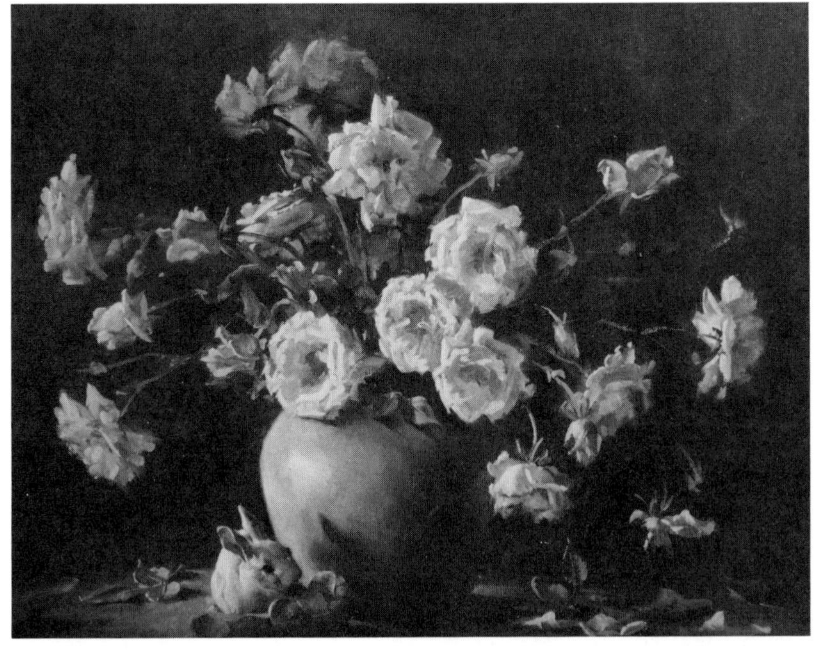

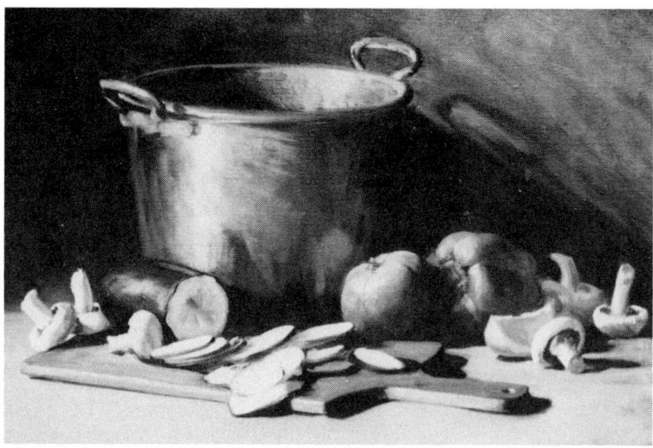

All the objects in this composition overlap each other. Nothing just touches. This overlapping can also bring to the composition a unity that supports the focal point. When subjects are apart from each other they are apt to be more distracting than supportive.

What are the most common mistakes in composition?

One of them is putting the importance of drawing over composition. Subjects in a composition can be well formed but can be arranged and placed with the other subjects in such a way that they cause confusion and ugly patterns. The mistake that's seen the most in many paintings is where two objects just touch each other, causing the eye to not see the entire beauty of each one and, instead, to see the two together. This mistake can also destroy the look of dimension, especially when, for example, a roof of a boat is painted into the same line as the horizon. Or, in portraiture, the fingers of a hand are just on the edge of a table. In still life, too, where the outer shape of two pieces of fruit that are on different planes just touch rather than overlap. I call this mistake in composition a "kiss," and the practice of doing it "kissing on canvas." As common as this mistake is in painting today among many beginners, and some more advanced painters, you will be hard pressed to find this mistake in any paintings of the past. Look for this compositional point the next time you visit a museum. The paintings of the thirteenth century, especially, never suffer from this mistake. I believe this is true because they didn't use strong contrast to show dimension. They realized that if they made their outlines touch each other, the figures would look as though they were on the same plane instead of one in front of the other, thus destroying any illusion of depth.

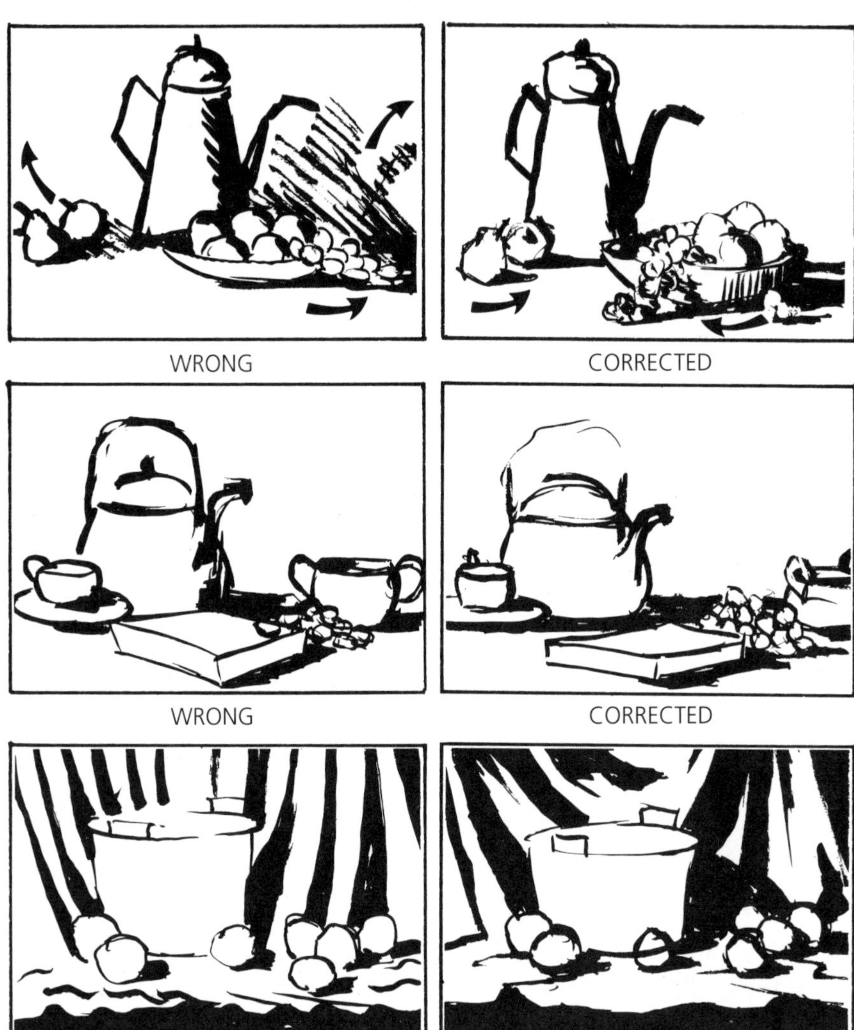

A mistake in composition is to have elements drain the canvas of interest. This can be avoided by being careful about how elements in a composition encounter the edges of the canvas. The arrows in the first drawing show how the fruit steals the attention from the focal point. In the second row of drawings, we see how objects that are just touching the edges of the canvas set up a disturbing scenario. The third row of drawings shows how the folds of the drapes drain the composition rather than accent the focal point.

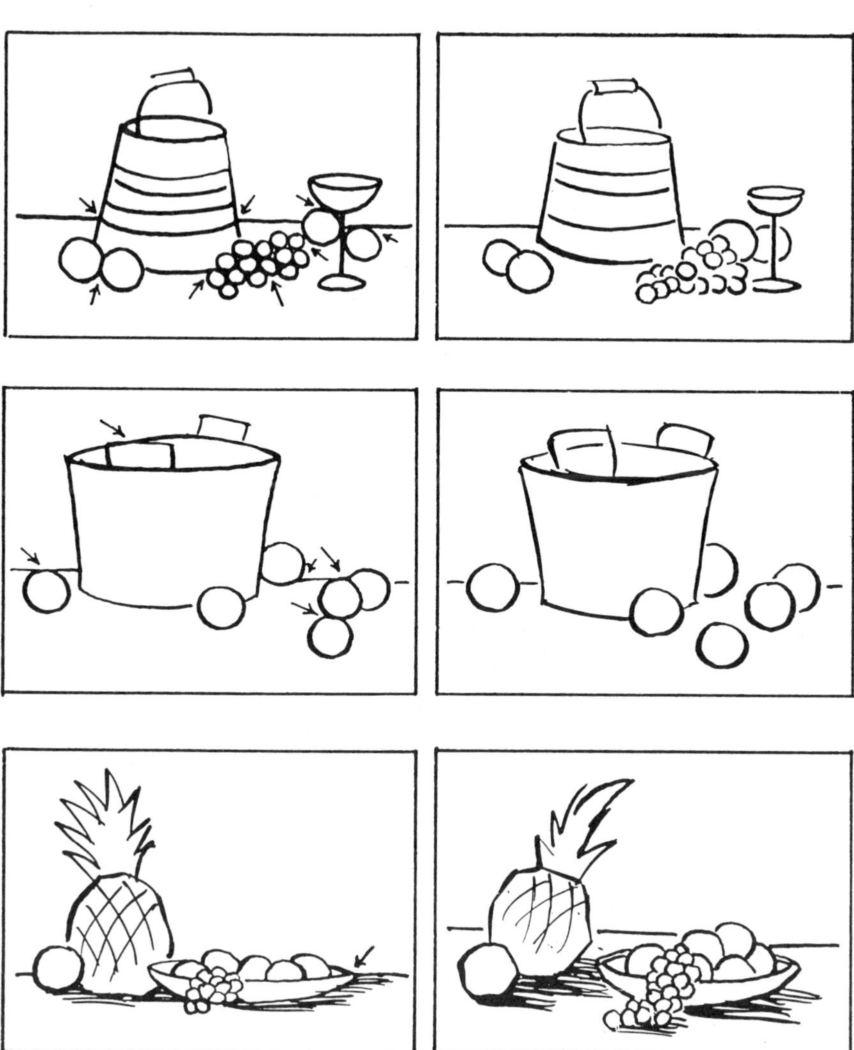

The most common error in composition is to let objects just touch each other. Since the depth dimension is almost synonymous with realistic rendering, you can see how this mistake destroys the illusion of depth. The arrows in the drawings on the left point out unfortunate meetings or "kisses." The drawings on the right show how much more depth is recorded by overlapping. While there is overlapping in the pineapple composition, the objects are too much on the same plane. The correction shows more feeling of depth and interest.

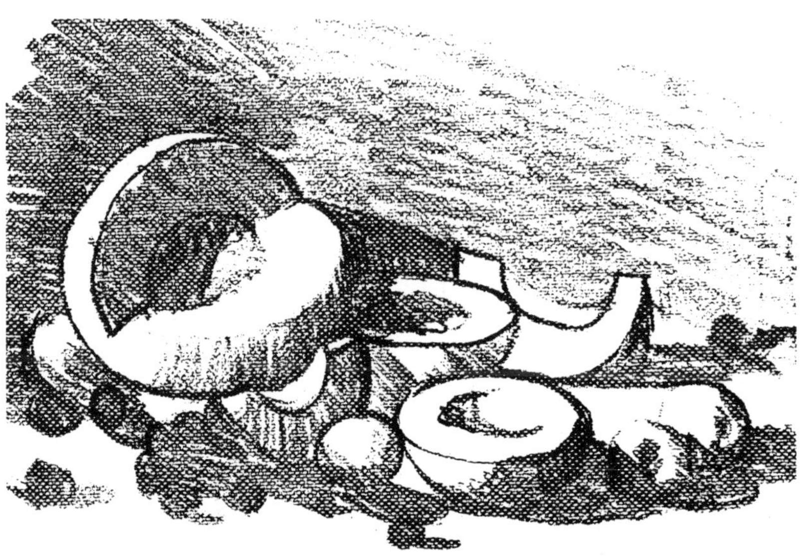

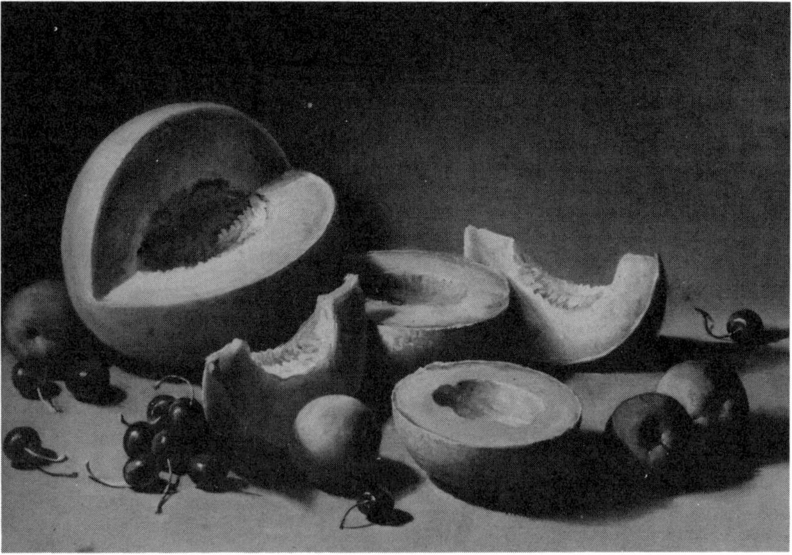

The dimensional effect from front to back, in a still life, is largely due to the placement of each element of the composition. The tonal drawing shows how unfortunate placement of one subject to another is misleading and flat-looking. This mistake can be avoided by always considering how each element of the composition is situated in its surroundings. In establishing a composition, all the subject matter are cogs of the overall effect and can never be drawn in as isolated elements.

COOL COLOR

Can cool colors be warm and warm colors cool?

Yes. Colors' temperatures are altered by graying them. An extremely grayed violet is a warm version of a cool color; a gray version of yellow is a cool version of a warm color. It's important to realize that a color's appearance is a relative condition. To see this plainly, mix a light gray by using black, white and Burnt Umber. Add to it a touch of Thalo Blue. Paint a one-inch square of this grayed blue on a canvas. Now mix Thalo Blue and white and paint around the square. See how the grayed blue area has become a warm gray.

When painting the effect of light, it's important to incorporate warmth into cool colors and coolness into warm colors. This is how your mixtures can record the luminosity of light.

Remember — cool colors (violet, blue, green) have to be warmed where they are in light; the warm colors (yellow, orange, red) have to be cooled in light. This is easily done by adding the color's complement.

COPAL VARNISH (see Varnish)

COPYING

Is there any benefit to copying paintings, such as by the Old Masters?

Many benefits can be had by copying paintings by others. The first one is that you will really appreciate the extent of the artistic worth of the painting as well as get an insight into the endeavor and labor of the painter. Also, painting well is very much a result of training your eye to see the elements that make paint interpretation not only sensible but beautiful. The scrutiny you will need to copy an Old Master is an eye-training experience as well as a chance to experiment with tones, color and shape and try to emulate the effects that the Masters got.

When copying Old Masters as a learning experience, it is not necessary to labor to get an exactness. Better to try to emulate the style in which it was painted and try to develop the paint as you think the Old Master did. Here are some guidelines:

- Copying Frans Hals portraits in just values of gray (black and white) will help you see features in simple brushstrokes.
- Copying Van Gogh will help you appreciate how the rhythm of brushstrokes

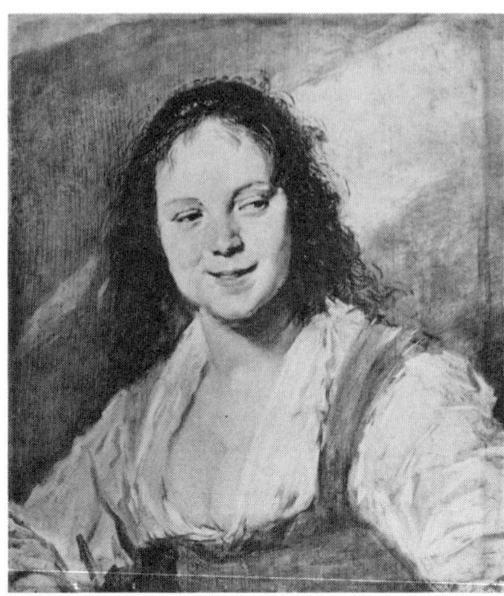

On the left is Frans Hals' painting of "The So-Called Gypsy Girl." Below is my copy of this marvelous painting. I did it more to emulate Hals' style than to make an exact rendering of it. To copy this way is a beneficial study of brushwork.

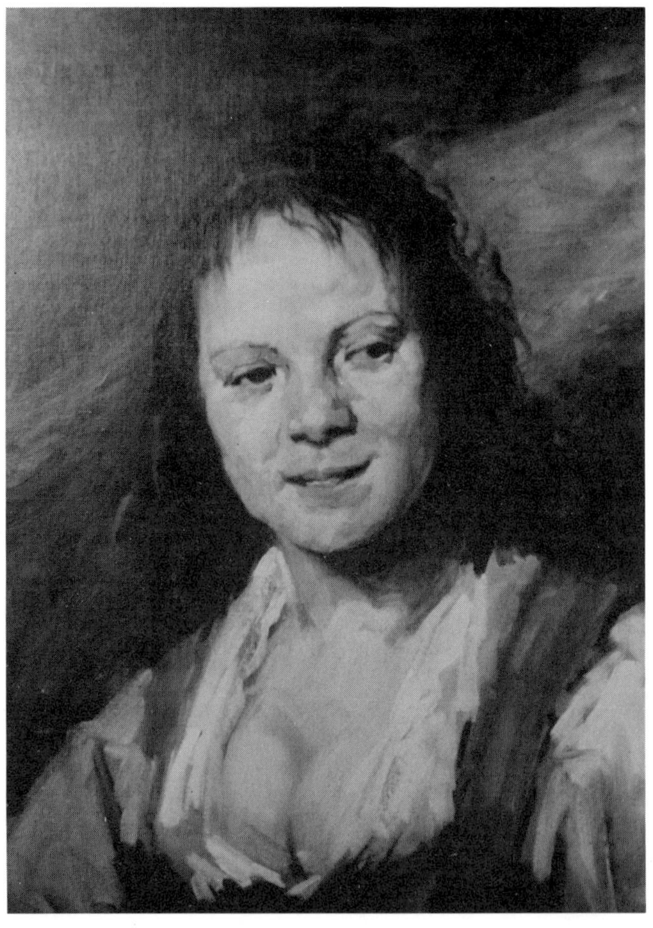

can influence a picture's impact.

- Copying Jacques David can help you practice blending.
- Copying John Singer Sargent will help you to understand that a loose, fluid style is not as spontaneous as it looks.
- Copying a Jan Vermeer will make you realize how the dramatization of elements of a composition have to be dealt with to give unity to the composition.
- Copying a Rembrandt will convince you that he was the consummate oil painter who used his mastery of the medium to express his outlook on his world.

While copying from prints is valuable, you might want to have the experience of copying from an original at a museum. All museums welcome you to paint there. Each one, though, has its own rules which you may get by calling or writing the office of your local museum. One rule that is consistent throughout is that your copy cannot be the same size as the original. *(See Original)*

What is a copy?

1. A copy is a painting that was completely inspired by another picture.
2. It is a picture that reproduces another picture, especially in interpretation and composition.
3. An oil painting of a watercolor (or vice versa) is a copy even though the medium for the copy was different from the medium of the original.
4. If an alteration is made, such as omitting an element, the picture still has to be considered a copy and not an original work.
5. There is nothing wrong with copying a painting if it's for study or for personal possession. Just designate it as such. Along with your signature, credit the source of your inspiration as "after such-in-such," or "copied from such-in-such" or "a variation of such-in-such." Your craftsmanship will then be valued by anyone who sees your picture. Even when you copy a photo that was taken by someone else for a commission because the subject may be dead and this is the only reference available, you should credit the photographer, if not on the front of the canvas, certainly on the back.
6. If you use photos as reference for technical and structural accuracy, your painting is not a copy.
7. If you paint from a photograph that you've taken yourself, then, obviously, your painting is original and not a copy.

How can I make a copy that's exactly like a photo or painting?

This project demands exactness and there are a number of means to use to accomplish this. To attempt to copy without the use of the copying apparatuses that are available is impractical and foolish.

To reproduce an image in any size, you could use a projector that projects from opaque subject matter, a slide projector or you could use a process that artists have used for centuries: gridding the canvas.

Gridding is a system of making squares on the subject and making proportionate squares on your canvas. Choose little squares for more accuracy; big ones for a broader viewpoint. If your print or photograph is valuable to you, cover it with a piece of acetate and draw the grids on the acetate with a grease pencil.

The size of the grid or squares on the canvas is determined by putting the number of squares on the print or photo into the dimension of one side of the canvas. For instance, with a photo that is 8″ x 10″ squared off each inch on the length, a canvas of 24″ x 30″ will compute as follows: Thirty divided by ten would make each square on the canvas three inches. The scale, then, is one to three.

Here is another way to use the gridding method to transfer an image on a canvas in the size you think is suitable to the canvas: When you want to paint a head nine inches long and you are working from a photo in which the head is three inches, grid the head on the photo with 1/2-inch squares, which make six squares on the vertical dimension. Now, on the canvas, put six into nine to get the proportion of the squares. This will give you squares of 1 1/2 inches, which will be the size of the squares on the canvas. These dimensions are only one example. You will have to rely on your arithmetical ability to adjust this example to your situations.

Often, the division of the number of squares into the larger dimension will not come out in inches and the usual fractions of inches — 8ths or 16ths. In that case, a caliper will help you to proportion the size of squares that will equal the amount of the squares on the photo. *(Illustrations on next page)*

Art is not a pastime but a priesthood.

— Jean Cocteau (1889–1963)

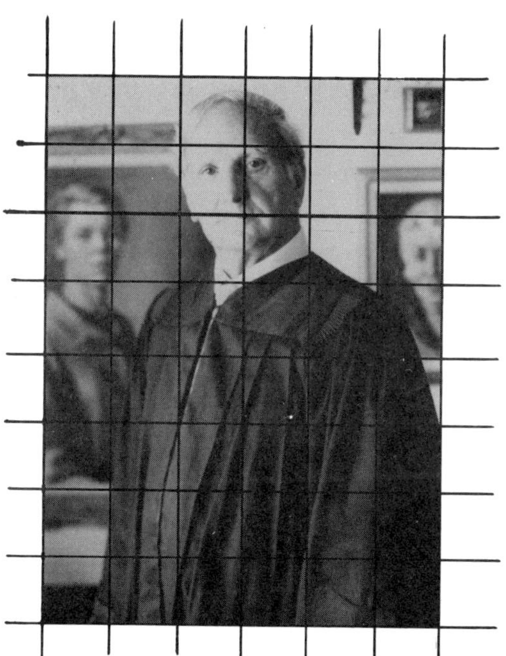

To enlarge this photo to fit a 24" x 30" canvas, the entire 6" X 8" photo was gridded into six squares across and eight squares down. The number of squares across, divided into 24 inches, results in four-inch squares. These larger-sized squares will guide you to draw onto the canvas shapes that are seen in each square on the photo in a larger, proportionate size.

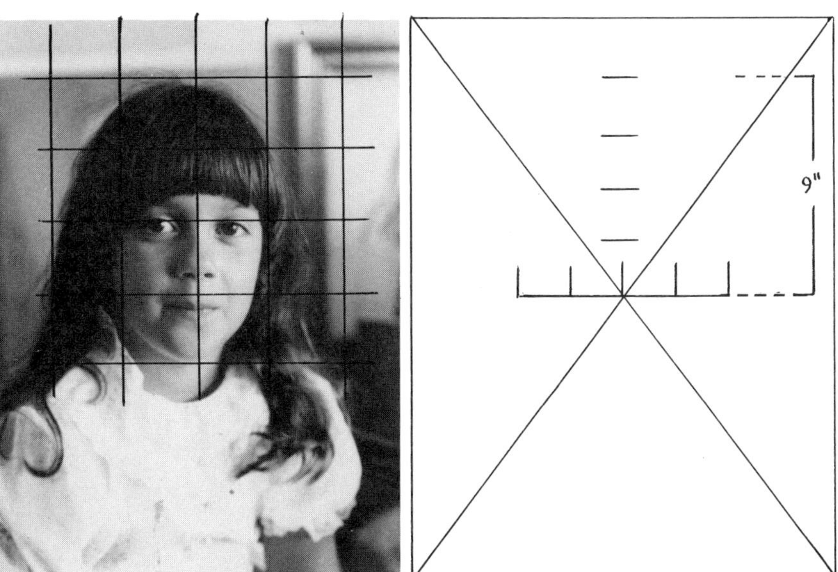

In the photo of the little girl, just the head is gridded: Four squares across, four squares up and down. The placement and size of the head is decided upon and then that area is gridded into the same number of squares.

COTTON CANVAS (see Canvas)

CRACKING

What are the major causes of cracking?

1. When fast-drying layers of paint are applied over slow-drying paint, this will result in alligator-type cracks that will eventually show up, usually within five years.
2. Extreme changes in temperature and humidity will affect a paint surface, whether it's on a canvas or a rigid support. The pattern of these cracks are usually in a spiral design.
3. The same kind of spiral pattern of cracks can also happen on a stretched canvas if, at one time, the canvas has suffered a shocking impact.

CROPPING

What does cropping mean as in: "Cropping the picture would make it better"?

Crop, or cropping, means to cut down, and the art world chooses this word to describe cutting down a canvas to improve the composition. Cropping a painting can make a world of difference since placement and size of the subject in relation to the size of the canvas is a major part of the composition's success. Cropping is a bother, especially with a stretched canvas. Here, I would like to urge you to never cut off or trim the excess canvas to a point that it's even with the stretchers. You may just need that excess canvas to restretch your canvas sometime in the future.

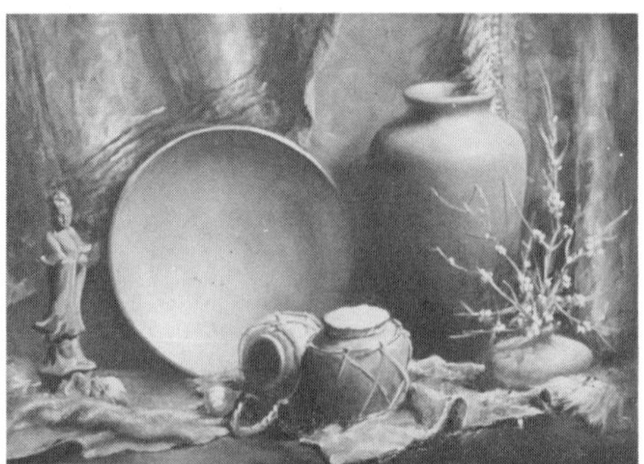

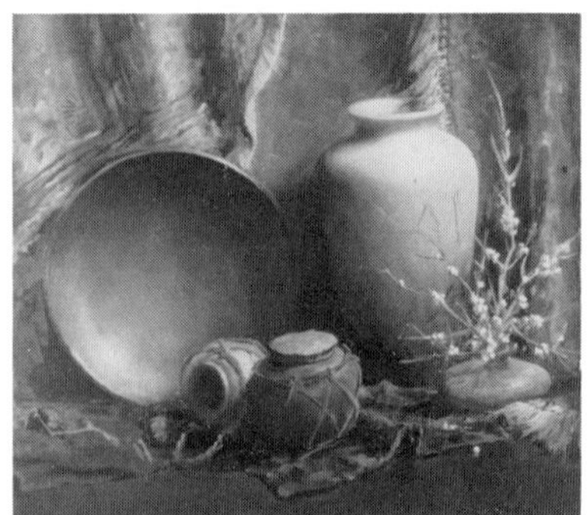

Compare the two. Notice how cropping has improved the composition.

CROSSHATCHING (see Blending)

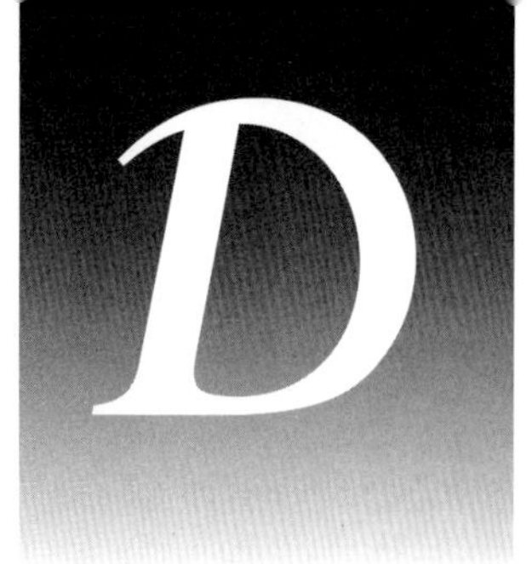

DAMAR VARNISH (see Varnish)

DARKENING (see Yellowing)

DESIGN

Is there a difference between design and composition or are they one and the same?

They are not, exactly, the same but are closely related. To design is to conceive or invent, and in painting the results are patterns. An artist has options to design the passages and forms in his painting.

Composition is a putting together of all the elements of the picture to form a whole. So composition refers to the entire design of the forms and patterns.

An overall good composition can have some unfortunate designs, for instance — in a portrait, the position and placement of the figure can be well composed, but the design of the folds of the model's sleeve could be confusing or too busy.

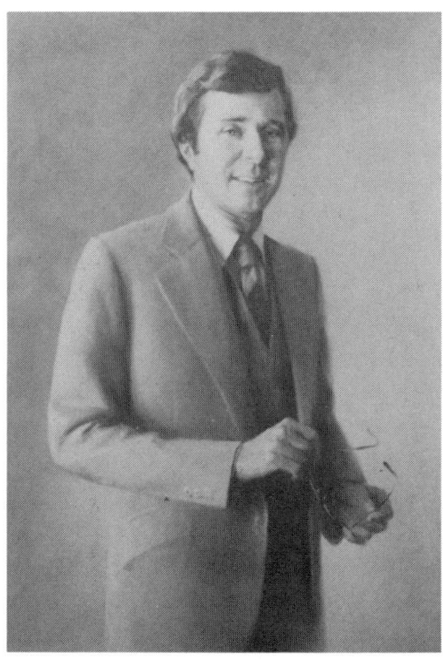

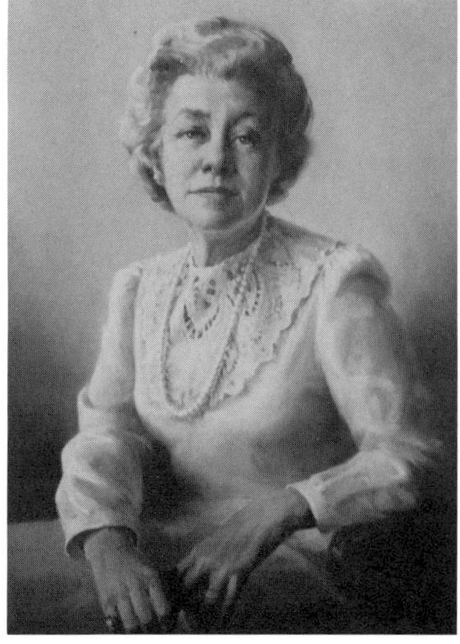

The overall placement of the figure on the canvas and the lighting constitute the composition. The folds of the sleeves and the placement of the hands were designed for the sake of the composition.

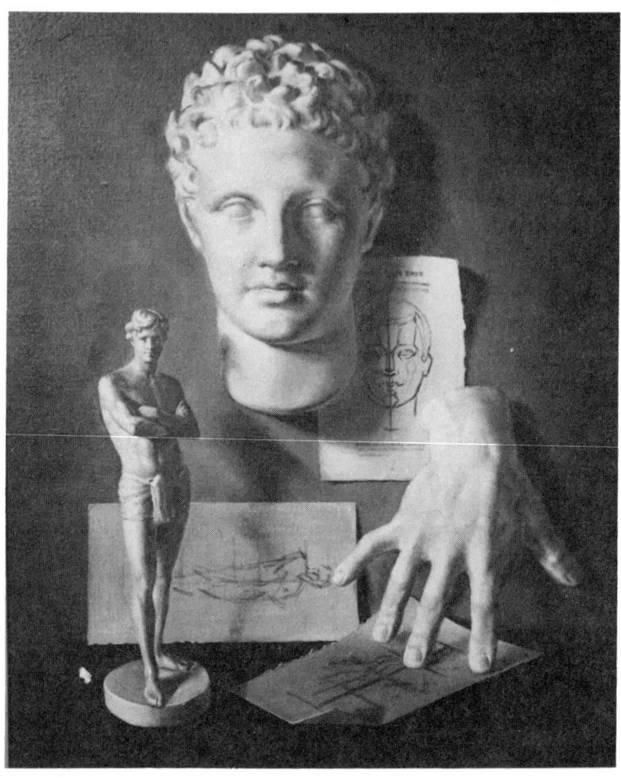

The contrast of light and dark in these paintings makes the subjects look three dimensional on the two-dimensional surfaces upon which they're painted. This dimensional quality makes them look real.

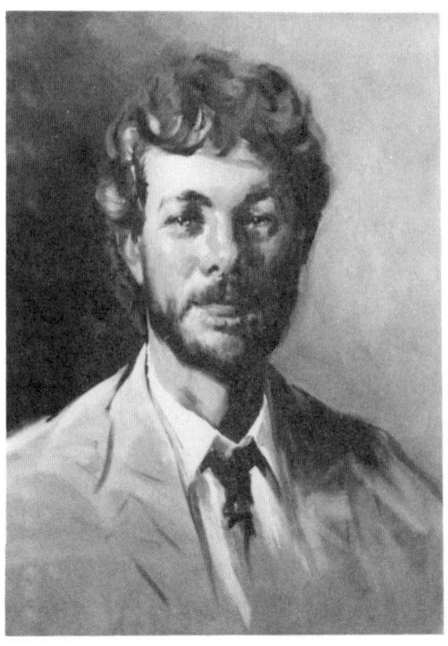

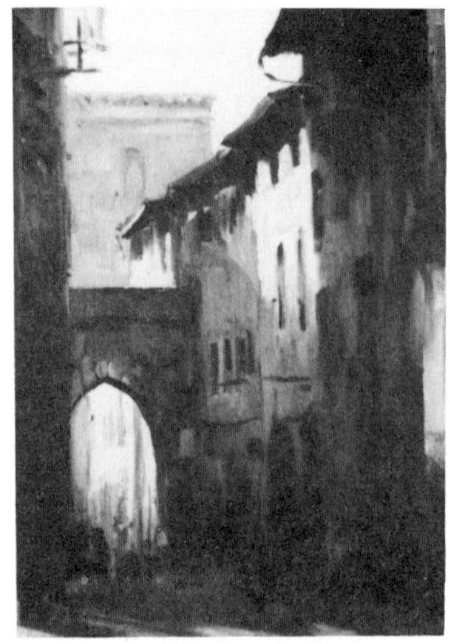

DIMENSION

My pictures look flat with no dimension. What can I do to correct this?

You probably don't realize how important it is to record any three-dimensional image with tone values that are caused by lighting. You must see the effect of the light and the subject instead of the subject itself. The painter's eye is trained to look for the contrasts of tone that will form his subjects on his canvas. It would serve you well to just practice painting something in tones of gray, made by using black and white. All the art schools used to have plaster casts of heads, the features of the face and statues for students to paint. Today, this important study seems to be bypassed by students. Instead, they just start out painting pictures. *Illustrations on page 64. (See Linear Perspective; Tone Value)*

DIRECT PAINTING

Does direct painting mean I can't draw in my subject first on the canvas?

No it doesn't. Direct painting refers to the application of paint, not to the entire procedure. Direct painting is the application of covering strokes of paint that somewhat spontaneously records the artist's observations. Of course, the artist has to have a progression of observation that is practical. Direct painting is done with opaque mixtures. It can also be used to further develop a painting that has been started with an underpainting and glazes, and, very common and effective, in a wet glaze. Beautiful direct passages are easily noticed in Rembrandt's paintings. *(See Alla Prima)*

DOUBLE-PRIMED CANVAS (see Canvas)

> A PORTRAIT IS A PAINTING WITH SOMETHING
> A LITTLE WRONG WITH THE MOUTH.
> — JOHN SINGER SARGENT (1856–1925)

DRAGGING

I've seen paint that looks like it's just skimmed over the surface. How is this done?

This effect is achieved by dragging paint over a dry or semi-dry area. Dragging color is a form of scumbling in that it's usually an opaque color and it should only influence an area but not cover it.

Dragging is an effective technique to use to paint the shimmer of light on water, fog or mist over mountains, sunlight flashing on a meadow, the dust on a table, the light hitting rough textures. You do this with opaque paint (always with white in the mixture) on a somewhat dry, large brush. Hold the brush in a position almost parallel to the canvas. With a light pressure on the brush, the tooth of the canvas will pull the paint off the brush, giving the effect of paint just skimmed over the surface, just as you described it in your question. The basic procedure of starting the values of your subject darker than they really are, will enable you to drag lighter color to record, for example, the shimmer of light. If you start the area with too light a tone, this effective technique can not be used. *(See Scumbling)*

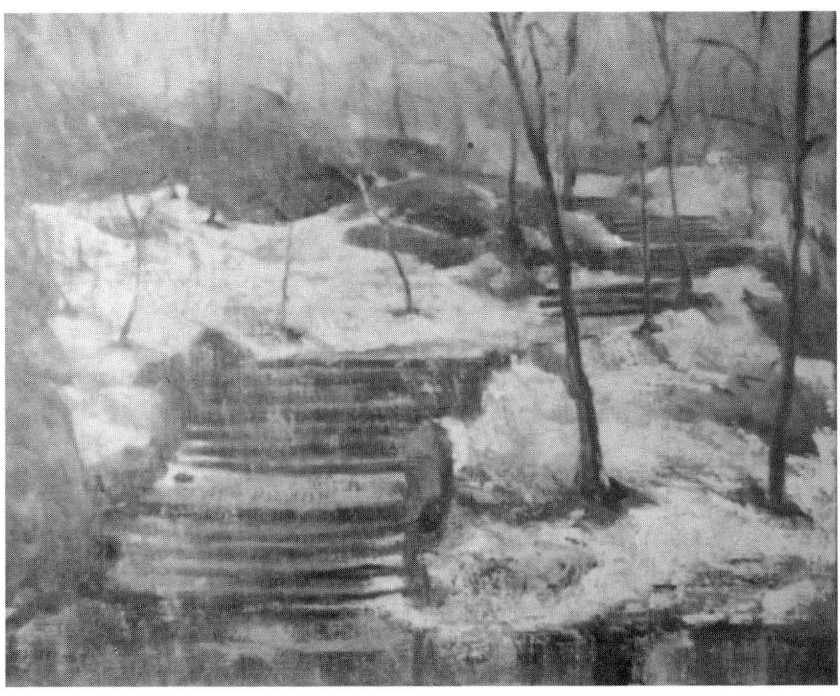

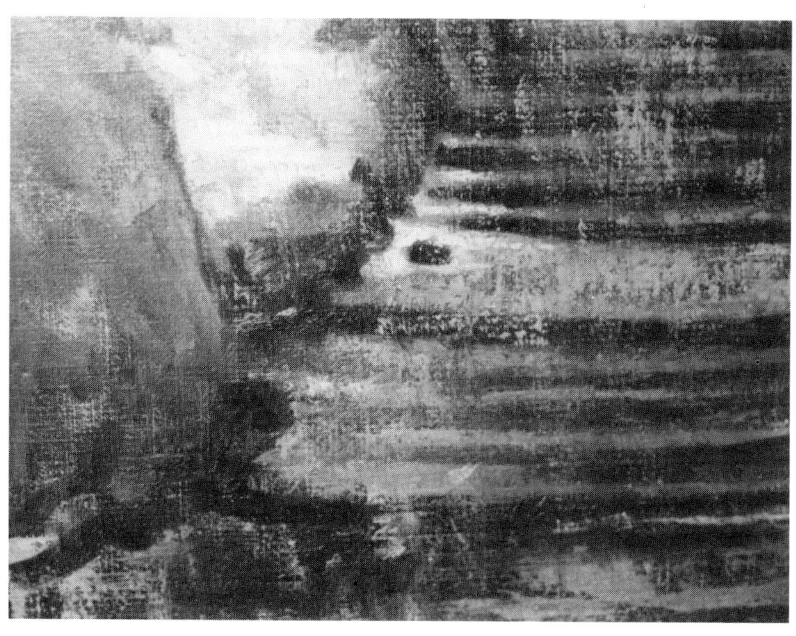

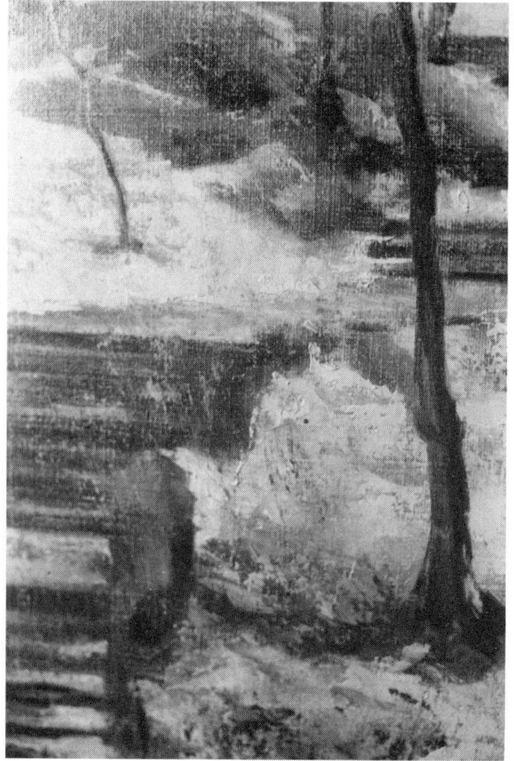

While driving through New York's Central Park, I was moved by seeing these steps in drizzling rain. I accomplished this effect by utilizing the technique of dragging. I always think of a picture's development in stages: Stage 1 — The scene; Stage 2 — The dragging of a light gray over the already dry first layer.

DRAWING

Do I have to know how to draw in order to paint?

If you understand that drawing is directed by your appreciation of proportion, perspective and anatomy, you will be well equipped to draw with paint. Making an accurate line, which drawing suggests, is not a part of the painting process. A shape in painting results from two contrasting tones meeting, thus making an edge rather than a line. So the painter has to contrive a way to make well-formed edges by bumping two tones together. This is very unlike drawing a line with a pencil.

Your preconceived idea, or memory, of what you are looking at, is the enemy that robs you of getting an accurate shape of the subject you're looking at. *(See Proportion; Perspective; Anatomy)*

DRAWING INSTRUMENTS

As a painter, am I permitted to use a ruler, compass or other technical devices as drawing instruments?

Of course. These are instruments that are designed to help you to make certain marks and shapes. The originality is in what you want to paint and how you want to interpret it. Any means to create your point of view can be used. Using these tools does impose quite an obligation to get everything as correct as a ruler makes a straight line or a compass makes a circle.

I have used measuring devices such as calipers and rulers but I have been told that it is not "allowed" in painting. Why have I been told this? Does it have any validity?

Many people who have come to study with me have mentioned this restriction. My answer: In painting, the end justifies the means. Any way you can find to resourcefully accomplish your idea for a painting is a valid procedure. I feel that the use of a caliper should be limited to checking to see if your freehand drawing is correct. It's better than measuring everything at first before you begin the drawing. The reason for this is that the absolute accuracy that's imposed by using mechanical measuring imposes an exactness that you must impart to the entire picture. Your freehand style makes your mistakes so homogeneous that the mistakes become hard to find. Once you mechanically make one object accurate, you have to follow through the accuracy with all the other elements of the painting. I'm a great believer in: "If you make everything all wrong it then becomes all right." I agree with the Swiss painter, Arnold

Bocklin, (1827 – 1901), who said: "A picture should have the effect of genial improvisation."

DRIERS

Do you ever add driers to your paints?

No, I am strongly against their use in oil painting. Most experts agree that oil paint is best used when it's rather unadulterated except for some discreet thinning with turpentine. Driers (called siccatives) make the painting surface brittle, which invites cracking. I prefer to use oil colors as pure as possible, using the faster drying colors in the initial layer and gradually employing the slower drying colors in the progression of the picture's development. *(See Siccatives)*

DRYING OILS

What are drying oils?

Drying oils are oils that manufacturers use to mix with pigments to make oil paints. Linseed oil is the best drying oil; others that are used are poppy oil and walnut oil. Drying oils do not dry because of evaporation, as water does, but by oxidation or absorption of oxygen from the air.

DULL SPOTS

What causes dull spots in my painting?

The earth colors dry matte or dull compared to the other colors of the artist's palette. Also, colors that have been thinned with turpentine and painted over a paint layer will dry matte or dull. You can avoid this by applying a painting medium to the area that is to be repainted or developed with more paint, or making your retouching applications with a painting medium other than turpentine. Dulled-out areas can be shined with retouch spray, or with a cloth that's been wetted with an oil-varnish medium, provided the surface is dry to the touch.

DUST COVER (see Framing)

DYES

Are the strong colors that stain my brushes dyes?

No. Artists' oil colors are pigments that have been mixed with a medium that is called a binder or vehicle. No colors that are designed for fine arts painting are made with dyes, not even the phthalocyanine colors that are so often accused of being dyes.

Pigments are fine, powder-like colored substances that are held in suspension by the vehicles that they are mixed with: Linseed oil, in the case of oil colors. Dyes, on the other hand, dissolve in their vehicles.

You have most likely heard the word "grind" in relation to the manufacture of oil paints. Grind is used to describe the mixing of the pigment with the vehicle. The process of "grinding" is actually a dispersion of pigment in the vehicle. This assures that each microscopic particle of pigment will be coated by the linseed oil binder.

The discoloration in your brush after using strong colors is really residue of particles of pigment.

In My Opinion:

ON PAINTING STYLE

The way an artist sees a subject determines the appearance of his paintings. Artistic pictures are done with an artist's eye. Learn to see in terms of your paint's capacities, that of

1. *beautiful shapes*
2. *modulated tones*
3. *harmonious colors*
4. *well-defined textures*

RECOGNIZE NATURE'S ORDER

Painters must be students of nature. A painting is an effect on canvas that is a record of the painter's choice of contrasts, of tones, of color, in patterns and shapes, either abstract or representational. Nature is in a beautiful order and we are accustomed to her benefits. So, in this world, the artist should recognize nature's order so his pictorial choices are just as beautifully organized.

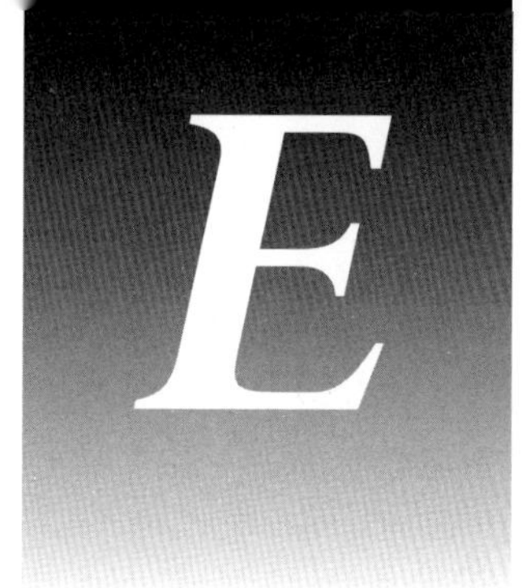

EARTH COLORS

What are the earth colors?

They are pigments that are derived from the earth. Earth colors are permanent and fast drying. Because of this and their low intensity, they are very suitable to use to begin the coloration which then can be brightened and developed completely with subsequent layers.

The most common earth colors are: Yellow Ochre, Raw Sienna, Venetian Red, Raw Umber, Burnt Umber, Burnt Sienna and Gold Ochre.

All the earth colors are warm. They are duller, darker versions of yellow, orange and red. I know it is difficult to realize that Burnt Umber is a yellow when you have a preconceived idea that yellow is only the color of lemons. But, nonetheless, it is true, and knowing that umbers are yellows awakens you to the fact that their complement is violet. Burnt Sienna is an orange and its complement is blue.

Incidentally, the sienna pigment comes from Sienna in Italy and the umber pigment gets its name from the Latin *umbra* (shade or shadow).

EASEL

What do you consider to be the best type of easel?

Obviously, one that is sturdy. Less obvious is an easel that will hold your canvas perpendicular to the floor and even allows you to tip your canvas toward you. This angle reduces the glare that is so disturbingly seen on a canvas that is propped up on a tripod-type easel. Another point of information is that your painting hand should not be higher than your shoulder. This enables you to look slightly down at your work, avoiding seeing a glare, as well as providing a comfortable position for your arm. Your easel should be sturdy enough to handle all sizes of canvas. It should also be heavy enough to withstand the artistic punishment you heap upon it. Even for outdoor painting, you should choose a sturdy easel and not be lured into buying one that is lightweight just for carrying convenience. Your easel is your workhorse, which the early Dutch painters realized: *Ezel* is the Dutch word for donkey.

EASEL PAINTING

I have heard paintings referred to as easel paintings. Aren't all oil paintings done on easels?

Originally, easel painting was used to describe pictures small enough to be done on an easel as opposed to a mural painting. Now, easel painting means a picture that is a self expression in contrast to commercial art, especially illustrations.

EGG TEMPERA

What is egg tempera?

Basically, it is paint that is made by mixing dry pigment with water and then with the yolk of an egg. As you know, when an egg yolk has been exposed to the air, it forms an extremely hard film. This quality makes it ideal as a binder for a paint. The artist paints with many crosshatching strokes which "blend" colors and tones together.

Centuries back in Italy, painting with egg tempera was called "*putrida.*" Considering that there was no means of refrigeration in those days, you can readily understand why these paints that were mixed with egg yolk were thus designated. *(See Painting Media)*

ELLIPSE

When I paint the opening of a jar, for instance, I make my ellipse by drawing a line across and making the top and bottom of that line equally spaced. But it never looks right. What am I doing wrong?

I describe an ellipse to be a shape that is a distortion of a circle as it's seen in perspective.

Many think of an ellipse as an oval. To me, it is quite different in that if divided in half, an oval is the same on both sides; an ellipse, on the other hand, isn't. That is what you are doing wrong.

It's very important to know the structure of an ellipse. It can be easily understood by realizing that a circular object can be put into a square box. Visualize the circle in a box, see the box in perspective and then the elliptical shape will be evident. *(See Linear Perspective)*

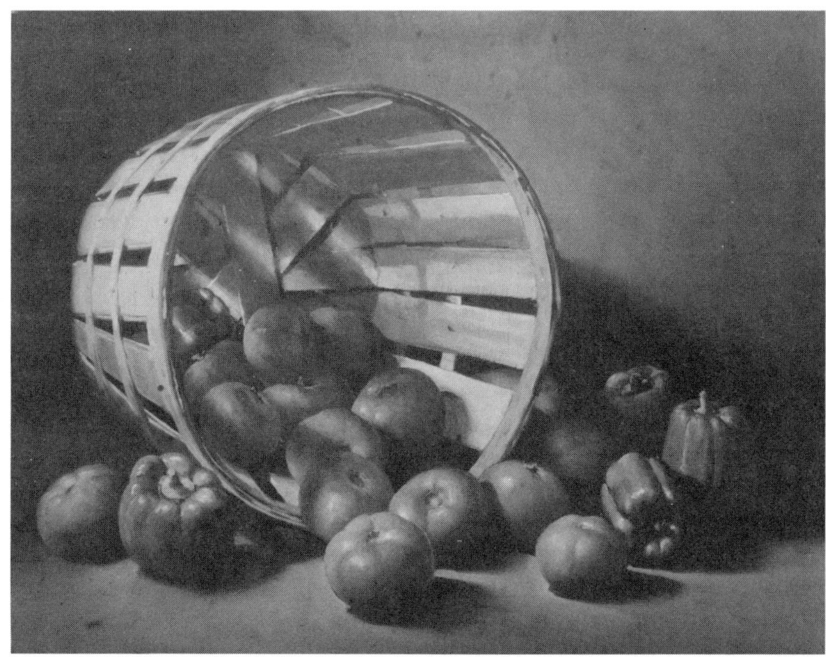

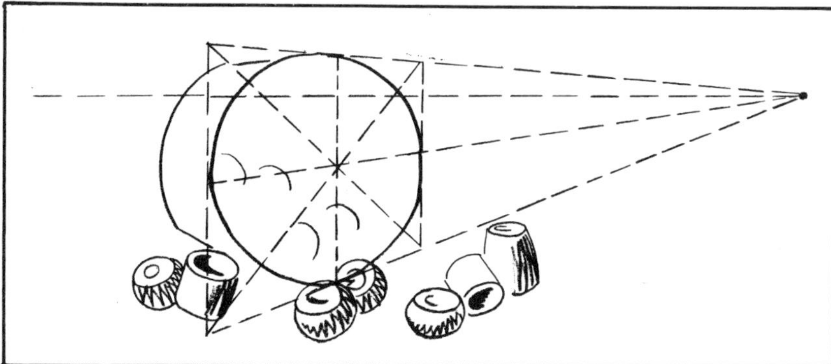

The correct way to see an ellipse is to visualize it as a form in a box that has been drawn in perspective.

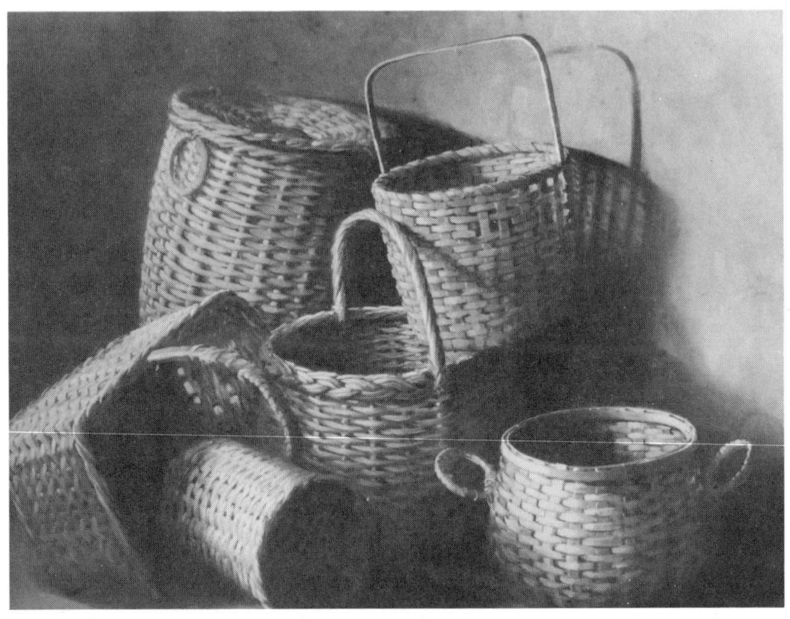

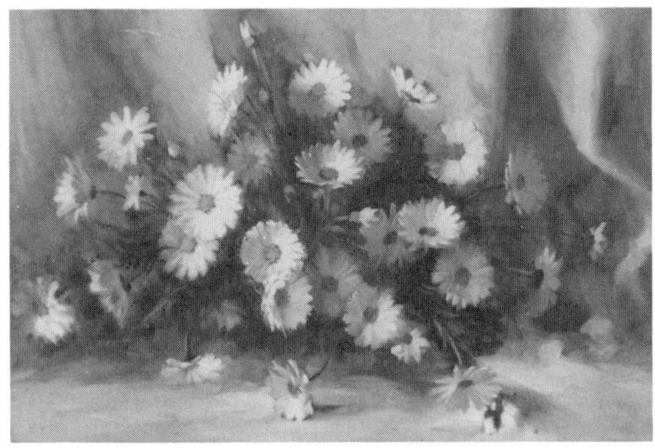

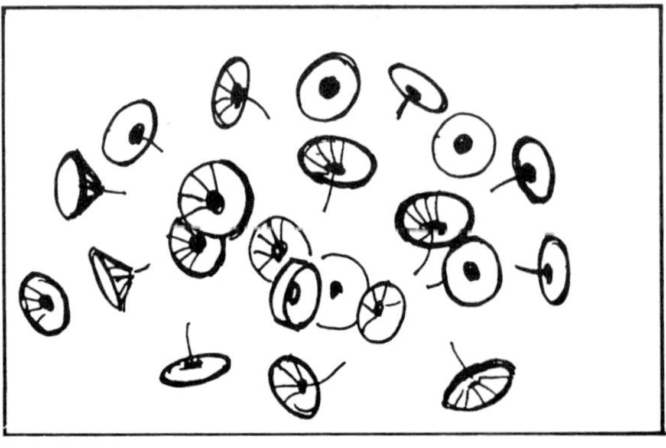

All round objects become elliptical shapes when seen in perspective.

EMERALD GREEN (see Greens)

ENGLISH RED (see Reds)

ENLARGING (see Copying)

EXHIBITING

What is an exhibition picture?

It has become a term that describes a certain type of picture that is appropriate to send to competitive exhibitions. To realize which pictures are suitable it's easier to list the kind of pictures that aren't good choices:

1. A commissioned portrait. Some judges seem to think that commissioned portraits aren't as creative as portraits that are personally initiated, such as self-portraits, or are done for study. A better reason to not exhibit a commissioned portrait is that general public opinion may discolor the sitter's appraisal of it. A commissioned portrait that is painted with as much universal appeal as personal appeal can withstand public exhibition.
2. A picture that emulates someone else's style. Or a copy of someone else's work.

An exhibition picture is one that shows you off as a painter and an originator. It's one that has originality and excellence of craft. Remember, it's not what you paint but how you paint it.

What kind of frame should I use for an exhibition picture?

One that is *plainly* suitable. Do not frame your picture with one that is ornate and that suggests a decor, especially Victorian or Baroque. Also, the frame should be securely attached to the painting with no protruding nails, and it's best if your frame is light in weight. *Illustrations on page 76. (See Framing)*

Can I exhibit classwork?

It depends on how original you feel the picture is. If you think your interpretation of the model or subject is uniquely yours, I would say yes. But if you make a good, hard, cold analysis of your painting and can answer "no" to this question: "Could I have painted this without the teacher's influence?" I would say don't exhibit it.

By the way, many judges can spot a classwork project a mile away. Even if it is a nice, valid picture, it might more often be rejected than accepted. This doesn't apply to nude studies done while sketching with a group or even a character study of a model, because there is so much leeway of interpretation in these circumstances. A classroom still life already has the instructor's influence in that it was he who set up the composition for you.

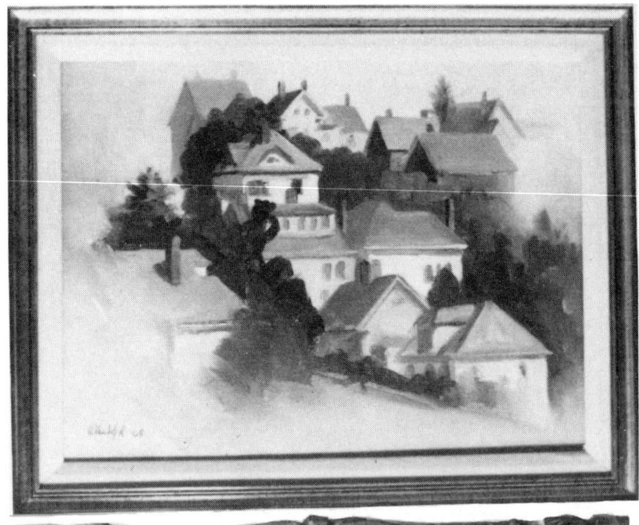

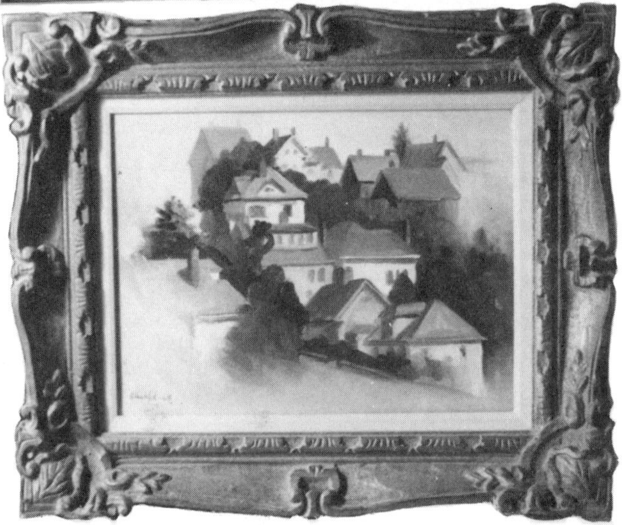

Here is the same painting in two different fames. The plainer frame is more suitable for a group exhibition. The ornate frame, while appropriate in a home decor, would be too distracting in an exhibition among many other paintings.

EYE LEVEL

How do I determine where the eye level is? Why is it important? Is it something that's different from the horizon?

The eye level is the horizon line but it is not where the land part of your picture meets the sky. Trees and mountains can be above the horizon or eye level. Determine the eye level, or horizon, by looking straight ahead not up or down. All the things you see on that line are seen straight on. Everything above or below this line has to be drawn correctly in relation to it to accurately record linear perspective.

A good way to appreciate the influence that perspective has on things above or below the eye level is to fix your eye straight ahead and then look at things that are going to be in your composition with your peripheral vision. Mistakes in perspective happen because a shape is drawn out of context to its situation. So you must always be aware of how the elements you have to draw are in relation to each other and to the eye level or horizon.

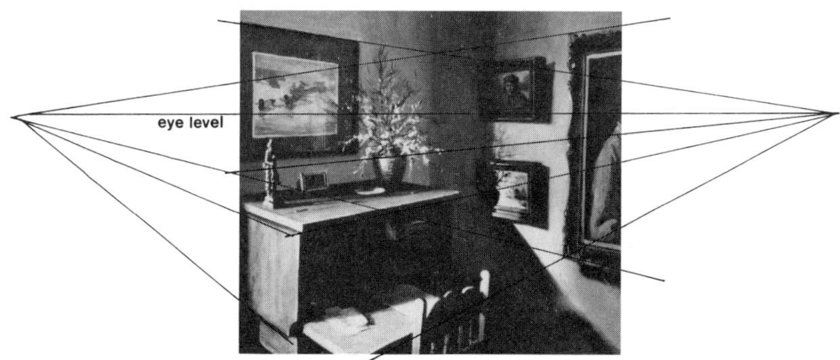

The desk and paintings on the walls are drawn in relation to my eye level.

How do you determine the point of view of your subject?

In a landscape this view is mostly determined by seeing the scene as it is. Your only way to alter it for drama or effect is to squat down to see if it looks better from the so-called worm's eye view of the scene.

In a still life, the degrees of view are more a matter of the artist's choice. I always start by looking at my still life setup from absolute eye level and begin to see how it looks below my eye level. Rarely do I put the composition above my eye level, except when I am painting a *trompe l'oeil*, such as looking up at a guitar hanging on a hook. Your point of view is your point of taste. Test your taste at every level of the picture's development.

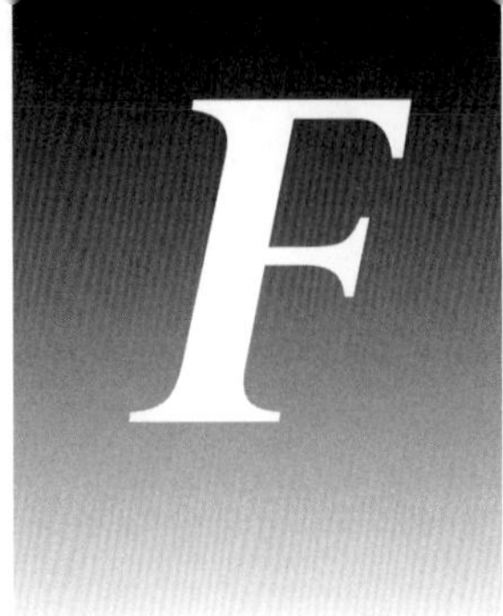

FADE

So many times I've finished paintings satisfied and happy with the way they look, only to be disappointed after they have dried — the colors fade away. The medium I use is:

> ***2 parts odorless thinner***
>
> ***2 parts linseed oil***
>
> ***1 part damar varnish***

No oil colors being made today, by any manufacturer, will fade under normal exhibition conditions. You will find colors that fade in painting materials that are made for commercial art, where permanence is not a factor. Colors that fade are made of what are called "fugitive" pigments as opposed to pigments that are "light fast" and permanent, those that go into oil paints, watercolors, acrylics, pastels, etc. I think what you really mean by the word "fade," are colors that go dead or sink in. That is a different matter. This is a condition that you yourself can correct.

First of all, your medium is not a good one. Use your odorless paint thinner only to clean up. As an ingredient in a medium it tends to break down the damar varnish. Use, instead, rectified turpentine. Another thing wrong with your medium is the proportion; yours is too lean, causing your color to dry matte, creating the condition that you call "fading." Here's a medium mixture that I recommend: One part turpentine, one part linseed oil, one part damar varnish. Of course, when your painting has dried, you should varnish it to show off the colors. For this purpose, I use a mixture of one part damar varnish with a half-part of turpentine. Finally, on this note, the colors in an oil painting have to shine much like a linoleum floor, which we all know looks better after it has been shined with wax.

Another cause of your colors looking dull may be that you may probably be painting in a lighting condition that is not conducive to using color well. Paintings that are done under a lot of light will lack contrast and seem to fade out under less light. What may have seemed like strong contrasts in strong lighting conditions, end up to be diminished under normal lighting conditions. *(See Fugitive Color; Sunken-in Areas)*

Do oil paints fade?

Many times this term is used to describe sunken-in areas on a painting. When this happens, the color is dulled by drying matte, giving it the appearance of faded color. An application of a varnish or a painting medium that will add a shine to the area will rectify that faded look.

As for oil paints fading as a result of exposure to strong light, sunlight, industrial odors, etc., most paints that are made today are extremely reliable. They will not fade nor change color due to the reactions of lighting and substances just mentioned. *(See Dull Spots; Sunken-in Areas)*

FAN BLENDER (see Brushes)

FAST DRYING

Why should I know about fast and slow drying colors?

The significance in knowing the colors that dry faster than others will guide you to use the faster-drying colors in the initial stages of a painting's development. Luckily, the fast-drying ones are all the duller ones. This fits in so nicely with the progression that it is easier to add brighter accents to duller areas. Of course, when fast-drying colors are mixed with white (slow drying) they then can be used in overpainting since they, too, become slower drying.

FAT COLOR

What is fat color?

Fat color is slow drying color. These can be colors with a lot of white, the cadmium colors or Alizarin Crimson. The word fat is usually used in the term "fat over lean" which means that slower drying (fat) colors should be painted over faster drying (lean) colors. *It's never the other way around.*

IMMATURE ARTISTS IMITATE. MATURE ARTISTS STEAL.
— LIONEL TRILLING (1905–1975)

FAT OVER LEAN

What does fat over lean mean?

Fat over lean refers to the correct application of one layer of oil paint over another. The fat, in this sense, means a slow-drying layer; lean means a fast-drying application. The development of an oil painting begins at the canvas's surface. The progression of layers of paint must be that of the fastest drying one first and each subsequent layer less and less fast-drying. If this progression is not respected, cracking will result. It's easy to understand that if the artist incorrectly paints a fast-drying layer over a slow-drying one, when the slow drying layer finally dries it has to crack the layer that rests upon it.

To achieve this proper progression, you must know which colors are fast drying ones and which ones aren't. You also must realize that the addition of turpentine will accelerate the drying rate of colors.

In the traditional oil painting technique, there is a built-in safe progression of applying colors:

1. Start with dull, medium-toned colors.
2. Finish with the lighter, brighter ones.

As it turns out, the dull colors are fast drying ones and the bright colors are slow dryers. Furthermore, since white is very slow drying, greatly lightened colors (with white in them) are classically the last to be applied and, fortunately, becomes the slowest drying layer in the painting.

FERRULE (see Brushes)

FILBERT (see Brushes)

FIXATIVE ATOMIZER (see Painting Mediums)

FLAG (see Brushes)

FLAKE WHITE (see Whites)

FLATS (see Brushes)

FLESH COLOR (Tubed)

Will tubed flesh color help me with my portrait painting?

Yes, if you use it properly and consider it just a base color. You can add colors into it to match up flesh colors that you see on the model, lighten it with white and darken it with more color and gray. I don't use tubed flesh color because I think I can get more sparkle to my flesh tones by mixing warm colors into white. Also, I feel the color control that it imposes doesn't give me a chance to pinpoint on the personal coloration of each of my models.

FLUORESCENT LIGHT (see Artificial Light)

FOCAL POINT (see Composition)

FORESHORTENING

Why is the foreshortening of a form so difficult to draw?

I think that the preconceived notion of a form robs the eye from seeing a form as it is in its particular situation. A book on a table is foreshortened because it is flopped back into the depth dimension that the flat canvas does not have. Exact measurement of an object's height as you see it in relation to its width will be the most helpful practice in getting objects to look foreshortened on that canvas.

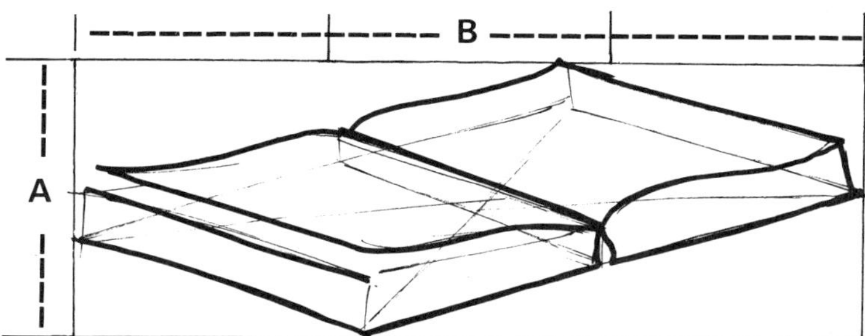

The proportion of an object's height in relation to its width is the clue to putting it in perspective. The illustration shows a book on a table. The entire height (A) of the shape was measured and then compared to the entire length (B) finding the proportion to be one to three. Correct proportioning is the solution to not only a foreshortened effect but the effect that linear perspective has on things as seen from front to back from where your eye is to the extent of your sight. (See Proportion)

FORM

I've heard the words form and shape used to describe some elements in paintings. What are they?

Form and shape are synonymous, although shape seems to suggest the object's periphery or outline. Form defines the object's three-dimensional quality or solidity. *(See Shape)*

FRAMING

How can I choose the right frame for my painting?

This is probably the most asked question at classes and lectures. Ah! "What a difference a frame makes." Put it to music and you'll have a hit.

An unframed picture will always look better than a painting that's been badly framed. How do we suitably frame our pictures? Here are some guidelines:

- Pictures that are warm in coloration should have warm-colored frames. Warm in this case means gold colors, tans or browns.
- Cool pictures, such as snow scenes, seascapes, etc., should be framed with cool-colored frames: silvers or types of gray.
- Neutral-colored pictures can be framed with a combination of cool and warm: silver and gold or grayed gold.

Generally, the frame should also be in keeping with the theme of the picture: Simple subject, simple frame. The exception to the rule, such as a contrasting frame, can often highlight a painting theme.

A reliable rule is: The smaller the picture the bigger the frame. Conversely, the bigger the picture the smaller the frame around it.

I prefer some kind of liner between the painting and the frame to stop the eye from including the frame too quickly. The comment "and the frame is so right" should be second to "what a lovely picture." Keep in mind, then, that your choice of frame should never provoke viewers to say, upon looking at your painting, "Oh, I love the frame."

Don't use highly decorative frames at an exhibition. These types of frames should only be used to fit a particular decor. Many judges, at group shows, have rejected pretty good paintings because the frames were too ornate. After all, you're putting your picture on exhibition not the frame.

Remember, a frame that suits the painting can be hung anywhere. Only when you work on commission should you consider the decor of the room.

Framing well, as in painting well, is much influenced by good taste. Although a personal quality, good taste can be developed by paying special attention to the makeup and characteristic of environments other than your own.

Someone told me that I should put a dust cover on the back of my oil painting. What are your thoughts on this?

You can, but you have to cut some holes in the cover to permit some air to get back there since a painting dries from both sides of the canvas. All paintings on paper, however, absolutely need a dust cover to keep out dirt and, more important, to prevent any oxidation that will do harm to the paper.

FUGITIVE COLOR

What is meant by a fugitive color?

The word fugitive is used to describe colors that are the exact opposite of permanent colors. Fugitive refers to a color's degree of lightfastness. Today, there are no oil colors that are made by any reputable oil paint manufacturer that are considered to be completely fugitive.

Years ago, Emerald Green was notorious in that it would turn darker, even black, when exposed to certain atmospheric conditions. But it has been replaced by a number of reliable colors: Viridian, Permanent Bright Green, to name a few.

Colors that are extremely permanent are:

- The earth colors
- The cadmium colors
- All the blues, greens and violets
- All the Mars colors
- All the whites; all the blacks

Of the popular colors in use today, Alizarian Crimson is moderately permanent. Years ago, before the synthetic Alizarin type of color was used, Alizarian Crimson would turn black when mixed with the zinc colors. There is no danger of that happening now since Alizarin Crimson, mostly used in admixture with more permanent colors, has had its characteristics strengthened.

Van Dyck Brown is not one of the very permanent ones either. However, its hue can easily be duplicated by mixing Burnt Umber and Ivory Black.

In My Opinion:

PLAUSIBILITY RATHER THAN ACTUALITY

I think that plausibility is more an artistic priority than realism. For example, a painting of a face showing every eyelash, every wrinkle, may look realistic, but if the face is larger than nine inches in length, it is not very plausible looking, because faces are rarely larger than nine inches. When plausibility is your painting goal rather than realism, your paint interpretations have a wide scope: Your pictures can be painted with thick or thin paint smoothly or roughly. They can clearly define subjects or just suggest them: They can interpret subjects with bright coloration or in more muted or low-intensity colors. You will be free to record how things appear to you not enslaved by their actuality.

MAKING A SUBJECT LOOK REAL

A subject needs more than an observation to make it look real on a canvas. It needs your understanding as well. Then its image will be convincing as well as real looking.

THE IMPORTANCE OF CRAFTSMANSHIP

Craftsmanship adds an important degree of excellence to creative expression.

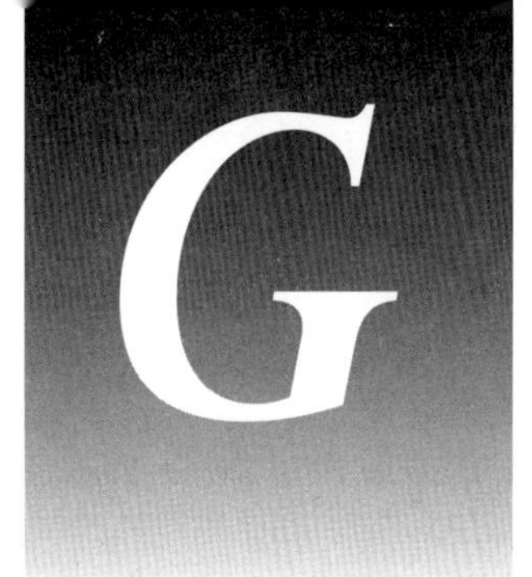

GEL

What is gel and when and where is it supposed to be used?

Gel is a painting medium that is not liquid but rather of the same consistency as the oil paint with which it's mixed. When mixed with color, gel has a tendency to lessen the color's covering power. Gel can be mixed with paint when subtle changes and developments are desired, especially if the application would be better if it weren't thin and runny. I personally don't use gel since my technique is *alla prima* and my style of painting is more loose than tight. I can see its value in the finishing touches if you're seeking a very smooth, realistic effect.

GENRE PAINTING

What is a genre painting?

A genre painting is one that depicts scenes of everyday life. Jan Steen, the Dutch painter of the 17th century, specialized in genre paintings and seemed to always inject a humorous note to the scene. Another genre painter, Chardin, on the other hand, painted scenes that suggested the plain and serene life.

GERANIUM LAKE (see Reds)

GESSO

What is gesso? What kind do you use?

Gesso is a suitable surface or ground for oil painting. Basically, gesso is glue, white and plaster of Paris or gypsum. Gesso should be slightly absorbent to hold the oil paint onto the surface but not absorbent enough to soak up all the oil, thus preventing the paint layer from filming.

I have great faith in acrylic gesso and use it on panels such as wood, Masonite and Upson board. I also use commercially sized canvas, but if I did buy raw linen or cotton, I'd use the acrylic gesso to prepare the raw material for painting. In preparing a gesso panel, I use two coats: The first one is thinned with water; the second coat is thinned with enough water to just facilitate the flow to even out the brushstrokes of my application.

GLARE

How can I stop getting a glare on my canvas as I work?

A glare often results from placing the canvas too high on the easel making you have to look up at it. The canvas should be at the level that your painting hand is, in line with your shoulder.

Also, if the easel is constructed in a way that you can tip it toward you instead of away from you, you will surely eliminate the glare. Of course, you can't do this with a tripod type of easel which means that you will have to lower your canvas even more than at your shoulder height.

I have found it common among students that they don't take the time to adjust the canvas height as they paint. You will be surprised how much this extra care will mean to your painting comfort and to the picture that you produce. Really, you have to give yourself every advantage because even under the most ideal painting conditions, it still isn't easy. *(See Easel)*

How can I stop light glaring on my oil paintings?

This is always a problem and can't be completely rectified. The best way is to hang the picture in such a way that the top is away from the wall so the picture is tipped toward the floor. This is done by putting the screw eyes a bit more than one-third down from the top and making the wire extend almost to the top of the frame.

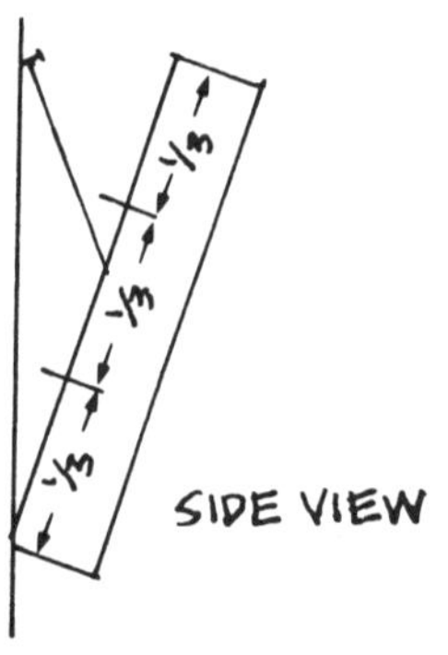

You will also find that hanging a painting in this fashion will prevent dust from collecting on the picture plane.

A painting that is hung on the wall that's opposite a window will reflect its light and glare except, of course, at night.

Luminously painted pictures will show up beautifully on walls where there is a little light. The best way to display paintings is to attach a picture light; its illumination cancels the disturbing influence of the light in the room.

By the way, oil paintings will darken if they're not kept in the light.

GLAZE

What is a glaze?

In oil painting this term means an application of a color that is transparent enough to not obliterate the tone it is applied over. A glaze is always painted over an absolutely dried area and is always a color that has no white added to it since white makes a color opaque. A glaze always darkens an area.

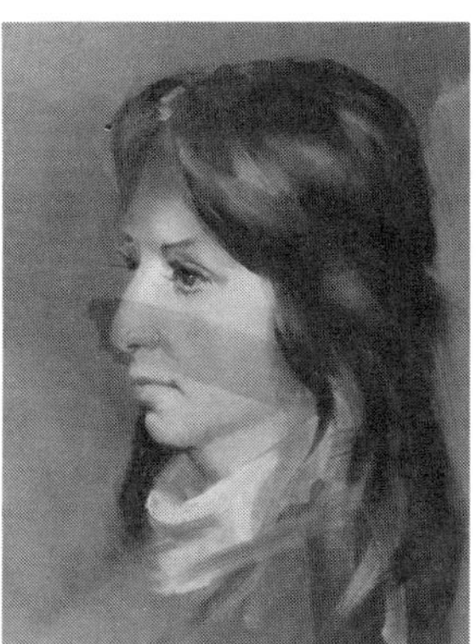

Important facts to know about glazing: 1) Always apply to a dry surface. 2) Glazing always darkens colors, as shown on the illustration where a glaze has been applied to the lower part of the face. 3) The secret of rich, luminous color in oil painting lies in using glazing in each stage of the picture's development. Paint and glaze, paint and glaze.

It's best to glaze with the most transparent colors but you can also use the lesser transparent ones by thinning them with more medium than you have used with the more transparent colors.

A glaze can be a heavy one, which imparts a lot of color, or a thin glaze that just adds a touch of color. The heavier ones have little or no medium; the lighter ones are greatly thinned.

If a color is too bright, use a glaze of the color's complement to tone it down as in a too-blue sky which can then be glazed with a slight amount of Burnt Umber.

A glaze can add color or diminish color, but in both cases a glaze always darkens a color. This is often advantageous to a picture's development, because if it is darkened, more light can be added on top of the glazed area to redefine and bring out the characteristic of the subject's texture.

Many people confuse oil glazes with pottery glazes. In pottery the glazes not only influence the color but also impart texture. Oil glazes only add color to a tone or area.

GLAZING MEDIUM

What medium do you use for glazing?

FOR A FINAL, FAST-DRYING GLAZE: One part stand oil, one part damar varnish, three parts turpentine.

FOR A WORKABLE GLAZE: One part linseed oil, one part damar varnish, one-half part turpentine.

GOLDEN OCHRE (see Earth Colors)

GOUACHE (see Painting Media)

GRADATION OF COLOR (see Backgrounds; Blending)

GRAYED COLOR

What is a grayed color and how do I mix it?

A grayed color is one whose identity can be called muted or diffused. Don't confuse a grayed color with a chromatically reduced or low-intensity color. Although they can be considered the same, it is in usage that there is a distinction.

A grayed color is used to paint shadowed areas on a color and is made by adding that color's complement to it. For instance, red is grayed by mixing a green into it, yellow is grayed with a violet, and blue is grayed with an orange mixed into it. A dull, or low-intensity, color can appear in light or body tones. For instance, Burnt Sienna can be used to record the body tone of a copper pot. This medium tone of a duller type of orange is then grayed by adding blue, its complement, to record the shadow on the copper.

Colors that record the light on subjects (the body tones) can be a vast variety of intensities of colors, from very bright and light to dark and dull. All these colors can then be grayed with their complements to shadow them.

To further explore grayness and intensity of color in recording nature's lighting, you should know that not only shadowed colors are grayed. Colors in glaring illumination are also grayed ones. These lighter, grayed versions of color are painted with less intense versions of the color rather than its complement. It is in this instance that grayness and dullness are the same. *(See Complementary Color)*

GRAY (Tubed)

What is the benefit of having values of gray on my palette?

There are many tubed grays available to the artist; they can be a valuable asset on a palette. Years ago, Grumbacher's Illustrator Grays and Reilly Grays (made for the late Frank Reilly by Grumbacher) were to the best of my knowledge the only pre-mixed grays on the market. The name Illustrator Grays has since been changed to Grumbacher Grays. Today, they are no longer available, having been discontinued along with the rest of the Finest line of oil colors.

To use these premixed grays correctly, you have to appreciate the importance of grayed color. When a color looks too raw or harsh, adding a gray of the same value to the mixture can correct it. Mixing a darker gray into a color can "shadowize" it.

Many fine painters who have been influential teachers have used a gray tonal control on their palettes to help establish the correct tone of color:

Frank Reilly used nine tones of neutral gray.

Frank Dumond used a tonal control from light to dark that was a gray violet.

The Grumbacher Grays were a series of four tones: From #1, very light, to #4, very dark. Even though I've used these grays for years, I've found that I can make students learn and appreciate the importance of grays in color more by having them make tones of gray by mixing black and white.

An ideal tonal range of gray could be made by mixing Cadmium Red Deep with Thalo Green with enough white to see the neutrality of the mixtures (not red nor green), then, with degrees of more white, light tones of this gray can be made. Making this tonal control, and using it on your palette to mix with color, would be a very valuable lesson.

Too many people who paint today do not experiment enough and should do exercises that would make them more adept at painting pictures.

GREEN EARTH (see Greens)

GREENS

There are so many greens. Could you help me narrow them down to a few?

The greens that I use on my palette all the time are:

1. THALO GREEN, because it is the darkest, most brilliant one. All lighter and less intense greens can be produced by admixture with yellows and oranges.

2. THALO YELLOW GREEN, because it is the extreme opposite of Thalo Green in tone and hue. I could mix it by using Cadmium Yellow Light, white and a touch of Thalo Green, but I like the transparency and convenience of having tubed Thalo Yellow Green on my palette.

3. SAP GREEN, because of its natural green look, that of a medium, yellow-grayed green. I could mix this hue, too, but it wouldn't be as beautifully transparent as tubed Sap Green is. I don't like to use Viridian, because it is weak. There are special uses for the other greens:

PERMANENT GREEN LIGHT. Mistakenly thought of as a natural looking green. Its medium tone and bluish hue make it quite impractical in intermixing.

CHROMIUM OXIDE GREEN. A very opaque, natural kind of a green, but because of its opaqueness, it has to be dealt with very carefully in mixture with the more transparent colors of the palette.

GREEN EARTH. Just the opposite of Chromium Oxide Green, although much the same in hue. Its extreme transparency has little tonal or color effect in admixture. It seems to be somewhat useful in portraiture in that a touch of it in flesh mixtures can mute the color without changing the color's tone.

To sum up, of all the greens that I use, I find Thalo Green the most versatile.

GREENS (Use Of)

Why do some landscape artists seem to have muddy dull greens that lack sparkle? How can you make a landscape come alive in the spring and summer, as opposed to fall greens that are starting to turn?

The tender greens of spring can be recorded by mixing yellowish greens into a good deal of white. Do so by taking white, adding Cadmium Yellow Light and then easing in a green such as Thalo Yellow Green, Sap Green or just a touch of Thalo Green. I stay away from Viridian; it is weak and chromatically reduced. As for the landscape painters you mention, they may prefer to work in a dull, dark key.

GRIDDING (see Copying)

GRINDING PAINT (see Oil Paint)

GRISAILLE

What does the word grisaille mean?

Grisaille is the French word for gray. In painting it is a term that describes the initial stage of a painting's approach, that of rendering the tones of the colors of a composition in tones of gray.

The *grisaille* underpainting is subsequently painted over with glazes, scumbles or direct painting. A *grisaille* is usually tones of gray whereas an underpainting of tone can be a monochrome of any color.

Underpainting is a procedure of division of labor. It relieves the pressure of *alla prima* painting and can be the clue to a successful *alla prima* rendering.

GROUNDS (see Canvas; Gesso)

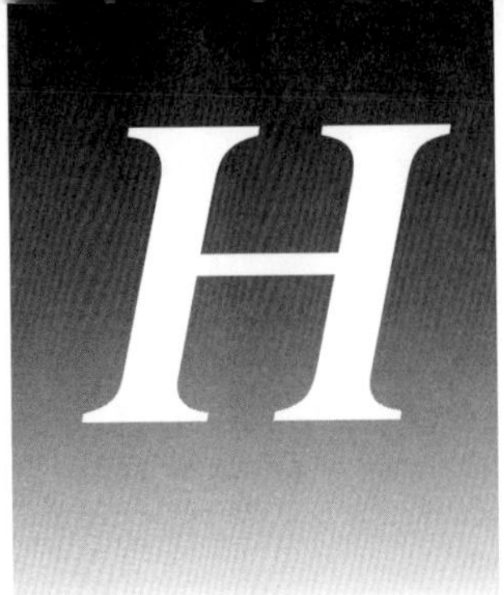

HALFTONE

What is a halftone?

A halftone area is what *I* call the body tone. This is the tone and color of the entire illuminated plane. This area meets the shadowed area, called body shadow, and gets blended into what I call the turning edge. The edge can be in strong contrast or be a larger area of gradation of tone. The body tone has lighter tones within it and a highlight area. These lighter lights relegate body tone to be darker, which is what many artists refer to as halftone. I don't like this term because it suggests darkening, or shading, a color. It is not seen in a shaded area; it is seen in a light area and should be an ungrayed color. *(See Tone Value)*

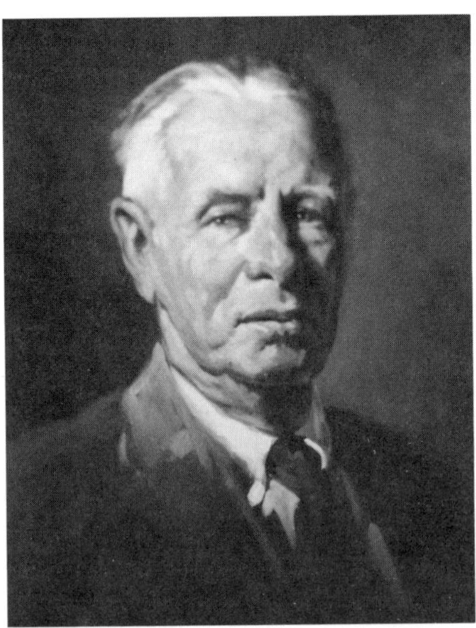

The body tone of the light side of the face has become the half tones because lighter flesh colors have been added to it on the concave and convex planes of the face.

HANSA YELLOW

I've heard the name Hansa Yellow, which I suspect is quite new. Is it safe to use?

Developed in Germany in the 20th century, Hansa Yellow is light fast and permanent. It is more transparent than the relatively opaque Cadmium Yellow.

HARD-EDGE PAINTING

To what style of painting does the term hard-edge refer?

I think this term came as a result of the increased use of acrylic artists' paints. Since these plastic-based colors dry too fast to blend them easily, the hard edges that resulted became characteristic of the acrylic paints, thereby creating a style. Artists have always had to work within the limitations of their media. That's why oil painting is so profound; so many effects can be achieved with it. *(See Outline)*

What are your feelings about hard-edge painting?

Hard-edge is a term that's been in vogue quite recently. It is an immaculately rendered delineation of two contrasting tones. Now we have hard-edge painting as a school or technique. It's interesting that so many people are impressed with a definition of technique. We get, therefore, phrases such as: "it's a palette knife painting" or "it's a hard-edge painting" or "an impressionistic painting." These don't truly describe the artistic merits, only the painter's technique. True, a painting's type of application is one of the contributing factors to its appearance, but this can't overshadow the other elements of composition, color, tone, drawing, originality.

Hard-edge painting is better done with a fast-drying medium, such as acrylic colors, since it is easier to butt a color up against a dry colored area without the two blending or smudging together. Oil paint was actually developed to enable painters to blend and model colors together.

HARRISON RED (see Reds)

HIGH KEY

What is high key painting?

A painting that is done in light, bright colors. A palette that is limited to light bright colors provides the artist with a good control to paint this kind of color interpretation. *(See Intensity; Low Key)*

HIGHLIGHT (see Tone Value)

HIGH SHINE (see Painting Mediums)

HORIZON

What and where is a horizon?

The horizon is synonymous with *eye level*. The horizon refers to the line of your sight that is directly in front of you without looking up or down. It determines what is below your line of vision and what is above it. It is necessary to establish this so you can realize that shapes and sizes of things are altered because of linear perspective. The higher up you are the higher your eye level or horizon will be. You will have more space to look at below your eye level, which will make it necessary to place your horizon near the top of your canvas. The lower you are to the ground level the lower the horizon will be on the canvas. Don't confuse horizon with where land meets sky. *(See Eye Level)*

HUE

What is meant by hue?

Hue is the word that many people use to describe a color. I like to use hue to particularly describe a color's characteristic. I feel that this identification proves to be more helpful in successful color mixing.

A yellow can have a greenish hue or an orange hue.

An orange can tend toward a red hue or toward a yellowish hue.

A red can be a violet red or an orangey red.

A violet can be quite reddish in hue or can be bluish in hue.

A blue can be a blue-green or a blue-violet.

A green can have a strong hue of yellow or be blue in hue.

These tendencies that the six colors can have, play an important role in coming up with a "color match." If you analyze the color you see and determine its hue, you will better know what paints to mix together. Let me cite an example:

You see a red. Look at the color and ask yourself what hue that red is, which will then direct you to add orange if it looks too red red, or a blue if it needs to be a violety red. A more subtle need to recognize the hue of a color is to make the color the right temperature, meaning warm-looking or cool-looking:

> A yellow that has a hue of green is cool.
>
> A yellow that has a hue of orange is warm.
>
> A red is warm with a hue of orange, but cool when its tendency is toward violet.

The awareness of hue and the warmth or coolness of a color is part of controlling color harmony and color unity.

In My Opinion:

ON COMPOSITION

One factor of good composition is how the subject is proportioned in relation to the size of the canvas, not too small, not too big. Just sized the way you artistically want it. This is easily done by realizing initially how important this factor is and establishing it at the onset of the painting process.

ART IS A COLLABORATION BETWEEN GOD AND THE ARTIST, AND THE LESS THE ARTIST DOES THE BETTER.

—ANDRE GIDE (1869–1951)

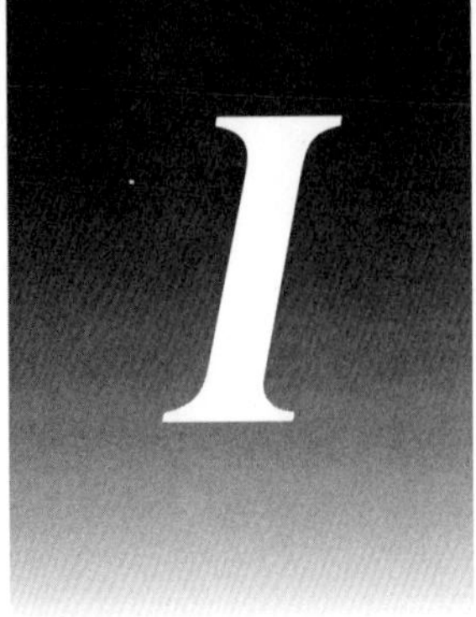

IMPASTO

What is impasto?

Impasto is an Italian word that means paste. In oil painting we use the word *impasto* to refer to obvious thick applications of paint. *Impasto* passages in contrast to thinner applications in the same painting can be the result of necessity and purpose. An entire thickly painted picture is called an *impasto* painting.

The many ways paint can look adds an element to the character of the interpretation. It virtually is part of the artist's vision of his subject. A word of caution: *Impasto* painting is best done on rigid supports: Canvas boards, Masonite panels, etc. A stretched canvas can't really withstand the weight and the lack of flexibility of very heavy applications.

Many people think that a palette knife painting is better just because it's been done with a palette knife.

No manner of application can ever disguise a shallow pictorial concept.

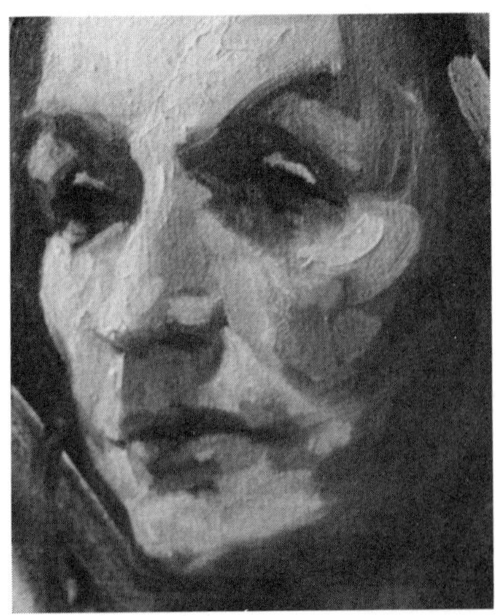

Often, impasto passages throughout a picture become the character of the painting technique, as seen in this portrait sketch. Impasto passages have to be part of the overall painting rhythm, not isolated to one area. An impasto painted sky and smoothly painted terrain is not a good way to use impasto passages.

IMPRESSIONISTS

Why are the paintings of the Impressionists so different and beautiful? What did the painters of this era do with the brush and paint to produce their pictures?

The Impressionists, fortified in the knowledge that color is a result of light, started to apply color differently from their more representational predecessors. The Impressionists painted a variety of colors in close proximity so they all reacted to each other, causing a vibration of color. Furthermore, in their subject matter and interpretation, they rebelled against the classic interpretation that had reached a stage where it was overdone and too stylized, especially in the salons of Paris.

How the painters of this era used their paints and brushes can only be answered by saying that all painters are motivated by taste, ingenuity and skill. These three traits can't be taught.

IMPRIMATURA

What is an imprimatura?

An *imprimatura* is a tonal or color adjustment initially applied to a canvas that the artist believes will benefit his procedure and pictorial effect. This is also known as a "toned" canvas. An *imprimatura* should never be made of slow drying paint. *Imprimaturas* are usually thin washes of color (color mixed with turpentine). Examples of *imprimaturas:*

1. A violet-toned canvas for a snow scene would enable an artist to start his composition by painting the light on the snow first. The violet *imprimatura* would serve to be the contrasting shadows at the initial stage of the picture's development.

2. A dark *imprimatura* for a picture that is to have a dark-toned background.

A practice seldom used now, but widespread in early days, was to apply the *imprimatura* on top of the composition and drawing. This would isolate the sketch from the painting surface as well as serving as the tone of the shadow pattern.

INCANDESCENT LIGHT (see Artificial Light)

INDIAN RED

Can I substitute Indian Red for Venetian Red or English Red?

No, you can't. You will see the difference between these two colors when you mix each of them with amounts of white.

Venetian Red tints out very pink and could be called frail in relation to Indian Red in covering power.

Indian Red tints out quite violetish. I am a great lover of Indian Red.

- I mix it with Alizarin Crimson to make a dark, strong covering red.
- I mix it with Ivory Black to make a very dark, warm color, suitable to backgrounds.
- I mix it into values of gray for cool red-violet reflections into shadows on flesh.

Indian Red is a workhorse on my palette; a little of it goes a long way. *(See Reds)*

INSPIRATION

How do you get inspiration for your paintings?

The answer to this question could easily be a whole book and yet, the best answer I can give you is that I really don't know. There is no formula for inspiration and it can't be taught. One thing that I think is an important key is that I don't see my subjects as they are but rather in terms of paint and paint's vast possible effects. Incidents in my everyday life sometimes provoke me, sometimes they don't. I don't know why. Possibly I am inspired to paint when my creative energy needs an outlet. Also, "necessity is the mother of invention." And sometimes, it's just challenging to try. *(See Original)*

INTENSITY

What is meant by the intensity of color?

Intensity is the term that's used to describe the characteristic of a color's capacity to be bright or dull or, in other words, the degree of brilliance of a color. This is also called *chroma*. Don't confuse the tone of a color with its intensity. Colors can be dark and brilliant as well as light and brilliant. It seems more obvious that colors can be light or dark. The intensity of colors is harder to identify. Intensity refers to a color's brilliance or lack of it. A yellow can be bright like the color of a lemon. But when yellow is dull it's the color of an oak table. I realize that it's difficult to think of an oak table as yellow when we usually associate the color with lemons or daffodils, but this is certainly true.

All colors (the six of the spectrum) have three characteristics: Hue, tone and intensity. Each of the six colors can vary in intensity, from bright to dull, but with no change in tone. Many students confuse bright with light, a good example being a student painting blonde hair: He is apt to use a bright yellow for the highlight in the hair instead of just lightening the duller yellow hair color. You have to analyze a color before mixing it. Ask yourself: "Is the color light and bright or light and not bright? Is it dark and dull or dark and brilliant in color?"

The bright, warm colors are the cadmium colors; the duller, warm colors are the earth colors: Yellow Ochre, Light Red, Raw Umber, Burnt Umber, Raw Sienna and Burnt Sienna. The brightest blue and green are the Thalos, even though they are the darkest. Lighter, bright blues are made by adding white to Thalo Blue. Since green gets more yellow in hue when it gets lighter and brighter, yellow has to be added to Thalo Green to lighten and brighten it.

Here are some facts about intensity of color:

1. The addition of white can brighten a color's intensity as well as lighten it, but only to a certain degree where the amount of white actually starts to reduce that color's intensity as it lightens it.

2. To brighten a color you must add a brighter version of that color, for example — Burnt Sienna is brightened by adding Cadmium Orange.

3. Don't confuse a low intensity color with a grayed color. A grayed color is one whose identity has been reduced by the addition of a complement. A grayed color is a neutralized one and is used in shadowed areas. A low intensity color is a dull version of a color used to record the body tones of things.

4. Many students think that bright means light as well. Not true. A dark-toned color can be bright or, better, described as having a strong intensity. For example — Thalo Blue, Thalo Green and Alizarin Crimson are all strong in intensity yet dark in tone. Students also only associate bright with light not realizing that dull colors can be light, too. The color of rocks is an example. To help you to further understand intensity, here are descriptions of the intensities of some readily recognizable subjects:

SUNLIT SNOW — Very light but low in intensity.

WHITE SKIN — Light orangey red or orangey yellow of a medium intensity.

MOST FLOWERS — Colors of bright intensity.

MOST WOOD — Medium-toned color of medium intensity.

SUNLIT GREEN GRASS — Light green of bright intensity.

DEAD GRASS — Light yellow of a medium to dull intensity.

Here are some generalities:

1. The brighter the general lighting condition the lighter the tones and the brighter the intensity.
2. When a color is described as "raw," usually its intensity is too bright in relation to its surroundings.
3. A painting's coloration is unified if the intensity of all the colors is geared to each other.
4. Colors described as "rich" are colors that are strong in intensity.
5. The intensity of a color is at its optimum as it is seen in the spectrum.
6. The duller, warm colors, such as the earth colors, can be intensified by adding the lighter, brighter, warm cadmium colors. Conversely, Yellow Ochre, Raw Sienna and Venetian Red can be dulled by adding the duller or lower intensity earth colors, such as the umbers.
7. The intensities of all the blues can be decreased by mixing them into grays made of black and white.
8. The intensities of the greens are increased by making them more yellowish by the addition of bright yellows and white.
9. The intensity of violet is the most difficult to work with. Violet is only intense when it is dark. It gets duller as it gets lighter. On the other hand, yellow is brightest when it is as light as Cadmium Yellow Light and gets duller as it gets darker.
10. Light colors of slight coloration are dull colors mixed with white, such as the color popularly called beige, which is Burnt Umber and white.

IVORY BLACK (see Black)

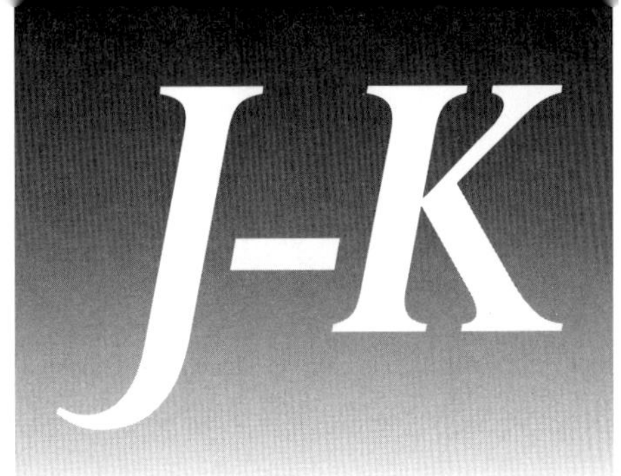

JAPAN DRIER (see Siccatives)

JUTE

What is jute? Is it good for painting?

Jute is a low grade, inexpensive fabric that is brittle and not strong enough to be durable. Jute has an interesting texture, the major reason why anyone would be attracted to it as a painting surface. The irregularities in its weave is much like good, rough linen, but the comparison ends there. Jute is the one material that I feel will not fare well as time goes by. Of course, once mounted to a rigid support, like Masonite, jute will perhaps last longer than if it were just spanned over stretchers.

Because of its extremely rough texture, jute is unsuitable for painting small pictures. A rough surface, in any material, is more suitable to larger paintings, but it is in these larger sizes that jute's brittleness is most dangerous; it can easily rip or be punctured.

If you're interested in trying various textures, jute will surely please you, but don't paint on it with any thoughts toward permanency. *(See Canvas)*

JUXTAPOSITION OF Color (see Broken Color; Complementary Color; Pointillism)

KEROSENE

Do you use kerosene to clean your brushes?

Absolutely not! I believe in staying within the pure confines of turpentine in my studio. Kerosene, though the least expensive of all the solvents, has an offensive odor and leaves an objectionable oily residue. I save up my turpentine that I dirty as I paint. The paint pigment settles to the bottom in about twenty-four hours. I then transfer the relatively clear turpentine to another container leaving the sediment on the bottom. This reclaimed turpentine is better than using kerosene and, in the end, much cheaper.

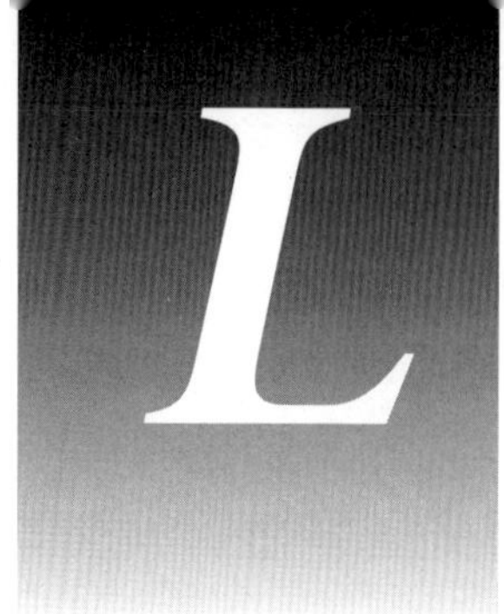

LAMP BLACK (see Black)

LANDSCAPES (see Greens; Pictures)

LEAD POISONING (see Toxic)

LEAN COLOR

What is meant by lean color?

Lean color is color with a minimum amount of oil in it. Color can be made lean by mixing it with turpentine. Lean colors are the faster drying ones. Lean colors, or lean mixtures, should only be used in the initial stages of a painting.

LEMON YELLOW (see Yellows)

LIGHTING (see Artificial Light; Canvas; Easel; North Light; Studio; Tone Value)

LIGHT RED (see Reds)

LINEAR PERSPECTIVE

What is Linear Perspective?

Linear perspective describes how the sizes of things change according to where they are in relation to your nearest point of view and the end of your point of view — *A Vanishing Point*. This illusion becomes easy to record if you realize that the proportion of things in relation to each other is the key to linear perspective.

Always establish the size of the thing nearest to you and then compare the sizes of all other things in the composition that are farther away from it. For instance — a tree in the foreground can be set down in a size that's suitable to the size of the canvas. Then, if there is a barn in the distance, its height should be compared to the size of the tree to make it look like it is farther away.

One way to realize how much the size of things are altered by linear perspective is to place two candles on a table, one on each side of a centerpiece. Then, from the long end of the table compare and measure them and see how much larger the one that is closer to you is in relation to the one that's farther away. The distance between them may be only three feet. Just imagine what a change in size or proportion would be if the candles had been placed thirty feet apart. *(See Vanishing Point)*

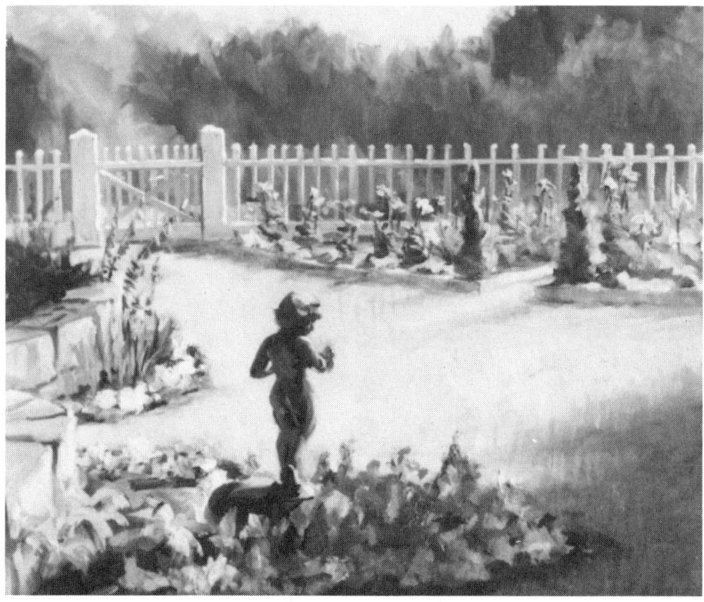

The painting, "Heini's Garden," shows how linear perspective alters the size of things as they are seen from close to far. The statue in the foreground is actually only two feet tall; the distant fence is actually four feet tall. But in the painting the statue is taller because it is in the foreground and the fence is in the distance. When painting this picture, I established the size of the statue on the canvas and then measured the height of the fence to it. Measuring is your greatest friend in getting your linear perspective correct.

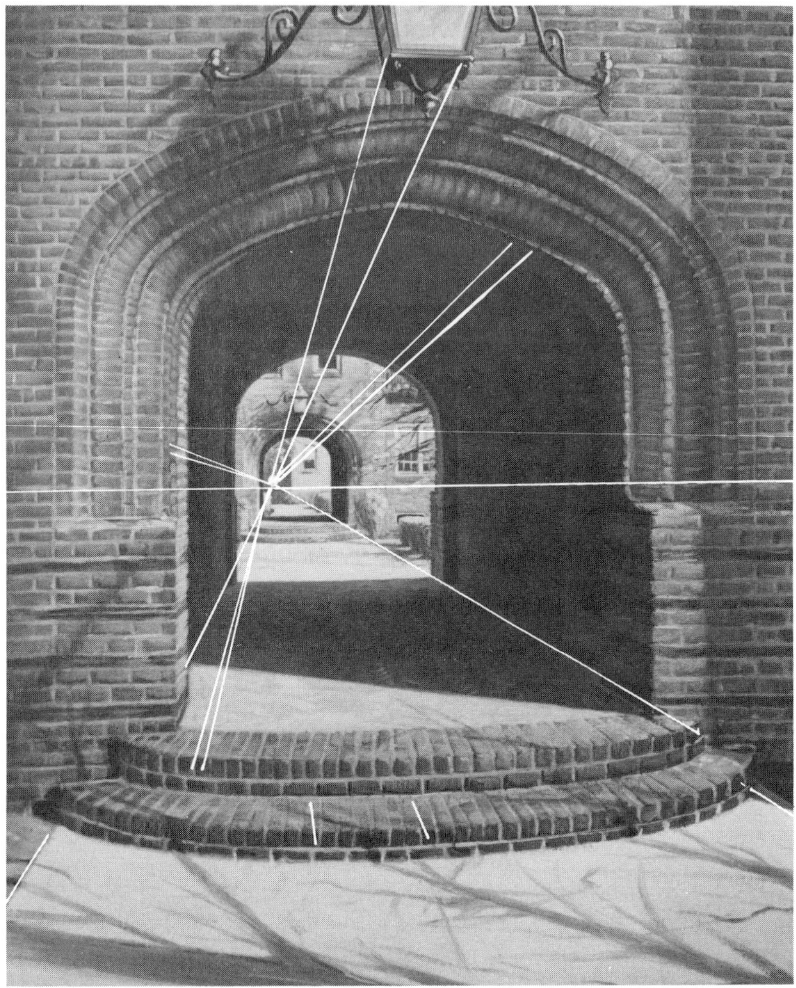

In my painting, "Arches," the open passageways of the foreground and distant buildings are actually the same, but because of perspective, the distant one appears smaller, and was painted as such. The vanishing point of these receding shapes is indicated by the white dot. The drawing of the bricks of the steps and the passageways converge up to that vanishing point. All the lines of the bricks of the arch above my eye level converge down to that vanishing point. All planes that are seen in perspective converge to that vanishing point which was my eye level and my direct point of view.

LINEN CANVAS (see Canvas)

LINSEED OIL (see Binder; Painting Mediums)

LOCAL COLOR

What is local color?

Local color is a slight change in color within a tone value, such as the body tone. The pink of cheeks, the redness of lips or a variety of colors in a fabric are all considered local color. Local color shouldn't alter the tone of the area it is on.

When you see streaks of rust on a metal barn roof, this change of color should conform to the general tonality of the roof, especially if it is in light.

LOOSE PAINTING (see Tight and Loose Painting)

LOW KEY

My paintings have been criticized as being low key. What does this mean?

Low key colors are colors that are not lightened to the optimum brightness. This tonal range can be a picture's purposeful interpretation but, at the same time, it can be detrimental to the painting's pictorial presentation, if it is done because of a fear of color on the artist's part. A low key picture can look like it has already aged and darkened because of age, even if it has been recently painted. Low key colors usually show up in the light passages because the colors have not been lightened enough with white. Of course, color that is lightened too much is accused of being chalky. *(See High Key; Intensity)*

LUMINOSITY (see Complementary Color)

In My Opinion:

EXPRESSING YOURSELF

When faced with a canvas, you don't have to try to express yourself; you will do so automatically. Your attention and efforts have to be focused more on a practical approach than on your emotional reactions.

WHAT YOUR ATTITUDE SHOULD BE

While painting any subject your attitude should be one of making your picture look better, not making the subject look perfect.

ON PAINTERS AND ARTISTS

An art teacher can make a painter out of a student, but he can't make him an artist.

ON ORIGINALITY

Each picture is a new experience. You can't ever do a repeat perfomance because the experience of your previous attempt will influence you. If you try to recreate past success, you are going to be inhibited by it. It is far better to recognize the degree of failure of every picture and not want to make the same mistakes again.

ON BACKGROUNDS

Backgrounds are like extras in a movie; they have no speaking parts.

TALENT

Talent is like a seed, it has to be fertilized with elements that will make it mature. Talent needs the nourishment of common sense, practicality, practice and dedication.

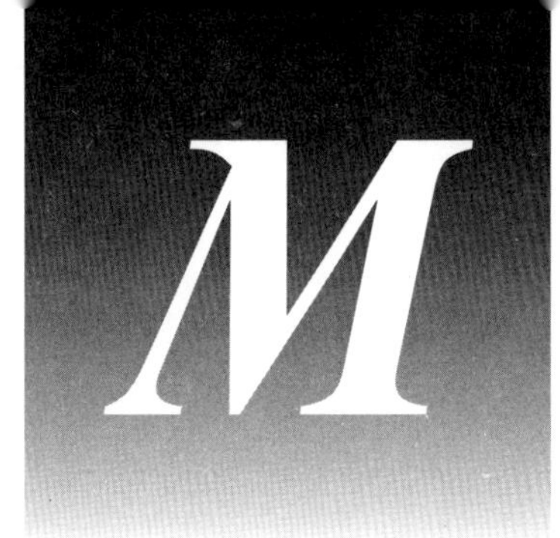

MADDER COLORS

What can you tell me about the madder colors?

The more available madder colors are Rose Madder and Brown Madder. Rose Madder has fallen into disuse since the development of Alizarin Crimson in 1870. Brown Madder is relatively new. Grumbacher's Brown Madder is a red violet, very transparent and is listed as moderately permanent. I consider Brown Madder to be a reliable color that is fun to have on my palette; but it's not essential.

MAGILP

What is magilp?

Magilp is a mixture of mastic varnish and linseed oil. The result is a jellylike, butter consistency that eases the application of paint. However, it is dangerous to use because it has been known to make paint layers darken, crack and blister. *(See Gel; Maroger)*

MAHLSTICK

What is a mahlstick?

A mahlstick is a painter's stick, from the Dutch *maalstok*. A mahlstick is a long rod that an artist uses to support his painting hand. The stick is held in the non-painting hand, rested on the edge of the canvas so the painting hand can rest on it when a steady hand is of the utmost importance.

Contrary to popular belief, a mahlstick does not inhibit loose, free brushwork. In fact, it enables a painter to be accurately loose about his strokes because the mahlstick offers a secure aim. You'll also find it spelled as maulstick. *(Illustration on page 108)*

MANGANESE BLUE (see Blues)

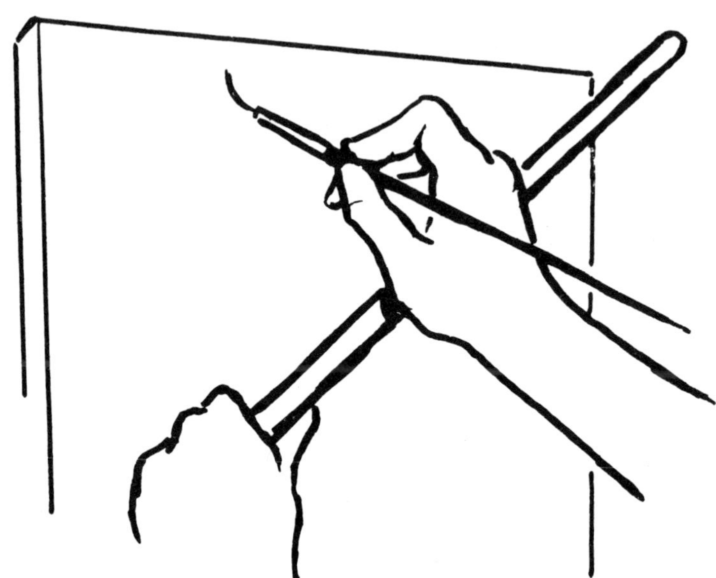

MANGANESE VIOLET (see Violets)

MANUFACTURERS' PAINTS

What is your feeling on intermixing different manufacturers' paints in each medium? Should I use only paints by one manufacturer or can I mix brands?

Although the "purists" say you should stick to one line, I can't see any danger in intermixing paints that are made by reputable manufacturers.

MAROGER MEDIUM

I was told that a lot of great artists got their beautiful effects by using Maroger medium. Is this true?

Maroger medium is a form of magilp except that it is made of black oil and mastic varnish. Named after its inventor, Jacques Maroger, it was developed to duplicate the techniques of the Renaissance, but it never succeeded in doing so. It is a gel-like medium of buttery consistency that is purported to impart an alluring look. It would be far better, however, to use more paint instead of extending paint with this additive, which I consider to be destructive. *(See Magilp)*

I want my colors and my paintings to be rich looking. What would you recommend using for a medium? What do you think of Maroger Medium for this purpose?

Ralph Mayer, in *The Artist's Handbook*, writes: "As frequently mentioned in this book . . . I do not advise the use of materials of this type (Maroger)." I, too, am vehemently opposed to Maroger. It is unreliable; it has a history of darkening with age.

To get to your question — no medium can add richness to color. All a medium can do is thin color to ease an application. While it is true that a colored surface that is shiny shows off the color's true intensity better than a matte finish, as evidenced by the look of a waxed floor in contrast to one unwaxed, richness of color is still very much a matter of the correct juxtaposition of color. This is done by putting warm and cool versions of a color next to each other in very close proximity.

MARS BLACK (see Black; Mars Colors)

MARS COLORS

How do the Mars colors differ from the earth colors when they seem to be similar in hue?

The Mars colors, synthetic iron oxides, are all permanent and all very opaque. Because of this, Mars colors will easily overtake the more transparent colors in admixture and can never be used as a glaze. Their use, then, is more suited to on-the-spot landscape painting because of their strong covering power. In relation to the Mars colors, the earth colors are transparent and are actually more versatile for oil painting techniques. The Mars colors are:

MARS BLACK — a warm black that's faster drying than Ivory Black.

MARS BROWN — can be called an opaque version of Burnt Sienna.

MARS RED — can be anywhere from a dull scarlet to a violet.

MARS VIOLET — a more violet version of Indian Red.

MARS YELLOW — an opaque version of Yellow Ochre.

MASONITE (see Rigid Supports)

MASS TONE (see Tone Value)

MASTIC VARNISH (see Varnish)

MATTE FINISH

I painted a large wall decoration using oil paints and my clients are unhappy with the shiny look. How can I correct that painting and also avoid this shiny look on future assignments?

A matte finish — a non-glossy one — is not characteristic of oil paint. You can knock down some of the shine in the painting by melting beeswax into damar varnish and varnishing the painting with that mixture. However, for any large, decorative paintings that call for an absolute matte surface, use acrylic artists' colors mixed with water or with matte medium.

MEDIA and MEDIUMS

I'm confused by the words media and mediums. Can you clear this up for me?

Pigments mixed with a binder make a painting medium. The pigments used for each painting medium are all the same: Oil paints, watercolors, pastels, acrylics, etc., are all made of the same pigments. Only the binders are different: Linseed oil is used to mix with oil paints, gum arabic is used to mix with water colors, an acrylic resin is used for acrylics, and so on. This medium, then, is a kind of paint that you brush and stroke onto canvas, board and paper. Its plural is *media*.

There is also a painting medium that the artist mixes with his paints to ease the flow of his paint. Its plural is *mediums*. Painting mediums for oil painters are: Turpentine, linseed oil and types of varnishes.

The watercolorist's *only* medium is water.

The acrylic painter has a variety of mediums, much like the oil painter has.

Basically, *mediums* are used to thin paints *(media)*. *(See Painting Media; Painting Mediums)*

MENDING CANVAS (see Canvas)

MINERAL SPIRITS

Can mineral spirits be used instead of turpentine?

In some instances. You can use mineral spirits to clean brushes as you work but it shouldn't be used in mediums, even the simplest formula for a medium of equal parts linseed oil and turpentine, which should be made with the finest rectified turpentine. I don't even use, for my mediums, pure gum turpentine and definitely not steam distilled. I use pure gum turpentine only for mixing with paint for the first application and for cleaning brushes as I work.

Many students get muddy color because they don't clean the brush well enough from mixture to mixture. This is remedied by having a large can (a coffee can is ideal) half-filled with turpentine nearby to vigorously swish the brush in it. You will also find that this will prolong the life of your brush because there is no need to bang the hairs (or bristles) on the bottom of the can to wash the brush, thus preserving those tender edges and points. *(See Turpentine)*.

MIXED MEDIA

Does the term mixed media mean that I can mix two painting media together?

This is a term of the 20th century and refers to using more than one medium to complete the picture-making process. It doesn't mean that one medium is mixed with another. That is a definite "no-no"!

Here are some examples of mixed media:

- A watercolor with pastel passages.
- The final appearance of added substances to acrylic, as often seen in collage.

Conversely, an oil painting that has been rendered on top of a tempera or acrylic underpainting, is not considered to be mixed media. The final result, in this case, is an entire oil painting.

If watercolors are added into tempera, the result is not mixed media either, since the watercolors become part of the tempera appearance.

I wish we didn't have all these labels because people, it seems, become more impressed with the labels than with the work.

Many of John Singer Sargent's watercolors have passages of opaque colors. They are not called mixed media; they're called *Sargents*.

Can I mix acrylics and oils?

This question has come up in almost every painting demonstration I've given and in many of my classes. No, you can't mix the two media because everyone knows that oil and water don't mix. You can, however, paint oils *over* acrylic providing that the acrylic paints are absolutely dry and the layer is not thick or too smooth. This can be done because acrylic is fast drying and lean which makes it suitable as a surface for painting over with slower drying oil paints. It's important to stress that the acrylic layer has to be thinned out greatly with water which, when dried, will still leave a considerable tooth on the canvas. This is the surface that oil paint will adhere to. I consider acrylic paints to be the 20th century's underpainting material, replacing tempera, which long had been an underpainting medium for the painters of the past.

MODELING

What is meant by the statement "The paint is well modeled"?

Actually, the term should be the "form is well modeled" because modeling in painting refers to the tones that seem to record the form in dimension, much like the way clay is worked to actually recreate a form. *(See Blending)*

MONOCHROME

What is a monochrome?

The dictionary definition of monochrome is "*one color.*" In painting, a monochrome is a painting done in *tones* of one color. This is done by mixing quantities of white into a relatively dark color, such as Raw Umber, Burnt Umber or black to vary the tones of that color. Underpaintings are usually monochromes.

A painting that records a subject in natural light cannot be painted monochromatically because a painting that records natural light must be done with the colors of light: Yellow, red and blue. A monochrome, then, can only record the dimensional effect that lighting causes, but doesn't record the luminosity of lighting.

Many students think that a white object, like an egg, can be painted with just black and white. Doing so would only produce a monochrome of an egg. To paint the *lighting* of an egg, the tones of the egg have to be colored, only slightly, of course. But adding just one color, such as yellow to the black and white would merely produce a monochrome of tones of yellow. To record the natural lighting on the egg, you would have to paint it with yellow and then incorporate violet (red and blue mixed). Yellow, red and blue are our color substitutes for the colors of our natural light. Therefore, when the light shines on the egg, the white becomes yellowish and where the white egg is in shadow, a shade of violet is used to gray the yellow.

Working monochromatically (using a dark color with white) is an excellent way to practice painting technique. It absolves you from worrying about color, and makes you concentrate on the all-important factors of drawing, brushwork, composition and, of course, tone. *(See Tone Value; Underpainting)*

What color would be a good one to use for a monochrome for portraiture?

The tonal underpainting for portraits is best done in values of gray. Any gray made of a color and its complement can then be mixed with white for tones of gray. A gray made of Payne's Gray and Burnt Umber, or one made of black and Raw Sienna would also be very suitable. A warm gray is a little easier to deal with than a cool gray, but don't use a dark tone that is anywhere near the color of brown.

These suggested mixtures should be greatly thinned with turpentine to make them fast drying, since all initial layers of oil paint should be fast drying.

The fast drying neutral gray you can make is of Burnt Umber, Thalo Blue and Flake White. *(See Underpainting)*

MUDDY COLOR

What is muddy color? How can I avoid it?

Generally, muddy color can be a result of mixing too many colors together. Proof of this is the muddy mixture you get when, in the process of cleaning your palette, all the colors are mixed together. You will be on your way to avoiding muddy color once you realize that color is relative. Color only looks right when it is in correct relationship to the colors that are nearby. So, a better description can be that color only *looks* muddy. In fact, chances are that it's a good color, but, alas, it's in an unfortunate place. Why is a color called muddy color? Often because it looks like a dark spot. But we know that "dark spots" are perfectly all right in shadowed areas. This leads us to conclude, then, that a muddy color could be a shadowed color where a shadow shouldn't be or couldn't possibly appear (shadowed colors can only be found where planes are not in line with the light). With this understanding in mind, here are ways you can avoid painting muddy areas:

It's essential that you establish what is in light and what is in shade, and mass in these contrasting tones initially. The tone of the light areas should not be massed in the lightest tone you see. Conversely, the dark passages should not be painted in as dark as the darkest you see. This will enable you to add lighter and lighter tones to the light passages and darker and darker tones to the darker passages. Never add dark to the light side or lights to the dark side (except for reflections). This procedure will help you avoid getting muddy colors in light passages and chalky colors in dark passages. Finally, don't overmix color on your palette. Constant grinding will only deaden the color. The quicker you mix colors together, the livelier and cleaner they will look.

In My Opinion:

GRAY AND ITS BEAUTY

Gray is a chameleon color; it will adjust to its surrounding colors and impart a feeling of atmosphere and dimension.

PICTORIAL HARMONY

A painter orchestrates a picture. He has to conduct his paint to present a harmonious effect. He has an advantage the musical conductor does not have: He can correct his sour notes, if he can recognize them, that is.

> FINE ART IS THAT IN WHICH THE HAND, THE HEAD, AND THE HEART OF MAN GO TOGETHER.
>
> — JOHN RUSKIN (1819–1900)

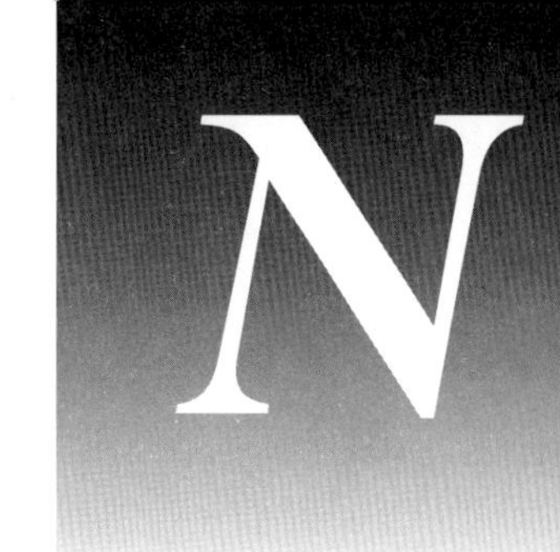

NAPLES YELLOW (see Yellows)

NATURAL LIGHT (see Complementary Color; North Light)

NEUTRAL COLOR (see Gray)

NON-OBJECTIVE

Should I read something into non-objective paintings?

A non-objective picture is a composition that does not suggest any natural form. It does not communicate to the viewer's mind or memory, it only provokes an emotional response.

Don't be narrow-minded by thinking that only realistic renderings are worthy. Exciting abstract patterns can be important parts of realistically interpreted compositions. *(See Abstract)*

NORTH LIGHT

Why do studios have to have north light?

North light is used because in this light there is the least amount of change of the shadow due to the movement of the sun. The beauty of natural light compared to artificial light is that natural light changes according to each day and each season. Sometimes the lighting that happens to be recognized on a particular day is the very spark of an inspiration for a painting. The painter really must learn more about how to see than how to paint. Seeing the lovely effects of light is the very essence of our sense of sight. Artificial lighting can never replace natural light. *(See Artificial Light)*

NFS

What are the occasions when you use NFS in exhibiting in competitions or group shows?

NFS, for those who don't know, means "not for sale." Each painter seems to have his own reasons for affixing these initials to his painting. The obvious one is that the picture doesn't belong to him, having been borrowed by the artist from the owner. To explain further, many artists are quite fond of paintings they have sold and prefer them to new works for exhibitions.

The second reason for using "NFS" is simply that the artist just doesn't want to sell his picture at that particular time. He is anxious to show it with thoughts of winning a prize that might add to the picture's pedigree, so to speak, thereby increasing its value when finally put up for sale.

"NFS" on a painting in a show seems to create a mystique about the picture and succeeds in causing a demand because something on the market that's not for sale very often provokes many people to want to have it.

Many small shows around the country rely on sales of paintings to help maintain their existence as a service to artists and the community at large. As a result, artists who exhibit in these shows should, whenever possible, put a price on their paintings which will hang on space that is costing the sponsoring group money to provide for them.

In My Opinion:

ON THE FINISHED PICTURE

To me, the finished picture is the residue of my creative experiment. Some residues are worthy of a frame.

PRODUCING AN OUTSTANDING PAINTING

Painting is not a difficult process. Making it produce an outstanding picture is just this side of impossible.

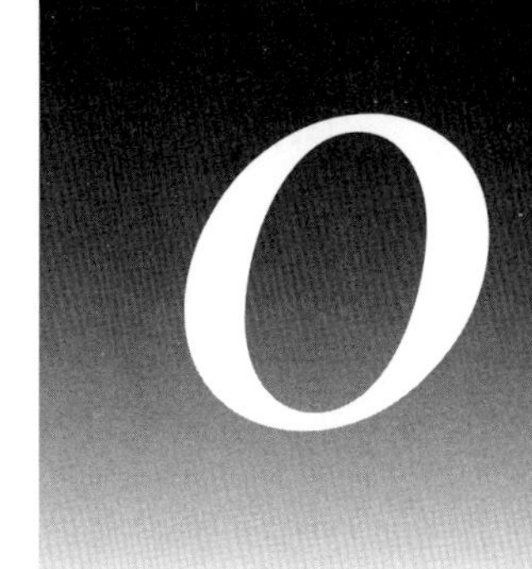

OBJECTIVE

I heard someone comment, "I don't like any objective paintings." What kind of work did he mean?

Objective painting refers to any type of pictorial expression that describes natural forms, from very realistic to highly interpretive. This is also referred to, in some quarters, as *representational, traditional, realistic*, and, to certain people in the art world, "old hat."

OIL OF CLOVE

I've heard of oil of clove in relation to helping aching teeth. What is its use in painting?

A small amount of oil of clove will retard the drying of oil paint. Some artists put a drop on each color on the palette to stop the paint from filming. A note of caution: This practice of using oil of clove in admixture encourages yellowing of color beyond the natural yellowing of oil paint.

OIL OF TURPENTINE

Is oil of turpentine different from turpentine?

Not really. They are the same. Oil of turpentine is merely an old reference to turpentine.

OIL PAINT

When did they first start using oil paint?

Oil paint, as we know it today, started to be used in the 1400s. The Flemish painter Jan Van Eyck (1385–1441) is popularly credited as the inventor of oil painting. He didn't invent something new; he just altered the formula that was widely used — egg tempera. He found that additions of oil to the egg and pigment mixture retarded the drying. Oil and egg mixed is much like mayonnaise. Eventually, he eliminated the egg yolk from the mixture leaving only oil and pigment. The result: A slow drying, film-forming medium that would insure permanency, and would suit his manner of painting. Oil paint has been a major medium of expression ever since.

The manufacture of oil paint involves mixing oil with pigment in such a way as to guarantee that each microscopic particle of pigment is completely coated with the oil. When pigment and oil are not thoroughly mixed, the result of just mixing and not grinding (or milling), agglomerates are formed. This is not desirable because turpentine will then break down the agglomerates, thus leaving particles of pigments that are uncoated by oil.

Linseed oil will film when exposed to the air, thus holding the pigment in the film. This highly concentrated paste of oil-coated particles is the very composition of oil paint which can stand being dispersed by additions of a thinner: More oil, turpentine, or a painting medium made of oil, turpentine and varnish. *(See Painting Media)*

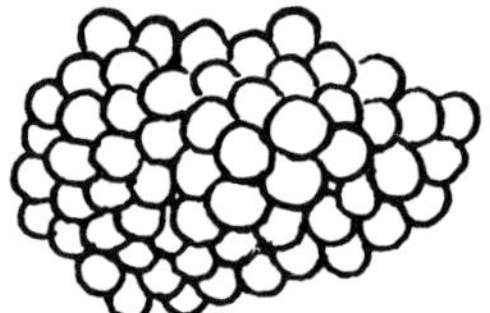

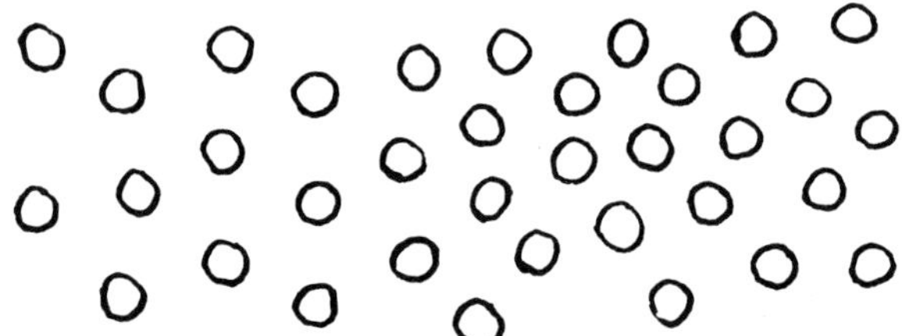

The diagram on top shows the result when pigment and binder (linseed oil) are merely mixed; agglomerates are formed. These are broken down, however, after the pigment has been ground on the color mill which disperses the pigment, guaranteeing that each microscopic particle is completely coated with oil (bottom drawing).

Is oil paint an adhesive as acrylic paints are?

Oil paint does not have any qualities about it that would make it adhere to a surface. You, as a painter, have to use it in a progression to make it have an adhesive quality. The first application of oil paint adheres to the surface because of the interstices of the canvas. The second application will then adhere to the first as long as this application is still wet. If this surface is too dry it should be wetted with a medium that has varnish in it. Another way is to mix the paint with a medium that has varnish in it.

How can I save my oil paint from lesson to lesson?

The best device is a 12″ x 16″ plastic box with an airtight lid that holds a 12″ x 16″ palette. By storing it in the freezer you can give it added protection. If you use another size or shape of palette, you can store it directly in your freezer. I have a box that my palette fits into. When storing my palette in it, I push the lid directly down onto my wet paints, stopping the air from drying them out. When I lift the lid, I scrape the paint that it had picked up and put it back into each color puddle on the palette.

The best way to be practical about your paints is to judge the correct amounts according to the picture that you have in mind. I've seen students squeeze out equal amounts of all the colors instead of estimating what they will use accordingly.

The way to waste the most paint, I've found, is to use a disposable paper, strip palette. It's just too easy to tear off a sheet and throw it away, with all that paint on it. Also, the mixing space can't be cleaned off easily, so puddles of paint are discarded when the filled, mixing area is used up. If you insist on using paper palettes, squeeze out your paints along the sealed edge of the pad and then you can tear away only the mixing area giving you a fresh sheet underneath but leaving your puddles of paint intact on the torn, sealed edge section.

How can I get oil paint out of my clothes?

First, it's necessary to remove oil paint from clothes while the paint is still wet, but this does not mean that you have to do it immediately. More clothes have been ruined by a haphazard, quick cleaning method while the artist is still at the easel. It's better to leave the paint in the garment until you have time to do it right, which can easily be done within eight hours after you've dirtied your clothing.

It's important not to rub the paint into the fabric. To avoid this, put some turpentine or mineral spirits into a soup bowl and dip the paint-soiled area of garment into it. Then, wiggle the material and work it with your hands to agitate it enough to flush the paint out of the fabric rather than rubbing it into the fibers of the material.

With paper towels or turkish toweling blot the turpentine out of the material and repeat the turpentine bath, if necessary. Now, while the garment is still wet with turpentine, pour a liquid detergent, like Wisk, on the spot and wash the garment. If the fabric is not a washable one, then take the garment to the dry cleaners before the turpentine you have used on it has had a chance to dry.

How do you clean an oil painting?

If you value the painting, send it to a restorer (or conservator, as this expert likes to be called today) to clean it because it is a job that requires patience, knowledge and experience. The dirt on an oil painting is often embedded in the varnish so the varnish has to be removed. This can only be done with a solvent that would endanger the painting were it is to be used amateurishly. One solvent could be five parts alcohol, three parts turpentine and one part acetone. Little balls of cotton have to be dipped into the solvent and squeezed out. Then, with little patting strokes, the varnish is carefully removed. It's important while working to stop the solvent action every step of the way. This is done with cotton that's been wetted with turpentine.

You might try a little ammonia in warm water on a painting that has not been thinly painted. Use this the same way with the cotton balls except that you cover a smaller area each time. My advice is not to try any method, except dusting with a feather duster while the painting hangs on the wall. You can help keep the dust off the painting by having the picture tilted toward the floor. Dust will be less apt to settle on the painting when it hangs at this angle.

A contemporary painting doesn't usually get dirty enough in one's lifetime to clean it. Old paintings are more the targets for restoration. For the antique value alone you should only permit a professional to clean and restore it, if necessary.

OPAQUE COLORS

What are the opaque colors? What are the transparent colors?

All manufacturers, whether on their tubes or in their literature, classify their colors as transparent, semi-transparent or opaque. These designations indicate each color's covering power. Actually, when using oil paint, think of colors that are mixed with white as being opaque ones and colors with no white in the admixture as being transparent.

I've listed below some hints to help you use oil paint transparently or opaquely for certain effects:

1. A glaze of color must be transparent, meaning no white.
2. The less transparent colors (semi-transparent) may be used as a glaze, but they need more thinning than the more transparent colors do.

3. The very transparent colors need little thinning for glazes.

4. A scumble must be an opaque mixture; therefore, it needs some white in it.

5. No matter how thickly oil paint is applied, it is not opaque unless it has white; it is merely transparent paint applied *thickly* enough to cover a surface.

6. Oil painting differs from watercolor painting in this major way: Oil painters establish their tonal values by using white paint, which makes the mixture opaque. Watercolorists use no white but rely on the whiteness of the paper as the lightening control of their colors. The same pigments are used to make both oil colors and watercolors. A color such as Indian Red, and even Chromium Oxide Green, which the manufacturers describe as opaque, are colors that appear in all lines of watercolors and are used by the watercolor painter transparently.

7. An important experiment for students is to add a medium (linseed oil) to a color and make a swatch of the mixture. Then, put a little white into that same color and paint a swatch next to the transparent one. Note how the white influences the color's covering power and intensity. By getting to know your materials through exercises like this one, you will put yourself in more control of oil paint and be awakened to its versatile properties. *(See Transparent Color)*

I have just read some literature that was put out by a paint manufacturer. I was particularly interested in their designation of opaque and transparent colors which differs in some respects from the way you have designated these colors in your books. Why does this difference exist?

A manufacturer only defines the property of a color without any reference to usage. This definition surely describes the covering power of each color. However, this property can only be appreciated by you upon your own experimentation.

As an artist and teacher, my definition of what is opaque or transparent is one that aids students to understand a basic use of oil color. The three types of oil applications are:

1. A glaze is transparent, made with transparent or opaque color without the addition of white.

2. A scumble is opaque, made with the addition of white to any color, but applied thinly.

3. *Alla prima* or direct painting is the use of paint, opaque or transparent, that's thick enough to cover.

It is true that there are degrees of transparency. For example, Chromium Oxide Green is not as transparent as Sap Green. In another example, Raw Sienna is more transparent than Yellow Ochre. Generally, however, all oil colors, when they are used without any addition of white, can be considered to be as transparent as watercolors. Even a color such as Cadmium Red, categorized by manufacturers as opaque, will make lovely, clean washes when mixed with water. The same pigments are used to make all media: Watercolor, oils, acrylics, etc. It's easy to see, then, that the same pigment can't be opaque in one medium and transparent in another.

The addition of white into color makes all oil colors opaque. It is a rare instance that any color is used pure (without the addition of white) in direct painting techniques. Of course, in order to use a color as a glaze, it is absolutely obligatory that this color be pure and free of any white.

ORANGES

Since orange colors can be made by mixing red and yellow, why is there a need for a tubed orange on the artist's palette?

I love the oranges I have on my palette and never want to do without them.

I use the Cadmium Oranges (different among various manufacturers because each has its own color control) in flesh mixtures; with greens for more natural looking greens; with grays for greenish warm background colors and also to pep up the intensity of reds that have been lightened with white.

Other oranges that I can't do without are:

RAW SIENNA for golden tones that are so prevalent in nature.

BURNT SIENNA is a color whose characteristics are invaluable and cannot be made by the mixture of other colors. Its lovely transparency is invaluable in glazing and its rich, dark warm quality makes painting dark oranges possible. Do not use Burnt Sienna to darken flesh. It's useful, however, in painting hair, copper, backgrounds and great for the inside of shadows.

ORIGINAL

How can I be original and different when it seems to me that it's all been done before?

Your question has to be answered more psychologically than physiologically. There is no need to try to be different because *different* shouldn't be confused with *original.* We can't really force ourselves to be different and remain sincere; sincerity, then, is your originality.

You shouldn't be concerned with what others are doing. You paint for your own reasons; conforming to others isn't fair to yourself.

Rembrandt and Michelangelo are both in heaven, neither one making light of your endeavors as long as you are sincerely just trying to express yourself, not trying to use your work to impress, compete or profit.

Remember, different is just different but it often isn't art. Oil paint has an individual characteristic, as do other mediums of expression. Writers, as we all know, don't try to change the alphabet to strive to be different; they use the existing language with its rules of grammar to express their points of view. You choose to use oil paint. Your *point of view*, therefore, is the difference. *(See Copy)*

OUTLINE

Making the outline with paint is very difficult for me. How can I do it more easily?

A painter has to master only four types of manipulations:

1. Fill in large or small areas of colored tone in an interesting manner.

2. Turn or alter a colored tone into shadow, either dramatically or subtly.

3. Add more colored tones on top of a painted area.

4. Make two contrasting tones come together to form an edge or periphery.

The last manipulation is what is so often thought of as the drawing, and many painters try to accomplish this by a drawing process rather than a painting process. This so-called outline is really an edge. The most efficient way to be in control of edges is to make them by an overlapping process. The first color should be painted in, overlapping the actual shape so the next tone that will record that shape can be moved into the overlapped paint. This overlapping technique necessitates a decision on your part to examine and decide what to fill in first. Here are some examples:

1. In portraits, the background should be painted to overlap the hair so the hair can then be eased out into the background color.

2. In flower painting, light flowers against a dark background should be painted in first and larger than they really are so the darker background can cut them down to size. Conversely, flowers against a light background demand that the light background be painted in so the darker flowers' silhouettes can be cut into that light background tone. Generally, all edges are formed by a well-thought-out progression of application. This will enable you to control the type of periphery you think is best to record the effect of the edge. The planes of things in their three-dimensional form are either projecting ones or receding ones. In recording hair, some parts of the hairdo are combed forward and some seem to fall back. The edge of the forward part is best recorded with a sharp — or found — outline, whereas the receding parts of the hairdo are best recorded with fuzzy — or lost — outlines.

The combination of found-and-lost edges records dimension far better than an outline can. The found-and-lost edge is best illustrated and explained when analyzing the outline of a portrait, since the outer shape of form is made up of many forms that should look separate from each other. Let's examine the outline of a typical portrait from the top down:

There is hair against the background which goes in back of the face. The neck goes down under the collar and perhaps the collar goes under the jacket or sweater. All these elements of the entire shape are best recorded with found-and-lost edges. The lost edges are where they meet each other and will stop the "pasted-on" look. All edges in painting should be a result of brushwork that is recording a form. For instance, brushwork should form the cheekbone area, including its outline, and then more brushwork should record the jaw and its outline. They should not be done as one, even though these two forms often are seen as an outline. *(See Periphery)*

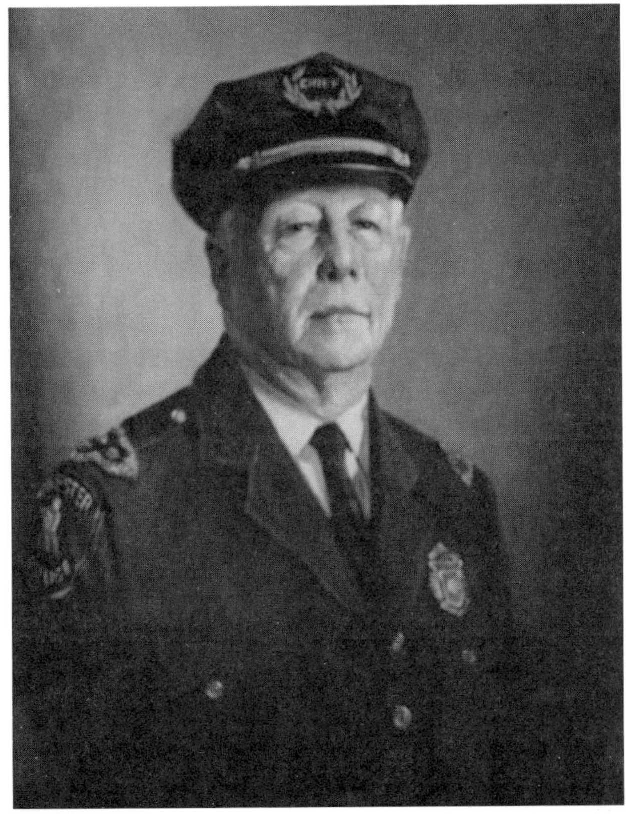

The outline of Chief Coyle's hat is fuzzier as it rounds his head than it is at the front where the emblem is affixed. Where his neck meets the collar there is a slight, lost, fuzzy appearance of the edge compared to the flat of the collar. His right shoulder outline (to our left) is sharper than the receding left one (to our right).

All colors are the friends of their neighbors and the lovers of their opposites.
— Marc Chagall (1895–1985)

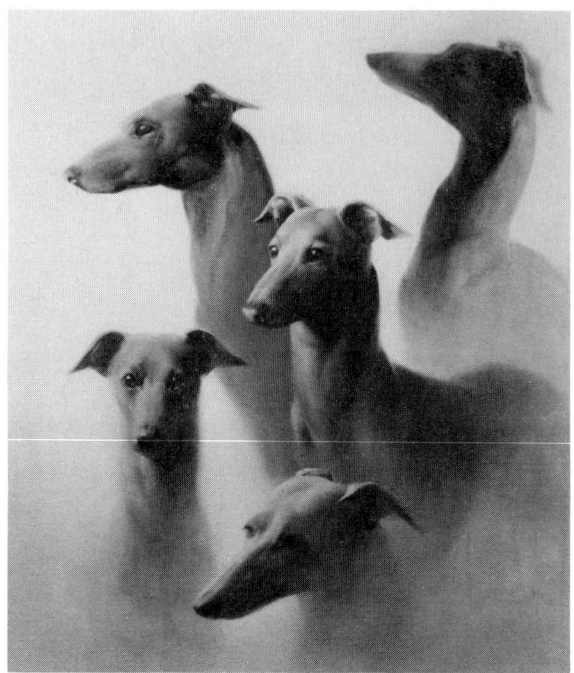

Notice the variety of the sharp and fuzzy handling of the outlines in "The Many Moods of Max." This control of outline was done by painting the background tone into the shape of the dog and then easing the dog's outline out into the background.

OVERPAINTING

What is meant by overpainting?

This is such a general term since oil paintings are most often developed in layers. Overpainting is a term mostly used to describe the character of a layer of paint on another layer of paint and how this layer should be formulated to be a correct application. Correct, in this case, means that the layer will adhere and will not crack. Overpainting can be done if this basic principle is always respected:

Start thin and fast drying. Each subsequent layer must then be slower drying than the one to which it is applied. This is easily done by starting dull and ending bright. Furthermore, correct each stage as you go, respecting the character of each layer. Don't make drastic changes that are out of context from the normal development of a painting done in oil.

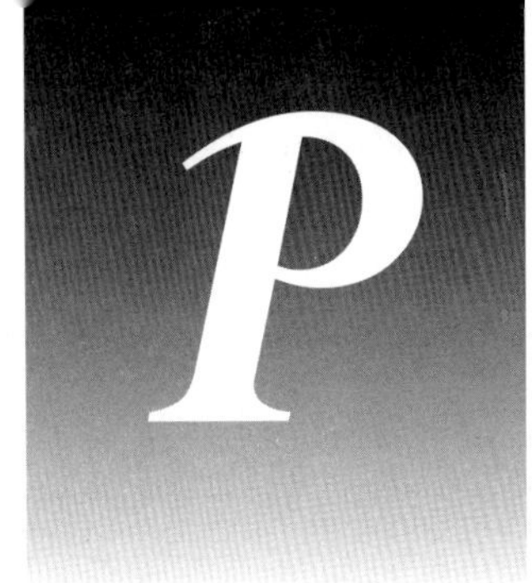

PAINTING (or PALETTE) KNIFE

Do you ever paint with a palette knife?

Yes, at times, especially to apply some final, very light accents. I also use one to scrape off paint passages that have, to my way of thinking, become too thick. Painting to me is getting effects with paint and I use any implement that will enable me to get effects. Don't be inhibited by painting tools. Also, don't put too much importance on them. I've heard of a painting described as done with a palette knife as though this was its artistic justification.

Incidentally, even though many artists use the words palette knife and painting knife interchangeably, there is a difference between the two: A palette knife, either straight blade or trowel-shaped, was designed to scrape paint off a palette; a painting knife is available in many sizes and shapes and is used by a number of artists with which to paint. This is not to say that a palette knife cannot be used as a painting tool; it is, and quite successfully by its practitioners.

PAINTING MEDIA

What are the differences among acrylic colors, casein, egg tempera, pastel, watercolors (or aquarelle) and oil paints?

The names that are used to identify the paints indicate the binders or vehicles that are used with pigment to make a substance that can be applied to a surface. In each case, the pigment is the very same, contrary to belief among beginners who are *sure* that the pigments vary from one medium to the next.

- Acrylic paints are pigment with a plastic-based binder.
- Casein paints are pigment with the curd of soured skim milk as binder.
- Egg tempera is a pigment with egg yolk as binder.
- Watercolors are pigment with gum arabic binder.
- Pastels are pigment with an aqueous binder that, when evaporated, leaves a stick of pure pigment.
- Oil paints are pigment mixed with linseed oil (and other oils) as binder.

All of these binders have a capacity to form a film, except for pastels, of course. Just leave an egg yolk out in the air and it will film to a hard finish, just as curdled milk will.

Watercolor pigment is embedded into the textures of the paper and held there by the gum arabic binder.

Egg tempera and casein should be painted on rigid supports. Oils and acrylics may be painted on stretched canvas.

What medium would you say is most like working with oil paints?

Oddly enough, it's pastel. When I work with that medium, I proceed just as I do with oil colors, the only difference being that instead of mixing all the colors, I use many sticks of color which contain quantities of white and quantities of black to give me a variety of tonal nuances of each color. I facilitate this by breaking my sticks of pastel into widths much like the widths of my brushes. I don't enjoy working in pastel as much as painting with oil colors. I find pastel to be unhandy, compared to the ease of oil paint applications.

PAINTING MEDIUMS

How do you apply an oil painting medium to an area without smudging the paint under the pressure of a brush?

I don't use a brush. I spray the medium on with a fixative atomizer to wet up the areas that I am going to paint on. It is quite a knack to use an atomizer, but once you get in the habit of using one the benefit from its use is worth it.

First, get a little jar, such as one for olives or spices, which is long enough to accommodate the shaft of the atomizer. Poke a hole in the lid with an awl so the shaft will fit inside. Now you can hold the bottle at an angle which seems to make it spray better. Keep a pipe cleaner nearby to run through the shaft after every use to keep the medium from clogging. You can mix your own medium as long as it's not too thick. I'm a great fan of Grumbacher Painting Medium II, which has a good consistency and is an excellent painting medium.

How can I avoid a high shine on my paintings?

You can avoid high shine by not adding large amounts of linseed oil to your mixtures while painting. Start your painting with color that's been thinned with turpentine. Then, subsequent applications should only be mixed with a medium made of turpentine, one-half part linseed oil and one-half part damar varnish. If you don't want a shine, by all means never use copal varnish or mediums that are made with copal. *(See Shiny Objects; Stand Oil)*

PAINTING RAGS

In all your books you insist on using turkish toweling for paint rags? Why? I use facial tissue and paper towels and don't seem to find anything wrong with their use.

A rag is as important a painting tool as a brush is for these reasons:

1. When the brush is used to mix a color on the palette, that brush is not loaded with paint in the particular way that it should be to apply the paint. A rag, then, is used to wipe the brush so it can be reloaded correctly.

2. So often, after a brush applies paint to the canvas, that application has to be softened and blended with the same brush that is not as loaded with paint. A turkish towel's roughness can ease the paint off the brush. The painting rag is the brush's assistant, not just a "cleanup" thing.

3. Often when painting onto paint, the brush picks up the color it's working on. It is easily wiped off with a rough cloth.

4. After a brush is washed with turpentine during a painting session, a turkish towel can absorb the turpentine better than any other kind of material.

I cut my toweling into five or six-inch-square pieces. Using one at a time, I find this practice not only conserves my towel supply, but it is much more efficient than using larger rags as I paint. As soon as you understand how beneficial it is to organize your materials instead of thinking that the quality of your work is solely dependent upon your ability, you will be closer to being a "pro," as they say.

With all of the above in mind, can you honesty say that your facial tissues and paper toweling could ever hold up to the demands made of a painting rag?

PALETTE

What is the best palette to use?

A wooden palette that is easy to hold is the best to use. Holding a palette puts color and color mixing close at hand (no pun intended). It makes mixing, matching and color evaluating easier because you can see your subject, your canvas and your mixing area in close proximity. Good color mixing is a matter of seeing a color and being able to quickly memorize its appearance and then experimenting with your colors to match what you see. This complex action is best done in one line of vision, which can only be accomplished by holding your palette semi-upright in line with your canvas and subject. This is far better than seeing your subject upright, seeing your canvas upright and then trying to mix your color on a palette that's resting on a table that's opposite from these viewpoints.

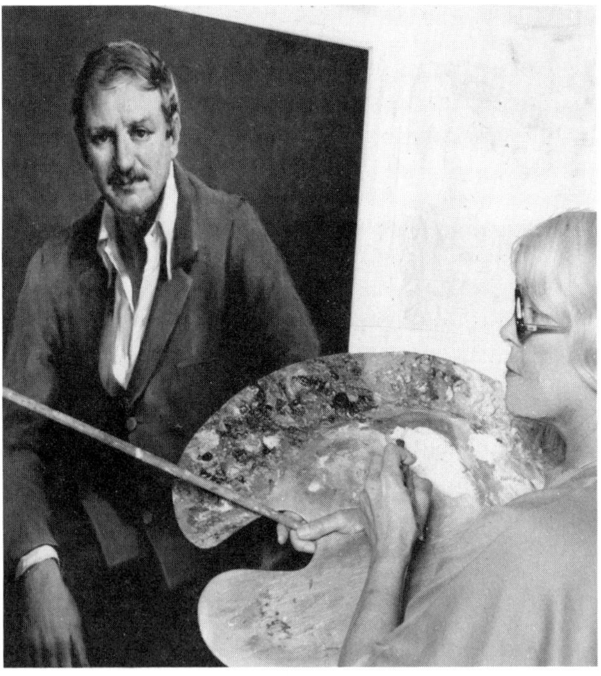

By holding a palette your colors are close at hand. A more important reason for holding a palette is that you see the color upright (or vertical) just as you see your painting and subject. This makes color mixing and matching easier and more accurate. The portrait on my easel is of Herb Rogoff, editor of this book. He is also my husband.

The tone of your palette should be a medium one. Why? Because this neutral tone makes it easier to judge the value of the colors you mix. If you use a white palette (the worst tone to paint on) all your mixtures will look dark in contrast to the white surface. The tendency, then, is to add more white unnecessarily which results in chalky color.

Watercolorists need a white palette because they paint transparently on a white sheet; they use that white to regulate the tones of their colors. Oil painters, on the other hand, regulate their values by adding white to their colors. A medium-toned palette, therefore, makes it possible for them to mix tone values more accurately. A very dark palette is as bad as a white one in that all the mixtures would look too light.

PALETTE OF COLORS

What is the least amount of colors I can have on my palette and still get a full range of colors?

You will need the three primaries — red, yellow, blue — along with white and black. The tones of your color, in that case, will be limited to a tonal range in that you will not be able to record rich, dark color. Correct color is a matter of color relationship to each other, so a limited palette can record subjects correctly within their tonal range. To have a chance to record the complete tonal range of color, the following is a list of the least number of colors with which you can manage:

WHITE
CADMIUM YELLOW LIGHT
GRUMBACHER RED
YELLOW OCHRE
VENETIAN RED
THALO BLUE
THALO GREEN
BURNT UMBER
ALIZARIN CRIMSON
BLACK

What is your palette of colors?

For general painting, I use the following colors, lined up on my palette, in the order they are listed, from right to left because I am lefthanded (righthanders should reverse this order, starting with white at the left):

WHITE
THALO YELLOW GREEN
CADMIUM YELLOW LIGHT
CADMIUM YELLOW MEDIUM
CADMIUM ORANGE
CADMIUM RED LIGHT
GRUMBACHER RED
THALO RED ROSE
YELLOW OCHRE
RAW SIENNA
LIGHT RED
ALIZARIN CRIMSON
THALO BLUE
THALO GREEN
SAP GREEN
MANGANESE VIOLET
BURNT UMBER
BURNT SIENNA
INDIAN RED
IVORY BLACK

I always use a wooden palette of medium tone. I detest paper, peel-off palettes and refuse to permit any of them in my teaching studio. There is absolutely no benefit to using one. It wastes paint, is white so the painter can't judge tone easily and, in the end, a peel-off palette is expensive to use. If, after reading this, you still don't want to use a wooden palette, and I've convinced you not to use a paper palette, a sheet of medium gray paper placed under a pane of glass on your painting table, makes a good mixing space and is easy to clean.

PAYNE'S GRAY

Can I use Payne's Gray to neutralize my colors?

Payne's Gray is not really a neutral gray; it is a grayed blue. It originally was exclusive to watercolor painting. Invented by a man named, of all things, Payne, it is a mixture of Ultramarine Blue, Black and Yellow Ochre. Unlike the neutral oil paint grays that have white in them, Payne's Gray is transparent. I use it sometimes on my palette as a source of dull blue in admixture primarily because my basic source of blue (Thalo Blue) is so intense. It is important to think of Payne's Gray as a *blue* not as a gray.

PEEL-OFF PALETTES (see Palettes; Palette of Colors)

PERIPHERY

In some of your books and articles, you've used the word periphery. I've heard of peripheral vision, meaning how and what one sees out of the corner of one's eyes. How does this relate to painting?

I like to use the word periphery to describe an object's outline, because the so-called outline is actually where we can no longer see the entire form since it is turning away from our point of vision. Realistic pictorial expression deals very much with getting a three-dimensional look. As a result, it is best not to think of an object's outline as a line but the place where you can no longer see the form. *(See Outline)*

PERMALBA

How is Permalba different from other artists' white paint?

Permalba is a brand name for an artist's composite white oil paint. It was introduced in 1920 by F. Weber. Its workable quality is that it is juicier than whites of some other manufacturers. Aside from this characteristic, I have found that Permalba isn't any different from other whites.

PERMANENCE (see Painting Media)

PERSONAL PAINTING PROBLEMS

How can I improve?

It is only natural to be impatient about improving. Even the very experienced painter still has the feeling that his work is not really what he wants it to be. It's this quality that makes all painters continue to paint and continue to get better at it.

It is beneficial to be in a workshop or to attend art classes if only to learn and develop, because you are with others who paint, too. The exchange of ideas and knowledge can be very helpful.

You will get better through practice. Here are some pointers to help you to practice more effectively:

Don't always paint pictures of subjects you are emotionally involved with (family members, pets, family heirlooms, and so on). Instead, set up study projects, such as a group of three apples or a cut-up lemon, and try to paint these subjects. Paint them against a dark tone first, then against a white cloth.

Is there a sure way you've found to overcome the intimidation of a blank canvas?

The blank canvas intimidates many, so be comforted by knowing that you are not alone with your problem. I, though, have never been inhibited at my easel because I don't expect to do any more than the best I can do. My approach to painting is a practical one:

First, I plan my procedure and then I try my best to execute each phase of my plan. I never have in my mind what I am going to get in the end, just the doing. I'm perfectly willing to be surprised and, sometimes, pleased with my result.

Why don't you interpret your initial caution as a benefit rather than something you think you should overcome? After all, the picture in the end is very dependent upon a good start. The start of any picture should be the placement and organization of the composition. Once you have isolated that concern, realize that you deal with just that by making singular decisions and establishing your composition accordingly.

My problem is that I run out of time or I'm too tired at the end of the day to paint. How can I set up some good painting habits to paint on a steady schedule?

Your question indicates that you are free only at the end of the day. The best way to discipline yourself to paint more is to always have your studio set up, ready to use. Try setting up your easel, your subject and your painting equipment on the morning before you attend to your chores or leave the house for the day. You surely will, all day, look forward to getting to your easel without having to think about the bother of setting up when you are physically exhausted. This will make your painting equipment as accessible as the switch on your TV set or any other of your diversions that may keep you from painting. Attending classes is also a source of discipline. After all, getting started is the hardest.

How can I be more involved in painting? I do more wanting than doing.

You will get more involved in painting by attending an art class. Being in the company of others with the same problems as yours, the same frustrations and the same relative degree of quality, will do much to increase your motivation. An important way to help you paint a lot is to set up a little studio at home that you will have ready at all times. Getting started by having to set up and arrange materials each time you want to paint is an effort that often discourages getting started at all.

Do I have to be talented to be a good painter?

According to the dictionary, talent means ability or facility to do something. It seems to be a word mostly used in the field of the arts. In so many other fields of endeavor, ability and facility comes as a result of aptitude, practice, study and a liking for the work. All of these factors make a person productive in his field. These factors, applied to an artistic field of endeavor, earns the label "talent." Someone's talent is always measured by the quality of his product. So why should talent be a prerequisite and an assumption. If a child shows interest in painting and is encouraged, he most likely will emerge as talented, if he applies himself. *(See Talent)*

PERSPECTIVE (see Aerial Perspective; Linear Perspective)

PHOTOGRAPHING PAINTINGS

What is the best way to photograph my paintings?

Photographing paintings well is very difficult. Even experienced photographers find it difficult at first. Light on an actual subject is light in space in contrast to the light on the canvas surface, which always glares at one or another angle, especially straight on. This makes using a flash an absolute "no no." The shiny canvas surface becomes a mirror of the light from the flash.

So now, with flash eliminated, you have to have the painting in adequate available lighting to take a time exposure. Of course, if you need photos of superb quality, let a professional photographer do it. But here is a procedure and instruction for those who have average photographic equipment and just want a record of their work:

1. You can use print or slide film.

2. Get film that is fast speed if you are going to handhold the camera. If you plan to use a tripod, slower film can be used and the resulting photo will have a more refined quality.

3. Set up an easel outdoors on an overcast day. Put the paintings a little lower than eye level so that you will be shooting slightly down at the picture. There will be a slight degree of distortion but not enough to notice except at the edge of the canvas which can be squared off and cropped.

4. Move the easel around until you don't see a glare on the canvas. Remember — glare is your biggest problem.

5. Focus the lens at the distance that makes the painting fill the frame.

6. Now for the second problem: A good photo of the coloration of the painting. If you have a camera whose lens you can adjust in speed and focus, take a variety of combinations. Sophisticated equipment will enable you to photograph your painting indoors, but a fixed focus lens, such as in the automatic cameras is best used in daylight.

PHOTOGRAPHS (Working from)

Do you have any hints on working from photographs? How do you know which details to leave in and which ones should be deleted? Do you think photos lack depth? I like the convenience since I'm a slow painter.

I can't answer what you leave in or leave out. This is a matter of taste which can't be taught. A knowledge of sound painting principles, that of the tone values and the forceful use of them, can help you interpret a rather flat-looking photograph into a dimensional painting. *(See Copying; Original)*

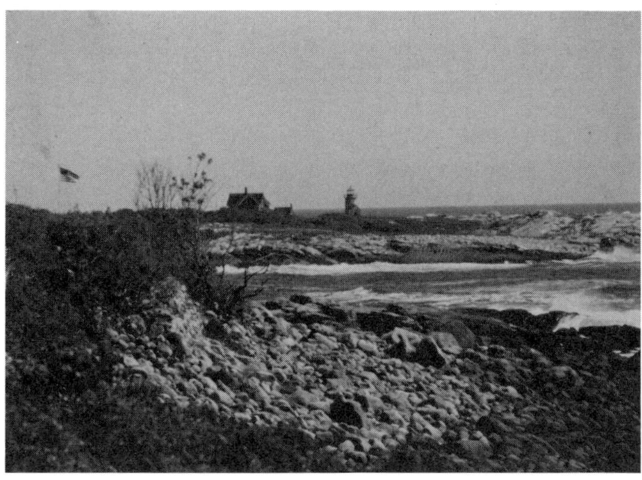

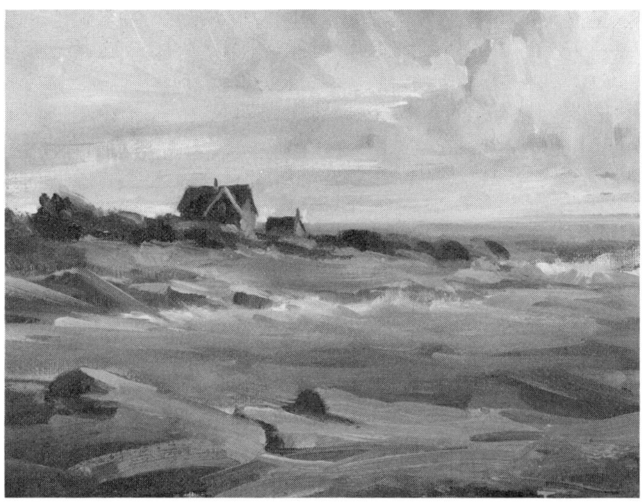

I take a photograph of what I want to be the focal point of my picture. I then broadly interpret the surroundings, never slavishly copying the photograph. You can see this broad interpretation by comparing the photograph with my painting.

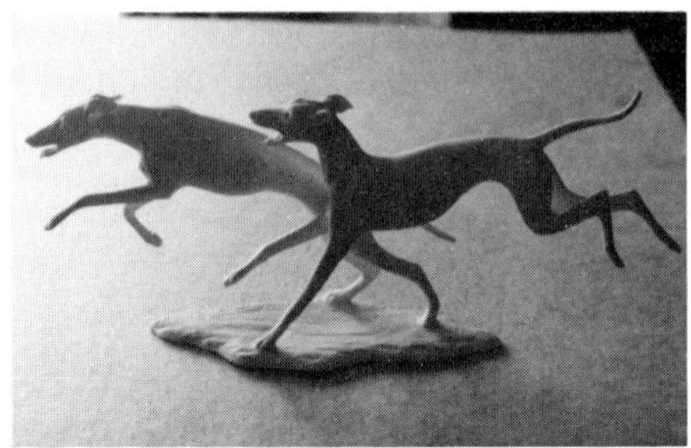
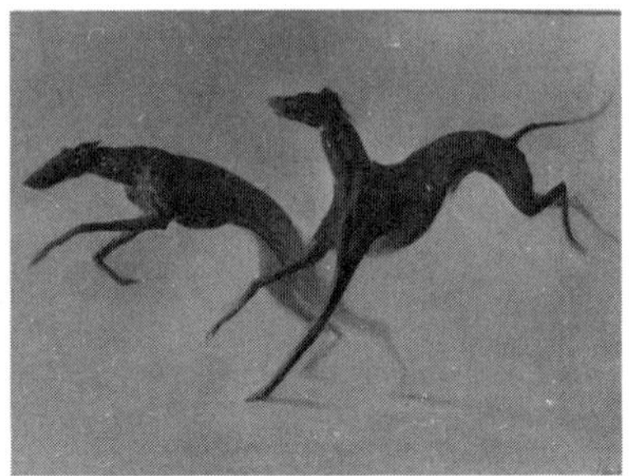

My painting, "Running Whippets," is a greatly exaggerated version of the action of the statue. Painting from photographs is more successful if the photos are of subjects that you know very well. The photos then supplement your knowledge of the subject. I have owned and loved whippets for years and years.

PHOTO REALISM

Is photo realism artistic?

It seems that critics, observers and dealers in art need names to describe the various schools and styles of painting. As soon as they find a designation, this seems to create a trend or direction for those who copy the innovators of the school or style. Photo realism, I feel, started as a protest against bad abstract painting. It manifested itself, logically, as its exact opposite: Extremely realistic renditions. What has followed the initial efforts, I fear, have been paintings, albeit realistic, but just as bad as the abstractions they were designed to replace. I don't think an artist should be enslaved by his camera. A camera should only be used to cut down on the time-consuming preparation for recording an original concept.

PHTHALOCYANINE COLORS (see Blues; Greens)

PICTURES (Naming of)

What determines the names given to pictures, and what are the types of pictures?

Paintings can be broadly classified as *people, places* and *things* pictures. *People* pictures are portraits, self-portraits, figures or figure compositions. Places pictures are landscapes, seascapes, snow scenes, views of interiors of buildings, and so on.

Things pictures are still lifes, florals, and any other objects that inspire one to paint them. Then there are genre and *trompe l'oeil* pictures (listed separately). The subject matter usually determines its title. Often this title is an automatic conclusion arrived at because of its pictorial message. Then there's always the system some modernists use, entitling their works with names like "Dimensions #4," "Motif With Red Line #l," and other names to provoke some interest in the non-objective offerings.

PIGMENT (see Painting Media)

POINTILLISM

Is there any difference between broken color and pointillism?

The two terms mean basically the same thing. The name *pointillism* was embraced by Georges Seurat (1859–1891), the acknowledged father of neo-impressionism. *Pointillism* is the noun form of the French verb *pointiller*, to paint small dots. Instead of mixing colors on the palette and then applying and blending them on the canvas, the *pointillist* applies his colors in small dots in juxtaposition on the canvas. It is then up to the painting's viewers to blend the dots, so to speak, into an overall effect. *(See Broken Color)*

POINT OF VIEW (see Eye Level)

POPPYSEED OIL (see Binder)

PRIMARY COLORS

Which red, yellow and blue are thought of as the primary colors?

The three primary colors are so called because they are the origin of all color. In light, the primary colors are: yellow-green, red violet and blue-green. In paint, the primary colors are: yellow (as in lemon), red (as in American flag) and blue (as in sky). When working with paint, light's primaries couldn't emulate nature's light. This is due to the fact that paint records not only the color of things but the tone that color is at the time. The three primary colors mixed without tone, as in light, make colorless white light. When the tones of the three primaries are mixed in paint the result is black.

The difference between light's primaries and paint's primaries has always been a point of discussion among artists, printers, photographers and all those who work with color. An understanding of color that makes color mixing easy is quite simple.

1. The primary colors are red, yellow and blue.
2. The secondary colors are green, violet and orange, and are made by mixing two primaries together.
3. The secondary colors are complementary to the primaries: red's complement is green; yellow's complement is violet, blue's complement is orange.
4. A color and its complement equals the three primary colors.
5. Since light is made of three primary colors to make color appear as it does, the painter must use three primaries to record that color.
6. This is achieved by using a color and its complement in juxtaposition *(See Complementary Color; Secondary Color)*

PRIME (see Canvas)

PROFESSIONAL

How can I become a professional painter?

A professional earns his living from his painting. This has nothing whatsoever to do with the quality of that person's work.

Some painters become professional by design but many an art student finds himself to be a professional by the demand for his work. Since he devotes all his endeavors to his painting and produces nothing else, his paintings are his product. He has to support himself so he sells the fruits of his labor. Some painters paint to sell, some paint to just paint, but subsequently sell. Commercialism in the arts is a difficult thing to put your finger on and to make blanket statements about. One has to wonder about this question of amateurs and professionals when we know that Vermeer was the owner of a saloon, and painted in his spare time. In a way, he could be thought of as a "Sunday Painter," but who would venture to call him that?

When a person's entire endeavor and dedication end up in his painting, he has to sell or have a patron in order for him to live from day to day. The portrait painter is the commercial artist in the fine arts field. While he doesn't (or shouldn't) exactly paint the portrait just to sell, he is faced with painting to satisfy. Any type of commission work provokes the painter's artistic and creative nature and this condition has given us some of our most revered artistic masterpieces.

Some amateur painters are better artists than many professional painters. Art is a matter of opinion not of fact. Professional status is usually bestowed upon a painter by the opinion of others. Thinking that you are always a student of painting is the best guarantee of personal improvement and professional success. If you sell a painting here and there, I don't think you can be considered to be a professional. It just becomes a lovely endorsement.

PROPORTION

How can I see things in correct proportion?

It is true that getting the various elements of a shape correctly proportioned makes that shape look correctly drawn. Moreover, getting one element in a composition the correct size in relation to other elements is the key to realistic, sensible rendering. In order to see things in correct proportion you should incorporate with your sense of sight your practical knowledge of arithmetic, especially fractions.

Proportioning is the simple matter of dividing a form into parts, or comparing the size of one form in relation to another. The sizes of things, as seen in dimension from near to far, are greatly altered, so proportioning of size comparison has to be made anew for each picture. It is said that the eyes are at the halfway mark from the top of the head to the chin. This is not true, however, if the head is tilted back. The eye often sees what it wants to see not what it actually sees, so constant measuring is essential to recording correct proportions and correct linear perspective as well.

A very important factor in getting correct proportion: You must first decide how large you want the entire shape to be on the size canvas that you are working on. Only then can you divide that shape into fractions.

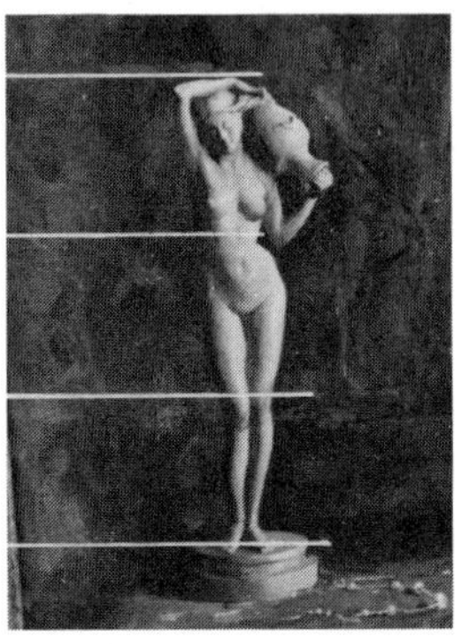

After deciding how large I wanted the figure to be on my canvas, I measured the size of her shape, from the top of her head to her waist, and compared it to the rest of her figure. I found that its size was the same as from her waist to her knees and, again, the same as from her knees to her feet. These three equal parts became the clue to her correct proportions.

To begin being in more control of the proportion of things in painting, you must decide and establish the size of the subject or composition on the canvas from the onset so you can compare all the elements of the composition to it. Proportioning is always a matter of making a comparison of one size to another so you have to have a starting point size. From there, you have to break down all the sizes of the things in the composition into fractions of the entire form. For instance, in portraiture, once you have established the size you want the entire head to be on the canvas, you can search out where the eyes are in relation to the top of the head and the bottom of the chin. You could compare the width of the head in relation to the height of the head, and so on with all the features.

In landscape painting, establish the size of the barn and compare all the components of the landscape to it. In still life, decide where and how big you want the chianti bottle so you can compare the size of the fruit around it in relation to it. In painting a vase of flowers, determine how much space the vase and flowers will take up on the canvas and then establish how much of the entire space is to be vase and how much will be flowers.

Getting everything in proper proportion must begin with judging how large or how much space on the canvas the entire subject is to take up. From there, it's just a matter of arithmetically dividing the whole into fractions to make everything fit.

A relatively correct drawing is a record of how something looks at the time you have decided to record it. It is not the way it is; it is the way it appears.

PRUSSIAN BLUE (see Blues)

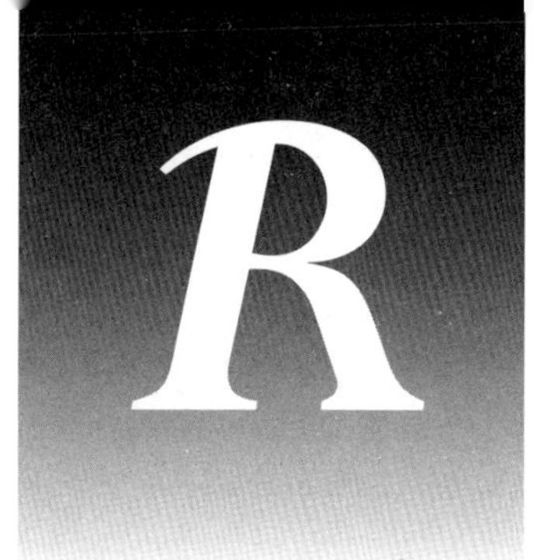

RABBIT SKIN GLUE

What is rabbit skin glue?

Rabbit skin glue is made from clippings of rabbit skin. It is an excellent adhesive and is unaffected by most chemicals and atmospheric conditions. Rabbit skin glue is an ingredient in most old primes or grounds for oil painting. Now that acrylics are on the scene, rabbit skin glue has become obsolete. Acrylics have excellent adhesive quality, which is important as a size, prime or ground for oil painting.

RASKO, MAXIMILIAN AUREAL

In all of your books and at your demonstrations, you frequently mention your teacher, M.A. Rasko. Can you tell me something about him?

M.A. Rasko was born in Hungary in 1884. He studied painting in Munich, Germany, and in Budapest and enjoyed a successful career as a portrait painter in England until his emigration to the United States in 1917. Here he continued his career, doing altar pieces as well as portraits.

I was only fifteen when I met Rasko at his studio on West 67th Street in New York City. At that time this was the area where many artists lived and worked. Rasko's studio apartment was impressive: It was large and two stories high with a grand north window that was easily seven feet off the floor and then extended ten feet in height. A balcony overlooked the studio which added a marvelous and romantic air to the overall look of the place. How was I to know then that four years later I would spend the most important part of my life studying with him in that very studio?

Mr. Rasko was short in height but tall in stature; he spoke six languages, had a quick wit, was extremely well read and was a fabulous painter. I considered him to be an excellent teacher; students who needed an ego trip, however, fell by the wayside. I was honored when he invited me to be a private student. My work crystallized under his severe constructive criticism. I kept in affectionate contact with M.A. Rasko until the day he died in 1961 on April 22—my birthday.

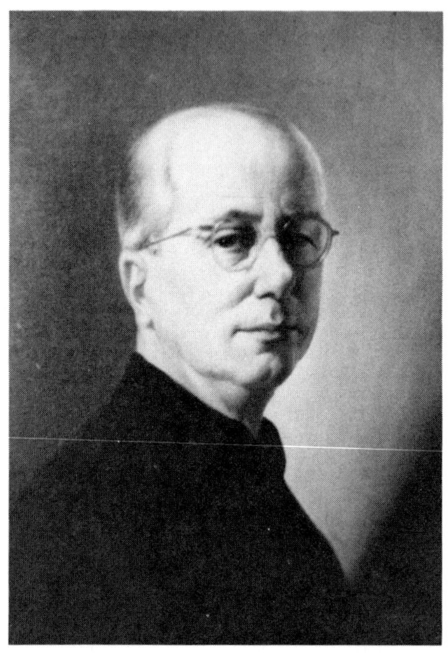

On the left is Rasko's self portrait, painted in 1948. Rasko's style tended to be classic and academic. On the lower left is Rasko's painting, "Bridle Path in Central Park," where Rasko, an avid horseman, rode often. Pictured below is Rasko's rendition of my mother, Alida DeBoer, painted in 1949 when she was fifty-seven years old. A valid likeness. I've painted her more casually and loosely.

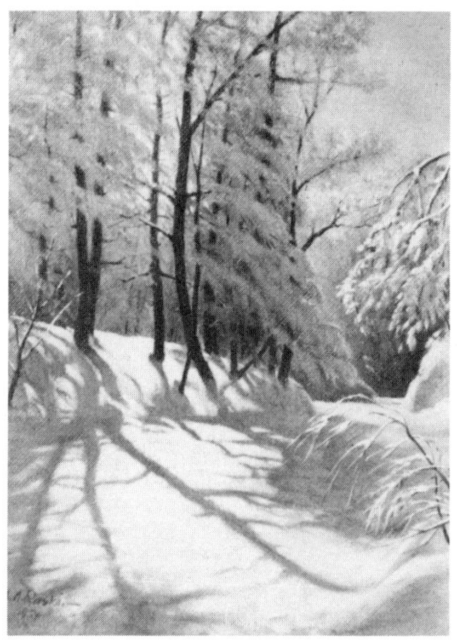

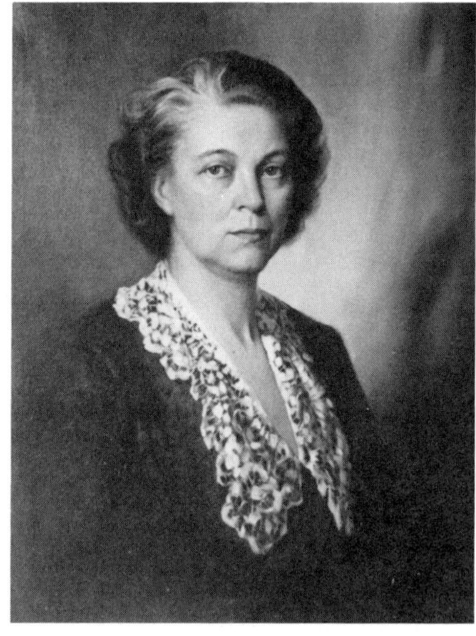

RAW COLOR

When an area of a painting, such as a sky, is criticized as being a raw color, how can it be fixed?

Glazing a colored area with that color's complement can impart a better balance of color. If a sky background looks too cool, often called raw color, a very thin glaze of Burnt Sienna can fix it. Of course, even the thinnest glaze of color always darkens the area slightly, so some lighter accents may have to be added into the wet glaze.

In painting the effect of light, cool colors have to be warmed more than the warm colors have to be cooled, since we live in a world of warm light. *(See Glazing; Intensity)*

RAW SIENNA (see Earth Colors; Oranges)

RAW UMBER (see Earth Colors; Yellows)

REALISTIC

Why are realistic paintings criticized with the remark, "It's just realistic"?

The word "realistic," which means natural looking, is overworked and often misused. I think that all paintings have a degree of interpretation and are a result of creative energy. Since art is a matter of opinion and not a matter of fact, anyone can comment or criticize a painting, but it is still opinion, and a word such as realistic only describes the viewer's reaction to the painting while someone else may think the same painting is unnatural looking. Real is real, paint is paint. Paint only interprets real and becomes another thing, but a picture is never reality by itself. To an artist, the paint world is real and the natural world is his reference.

The artist's picture plane is real even though it is only two-dimensional. Nature's pictures are three-dimensional and it is the transition from the three-dimensions of reality to the two-dimensional surface that taxes the creative interpretation.

REDS

Which of the red colors are permanent?

All the cadmium reds are permanent, although when they are tinted with white, they tend to change in hue: Cadmium Red Light tends to be orangey and Cadmium Red Medium and Cadmium Red Deep turn very violet.

GRUMBACHER RED is a permanent, bright red that doesn't tip from its brightness when mixed with white.

The earth reds or iron oxides: VENETIAN RED, TERRA ROSA, LIGHT RED (also called ENGLISH RED). These reds are all medium in tone and medium in intensity. They all make dusty pinks when mixed with white and they are permanent.

ALIZARIN CRIMSON is actually a violet but is very useful to darken the other reds. Alizarin Crimson is permanent.

THALO RED ROSE is a permanent, bright, violet red. This is a proprietary color in Grumbacher's lines of oil colors.

INDIAN RED is a permanent, dull, medium-toned red that is quite violet in hue. Indian red is very opaque and a touch of it into Alizarin Crimson will make a strong, dark rich red.

HARRISON RED is a bright, cherry red that is not considered to be permanent.

GERANIUM LAKE is an intense red that fades under daylight exposure.

ROSE MADDER and MADDER LAKE. Very old colors, dating back to the Egyptians. Its color has now been replaced by Alizarin Crimson.

I have trouble making red lighter and brighter.

In paint, red is a primary color; in light, it is a red violet. Red is a middle-toned color and one of the most difficult to lighten into brilliant illumination without losing its intensity. To do so you have to sacrifice its hue and accept a more orangey hue. For example — Cadmium Red Light is best lightened and brightened by adding white and Cadmium Orange. Alizarin Crimson, when used as a red, can be lightened and brightened by adding Grumbacher Red and a slight amount of white. To deal with reds, either to lighten or darken them, first adjust them with a brighter red to go lighter, or a darker red to go darker, before adding white for the lighter tones or green for its darker shadowed values. This adjustment is necessary because of red's middle tone nature in the spectrum. *(See Alizarin Crimson)*

REDS (Earth)

How do English Red, Light Red, Venetian Red and Terra Rosa differ?

They are all reds that are quite the same in hue and tone. As they come out of the tube, these iron oxides can be called "brick" reds. Each one's subtle difference is exposed when it is mixed with white and then compared. Actually, all of these reds can substitute for one another, but not so with Indian Red, Mars Violet and Mars Red, all of which are different from them in hue and opacity. Incidentally, English Red is the same as Light Red; most manufacturers list both names on their tubes as follows: English Red Light (Light Red) or Light Red (English Red Light). Another confusion among many painters is the thought that Light Red can be substituted for Cadmium Red Light. These two colors are radically different in hue and intensity. Cadmium Red Light is a bright, light red. Light Red is the name for a duller, red oxide, and bears absolutely no relationship to the cadmium color.

RED SABLE (see Brushes)

REFLECTED LIGHT

What is reflected light?

Reflected light is caused by the general illumination in the room and adds color to the shadowed areas. If it weren't for reflected light, shadows wouldn't have any color at all. Reflected light influences the color of the shadow. Make sure that this color is the tone you want to influence the shadow. Don't confuse reflected light with reflections. A reflection actually makes a tonal change in the shadow. *(See Tone Value)*

REFLECTIONS

How do I paint reflections, such as in water and on tables?

Reflections in shiny surfaces, such as the ones you refer to, should not be confused with a reflection, one of the five tone values that are caused by one source of light on an object and is one fifth of the clue to dimension.

These shines are not actually reflections; they are diffused highlights that are caused by a general light source. They are always a lighter gray color, made by using the complementary color to the color of the surface it is on, mixed with black and white.

Reflections are best painted first with downward strokes and then blended with horizontal strokes.

REFLECTIVE AND NON-REFLECTIVE (see Textures)

RESIN (see Varnish)

RETOUCH SPRAY (see Varnish)

RETOUCH VARNISH (see Varnish)

RE-USING CANVAS

How can I use old canvases? What should I cover them with to be able to paint over them?

I don't think that you should ever re-use canvases. Since the initial coat on the support is so important to the permanence of an oil painting, each picture should be done on an ideal surface which certainly is not an old painting. I realize that it's hard to just throw out canvas that you have suffered over, but why waste new energy by painting over past failures or obsolete experience?

My advice, therefore: Always start fresh. Your new idea is worth it.
(See Canvas)

RIGID SUPPORTS

What is the correct way to prepare an unfinished rigid support to paint on with oil?

This procedure can apply to Masonite, pressed wood panels, or any other rigid support.

Masonite (untempered *only*) can be sized on either side — the smooth or rough — depending on your preference of surface. First, clean the surface with a damp cloth and then apply a thinned coat of gesso (any prepared acrylic gesso will do). When it has dried for about six hours, apply a thicker coat of gesso (less water mixed into it). You can use a wide, house painter's brush or a roller, both available at hardware and paint stores. A soft-textured roller will give you a slight texture on the smooth surface, which is sometimes advantageous for easy application once you begin to paint. If your rigid panels are larger than 16" x 20", you should size both sides to prevent warping. Only one coat is needed for the back surface.

Many people use flat, water-based house paints to size their rigid supports. I can't sanction this practice. These house paints are not made to withstand overpainting and, thus, should not rest under your precious applications of oil paints. *(See Gesso)*

ROSE MADDER (see Madder Colors; Reds)

ROUND BRUSHES (see Brushes)

RULER (see Drawing Instruments)

In My Opinion:

WHEN FACING A NEW CANVAS

A painter facing a new canvas is much like a boxer fighting to win. The boxer doesn't know what punch will come his way. He has to respond to them with his intuition and training. The painter doesn't know how his attempt to record his impressions will look. He has to battle with his shapes, tone and colors, hoping his picture will respond to his jabs with his brush.

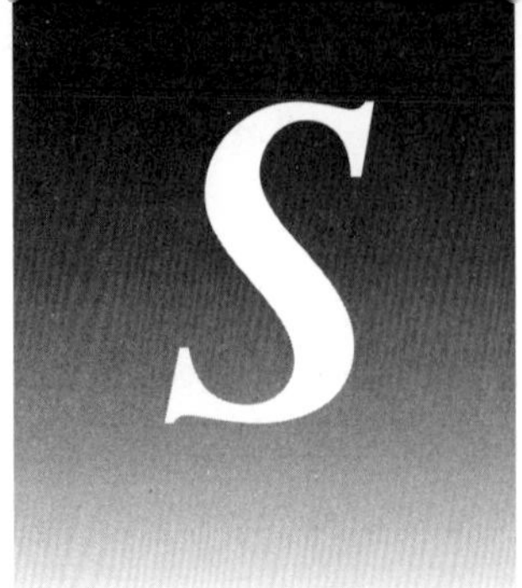

SABLE BRUSHES (see Brushes)

SAP GREEN (see Greens)

SCREW EYES (see Framing)

SCUMBLE

What is a scumble?

A scumble is an application of a film of opaque color over a dry, painted area. A scumble is usually a lighter tone than the area over which it is applied, not only to lighten it but to impart a new dimension to the color. Scumbles are often used on a large area, such as a sky or a background.

The mixture of a scumble is usually made of a grayed version of the color it is to be applied to. It's also often used to impart a better gradation of tone from light to dark.

You will want to scumble to lessen a color's intensity, and scumbling can be used to give a dusty look to a surface, to paint fog or mist over mountains or, in portraits, to paint a gossamer veil over skin.

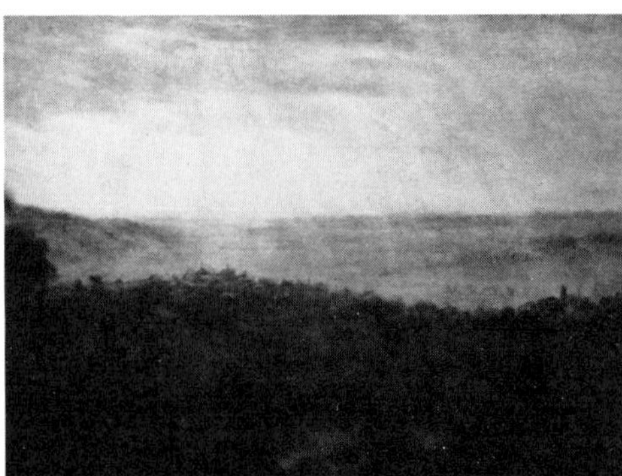

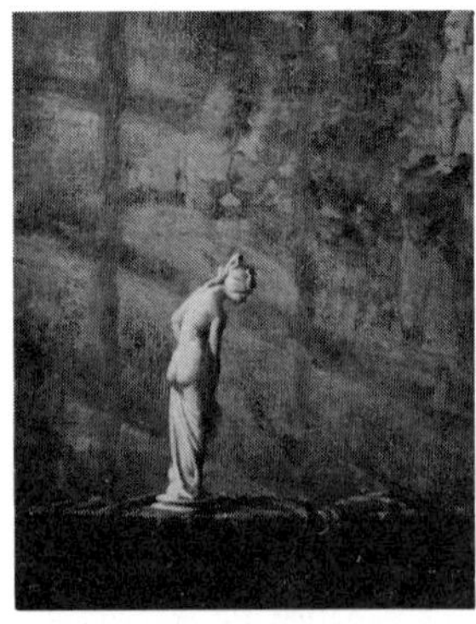

Scumbling has contributed greatly to generating the mood of these pictures.

SECONDARY COLORS

Are the secondary colors and complementary colors one and the same?

Yes. The secondary colors are the results of mixtures of two of the three primaries. Therefore, orange is a secondary color because it's a mixture of red and yellow; green is a secondary color because it's a mixture of blue and yellow; violet is a secondary color because it's a mixture of red and blue. These secondary colors are complements of the primary colors which were not part of their mixtures: Orange (mixed with red and yellow) is the complement of blue; green (mixed with blue and yellow) is the complement of red; violet (mixed with red and blue) is the complement of yellow. *(See Complementary Colors; Primary Colors)*

SELF PORTRAIT

How does one go about painting oneself?

Many people think that a self portrait is a difficult portrait to paint. Actually, it's easier to do than one of a model. The obvious reason for this is that you have in yourself a very cooperative model, one who understands your working conditions and working problems.

Start your self portrait by holding a mirror, and find a lighting condition on your face that you feel is suitable. Then, set up a large mirror at that place, and one convenient to your easel, just as you would with a model other than yourself. It's important that you don't place your mirror too close to you. This may result in your getting to paint the detail too soon rather than seeing the all-over effect that comes from viewing a model at a distance of not less than five feet from you.

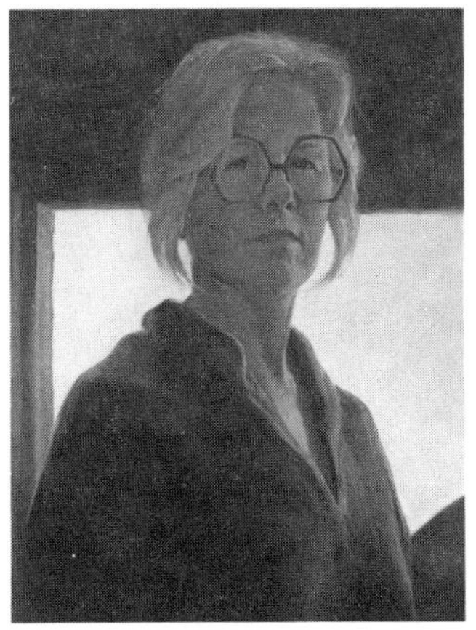

Doing a self portrait is the professional portrait painter's way of going back to school. Alone in a studio, with no concern for the model's comfort or of the likeness, the artist feels free to take time and license with paint and interpretation.

Proceed as usual: Look and paint, look and paint. Don't try to look at yourself and paint at the same time. Although this may sound silly, more painters than you can imagine try to paint just this way.

Using one mirror, you understand, will give you a reverse image. Don't try to adjust this to what is the actual. This means that if you are righthanded and hold your palette, you will be painting yourself holding your palette in your right hand instead of in your left.

Should you want to paint yourself as you actually are, you will have to use two mirrors. However, your eyes will not look out of the picture at all viewers as they will do with the use of one mirror.

Since so much of painting well comes from hours of self-study and practice, doing self portraits is an excellent way to study portraiture. It is hard to impose upon the patience of a model while you practice and experiment with your paints for certain effects.

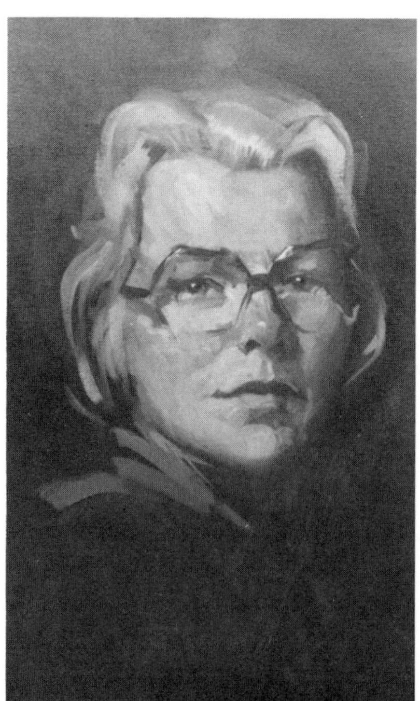

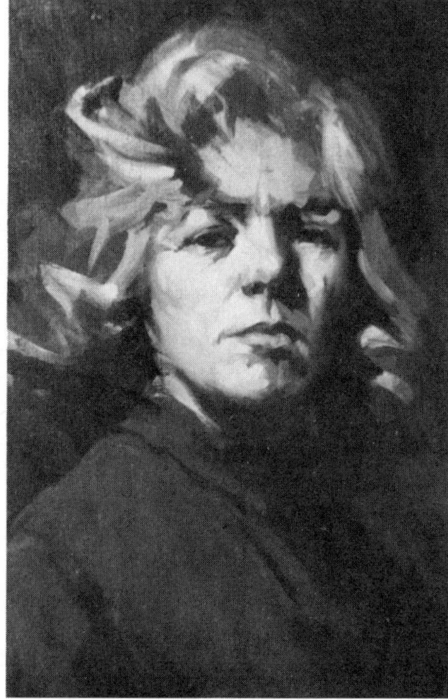

Two self portraits by the author. Two different moods; two different times.

SELLING AND PRICING

I have been painting for several years now and have been asked to sell several of my paintings. How does an amateur go about pricing his works?

Here are some considerations that can influence the prices you charge for your paintings (from time to time, I've used them all):

1. If you like the picture a lot, the price should be high.
2. Conversely, if you want to get rid of it, sell it cheap.
3. If you need the money, sell it; if you don't need the money, keep the painting.
4. If someone really loves the painting, consider that person's financial status, and then price the picture accordingly.
5. Of course, you should value your frame, materials and your time.
6. Ask yourself how much one would have to pay today for a framed print or a large photograph.
7. Once you've established a certain price range, you are forced to stay within that range. As demand for your work increases, this price has to be adjusted. As soon as you are pressured to produce too much, your quality is going to go down. Don't ever be in a position to hack your work out; it may seem profitable but in the end you will never be able to rise above a label that is so easily affixed by the public.
8. Keep in mind the fact that people seem to value things they have paid a lot of money for. Always make sure that you give them their money's worth.
9. Finally, as tempting as it is, don't give any paintings away. A token amount is going to make the recipient value it. *(See Professional)*

SHADOWED COLOR

What is a shadowed color?

A shadowed color is a color that has been darkened and dulled in intensity to make it appear to be in shadow. This is done by adding a color's complement. Ideally, when painting *alla prima*, a shadow or shaded color is best made by first darkening the body tone with its own color and then adding some of the color's complement that is darker than the color. For example:

1. If the body tone of the flesh you're painting is made of Cadmium Yellow Light, Cadmium Red Light and white, first add some Yellow Ochre and some Venetian Red to the mixture before adding Sap Green or Cobalt Blue.

2. If your beach sand is Yellow Ochre and white, first add some Raw Sienna before adding its complement — violet (a mixture of black, white and Alizarin Crimson).

3. If a rose is Grumbacher Red, first add a little Alizarin Crimson before adding a touch of Thalo Green to paint in the shadows.

4. When painting the sunny greens on trees and grass, add more green into the mixture to lessen the amount of white in the mixture before adding Alizarin Crimson or Cadmium Red Medium to make the shadows.

SHADOWS

Is there a formula for painting shadows?

There's no set formula for painting shadows, but there is a basic principle that can guide you to mixing the correct shadow color on any object. Here are some simple observations that will help you understand shadow colors and be able to mix them:

1. Shadowed areas on objects are where the light can't directly strike.

2. There are two types of shadows: *Body Shadows* — these are where that portion of the object is not in line with the source of light; *Cast Shadows* — these are the ones seen when something is in the path of the light, robbing the light from striking.

3. Both types of shadows are darker tones than the objects they are on: Very dark in very direct lighting; not as dark in muted lighting.

4. Because color comes from light, and shadows are areas where light can't strike, shadows are somewhat colorless.

5. Since direct light also causes general illumination, there is always a degree of reflected light in shadows, causing some color to appear in a darker tone value than the area in light.

These observations of mine bring me to the conclusion that shadows can be made by:

1. Painting the shadow color in a gray tone made of black and white and the color's complement, or graying the body color by adding its complementary color.
2. Then adding a reflected color into the shadow tone. *(See Tone Value)*

SHAPE

I see shapes but can't seem to draw them right. How can I get them the way I see them?

I'm a great believer that when you look at shapes if you analyze them before drawing them you will be able to draw them somewhat correctly. You will never get them really right but you will be able to make them look right.

Always dissociate yourself from your personal relationship to the shape, and see its proportion in the perspective you are looking at it and try to understand its structure.

A very elementary way to approach getting a shape relatively right is to visualize any shape in a proportionate box. Draw that box and then draw the shape within it. *(See Anatomy; Perspective; Proportion)*

SHINY AND DULL SPOTS

My students seem to have problems with shiny and dull spots. How can we get away from this? I don't like them to use retouch varnish.

A certain degree of shiny and dull spots in one painting is characteristic of the oil painting process. It is due to many reasons, the first being the fact that some colors dry matte (such as the earth colors) and some dry shiny (such as the cadmium colors as well as colors that are mixed with white). Since the addition of white makes colors shine, the matte finish will be more evident in the shadowed areas where there is an absence of white. Paintings that are developed in classes that usually meet once a week are much more apt to have this condition because the paint process is interrupted by time. An artist in his studio regulates his painting sessions and his picture's development in stages that avoid this condition.

Now, how can this shiny dull condition be dealt with?

First, use only turpentine as a medium in the initial stage of the painting, meaning the first, entire paint layer. This makes the paint layer fast drying and relatively matte all over. After working over this layer, a retouch varnish can be sprayed over the entire surface and the further development can be made with or without a medium.

At this point, I would like to discuss retouch varnish. There's nothing wrong with using this material. It's wonderful to even out the shine. But it should be used properly, as follows:

Hold your canvas at a forty-five-degree angle and then start spraying the retouch varnish, starting in the air above the canvas edge and then lowering your aim down into the dulled surface. Spray your varnish at an angle rather than directly at the canvas. You should ease the spray on rather than pushing the valve all the way down at "full throttle," so to speak. Aiming the spray directly at the dull spots puts too much of a concentration of varnish on it, resulting in too much shine.

You have to be patient with an oil painting. For your painting to have an overall finish, you have to wait a month. Then, using a lint-free rag, apply a very thin coat of medium. The medium I use is made up of equal parts of turpentine, linseed oil and damar varnish.

Finally, it is much better to be able to shine up a dull surface than to try to dull down shiny spots.

SHINY OBJECTS

What medium can I use to create textures such as glass and other shiny surfaces, principally shiny tables?

There is no medium that can create these shiny textures, or any other textural effect either. Textural effects are all a record of the tone values that make up these textures. The appearance of texture and dimension is completely a matter of tone value. A medium can only thin paint and add a property to the paint texture or character. A medium can't impart a property that records the characteristic of any subject. Confusion about a medium's power is usually in the area of shiny textures. I'm never asked about how medium can help the painter to create a dull texture, such as the one of a clay pot or the matte finish of a cloth bound book. Keep in mind that shiny paint doesn't record shiny objects just as a matte finish paint doesn't record dull surfaces. *(See Textures)*

SICCATIVE

What is a siccative?

A siccative is any substance that is added to a paint mixture to accelerate its drying time. Using any of these siccatives — or driers — encourages cracking or, in time, darkening. Why are they used? Well, painters are tempted to use driers in glazes to make them faster drying. But it's far better to add more varnish to a painting medium to make your glaze dry faster than to resort to a siccative.

Another reason for their use is to make it possible to drag more paint over painted areas for effects such as adding the shimmer of light on water or adding fog and any other special effects that need two separate applications.

If you want to try these effects, remember that caution is the word. Always keep in mind that paint that's forced to dry fast is not as healthy as paint that has been permitted to dry at its own pace.

SIGNATURE

How should I sign my name? And should I date my paintings?

Your actual signature is a personal thing. I have some views on where you should sign the picture and how it should look. Here they are:

Sign your name in one of the four corners, writing in a straight line. The corner to choose is the one that's the emptiest (there's no sense in writing your name over a lot of busy stroking: details, textures, etc.). The two bottom corners are more preferred than the two top corners. John Singer Sargent very often signed his name at the upper right corner, which became as distinctive as his signature itself.

When choosing a color for your signature, use a tone that's not in strong contrast to the tone of the spot you've selected and in a color that's not bright in intensity. And make sure that you are aware of where the frame's edge will be, thereby signing your name with enough clearance. Design the size of the letters to be in proportion to the size of the painting, never larger than five eighths-of-an-inch. Of course, should you use capital and lower case, the capitals will be larger than the other letters.

The actual technique of putting your name on the canvas is best done with paint thinned with enough medium to make it flow from the brush, much like ink. You will also find that it's easier to make all of your letters look neat and professional if you use straight lines, rather than curved shapes, to make all of your letters, even the letters o and s.

HERB ROGOFF

Your paint signature does not have to be your handwriting signature.

Don't date your paintings on the front of the canvas. You may want the date to appear as a record, and in that case place the date on the back of the canvas. And while you're at it, it's a good idea to also sign your name on the back of the canvas in large letters which makes it difficult for anyone to remove or paint over your signature, as your signature on the front can be. This is just another way of validating your work. A date on the front can affect the picture's appeal and saleability; people always seem to want the artist's latest work.

A portrait is a different matter. You should sign and date it on the front. On the back, for posterity's benefit, write your name, that of the sitter's, the date and location where painted. Portraits not only function as a painting, but also as a record of a person. This information, therefore, becomes part of the picture's value.

If you do a portrait from a photograph, the photographer should certainly be credited on the back and, if you choose to do so, on the front. Under your name, write: "From photograph by ______________________________ ." Obviously, this does not apply if the photograph you used was your own.

SILHOUETTE (see Outline)

SINGLE PRIME (see Canvas)

SIZING

What is the difference between sizing and priming?

Sizing prepares a surface for oil painting. Priming usually refers to a coating that will affect the appearance of the oil painting or dictate a specific technique. *(See Canvas)*

What should I use to size Masonite?

Use two coats of any commercial gesso. I don't think any of the water-based latex house paints should be used. Most of them have additives that serve purposes counter to the demands of a fine arts material which places the stress on permanency. Home owners never expect the paint on their walls to last longer than a few short years. *(See Gesso)*

SKETCHING

What should I use to sketch in the drawing before I paint?

There are a few ways to initiate the painting process. The way I prefer is to wash the canvas with turpentine and use Ivory Black or Raw Umber greatly thinned with turpentine to sketch in the composition. A good brush to use for this is a size three white bristle. Its firmness records the conviction of your drawing. A cloth that has been wetted with turpentine can function as your eraser. Many students use a little round brush for their drawing, but what this does is inhibit you to make a neat, immaculate drawing which is unnecessary at this point. After all, the drawing just works as guidelines for the painting process. Since your drawing is going to be covered by your paint, if it's too neat and pretty, you're going to hesitate to work over it.

For the drawing stage you can use any color of pastel. Because pastel is pure pigment, it will become part of the first application of oil paint. Charcoal, on the other hand, is a coal tar substance and can only be used if it is greatly dusted off, leaving but a slight amount on the surface. It is my belief that if a lot of charcoal is painted over, in time the charcoal will come to the surface, thereby dirtying your color.

You can also use a soft graphite pencil for your preliminary drawing. Particles of graphite seem to dissipate in turpentine so you can use a brush soaked in turpentine to erase any unwanted lines. The remaining pencil lines under the paint will not come to the surface as charcoal might.

SLOW-DRYING COLORS

I know of the procedure of applying slow drying colors last in the development of an oil painting. What I don't know is how can I be sure that these are the slow drying ones?

All colors that are mixed with a lot of white are slow-drying. So if you start light passages of the composition in tones that can be subsequently painted lighter and lighter, you will be guaranteed that the last, lightest application will be the slowest drying. Another guarantee: Start your painting with thinned paint and finish with thicker paint. *(See Alizarin Crimson; Cadmium Colors; Whites)*

SMOOTH PAINT

Can I paint one part of my picture, such as the sky, smooth and paint another part rough?

Many people do this but I think it is really better to make the paint application more homogeneous in appearance: All smooth, all rough, or smooth and rough somewhat evenly dispersed.

The paint is trying to record a mood or impression and a unified presentation is all important. The appearance of the paint contributes greatly to a successful composition.

STAINING COLORS

Why can't I get the Thalo colors out of my brushes?

If you are cleaning your brushes properly, you are getting the paint out of them. Colors such as the Thalos, Alizarin Crimson and Prussian Blue will stain the white bristles of your brushes. But your brushes will be clean. These colors stain because they are organic ones that today are made synthetically. Even though they are staining colors, they are perfectly safe to use and are permanent. The inorganic colors, such as the earth colors and the artificial mineral colors such as the cadmiums don't stain, probably because their pigments are not as fine as the organic type of pigments are. *(See Thalo Colors)*

STAND OIL

What is stand oil? Is it the same as sun-thickened oil?

Stand oil is linseed oil that's been heated for a length of time. It thickens and changes in character in that it becomes fast-drying. Stand oil can be mixed with turpentine as a painting medium and will not yellow as much as using plain linseed oil.

The fast-drying property may not be advantageous to a wet-in-wet technique. Also, mixing stand oil with paint makes the paint "long" or having a leveling property like house painters' enamel.

Sun-thickened oil is very much like stand oil. Linseed oil is heated in natural sunlight instead of mechanically.

STILL LIFE (see Pictures)

STORING AND SAVING PAINT

What is the best way you've found to save paint from week to week?

The best way to store paint is to put your palette in an airtight container. But since this is not always practical, putting the palette into your refrigerator or freezer will do the job very nicely.

Paint that has filmed on a palette is not good to use because the oil, the all important binder, has surfaced, leaving the paint in an unsatisfactory condition. Another factor in using paint efficiently is to determine how much of each color you think you will need for each painting session. This will also make you put some thought into your procedure, which is so important to a successful technique.

STRETCHING CANVAS (see Canvas)

STRIP PALETTES (see Palettes)

STUDIO

How important is it to have a real studio?

I think that it is most important to have a place that's ready to work in at any time and where you can leave your work unfinished. Inspirations are fragile. To have to put time into an elaborate setup arrangement can dampen or even extinguish the urge to paint. A ready studio is the positive answer to this problem. A studio can be just an easel, a taboret, a portable spotlight and a place to put a subject in a place that can be left as it is. Being able to get back to the painting to finish it while your interest is still alive stops you from piling up

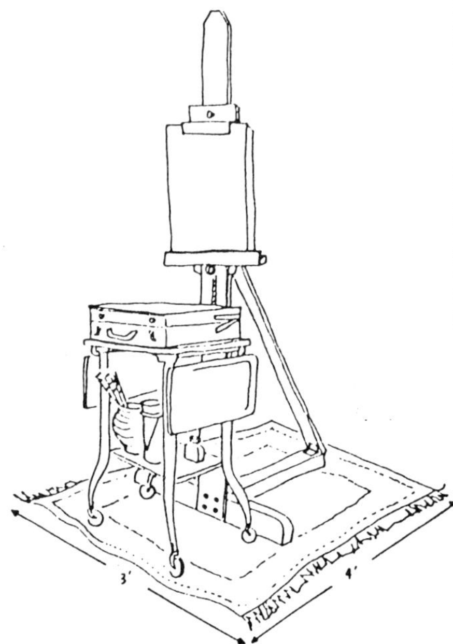

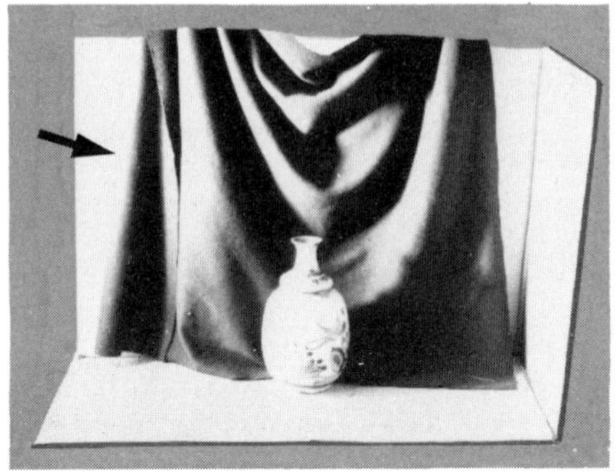

A typewriter table makes an ideal taboret. Placing your subject matter in a shadow box (two sides and a bottom of a cardboard box) makes arranging a view of your subject in relation to the light easy to do. Different toned drapes can be used to alter the tone of the background. The open side should be toward the light source.

unfinished pictures. Try to finish everything you start. Leaving paintings unfinished is a clue of insecurity. You enjoy the possibility of it rather than exposing the extent of your ability. Ones you don't want to finish should be destroyed — out of sight, out of mind — and don't be tempted to paint over them unless the paint layer is merely a wash.

STUDY

Why are some paintings called a study?

Many paintings in the past were commissioned work so when an artist did an uncommissioned work, he labeled it a study. So often we paint something just to see if we can do so. These studies are very intriguing and enlightening, especially to people who paint.

STYLE (see Technique)

SUNKEN-IN AREAS

What are sunken-in areas? What causes them?

Some colors, especially earth colors, dry flat or matte. This condition is referred to as sunken-in areas. All colors look better if they have a degree of shine.

Sunken-in areas also appear when paint that has been mixed with a lot of turpentine has been applied. If paint has to be thinned to any degree after the initial layer, it should be thinned with a painting medium.

Sunken-in areas are remedied by additions of retouch varnish or a painting medium.

SUPPORT (see Canvas)

SYNTHETIC HAIR (see Brushes)

In My Opinion:

ON DRAWING

Try not to be mechanical about drawing. It is tempting because you sometimes feel that you don't draw correctly enough. But by drawing spontaneously you have the beautiful chance to offer to others the way you were impressed at the time.

ON LEARNING

Did you ever wonder why a music student starts with a simple melody while a painting student wants to start with a symphony?

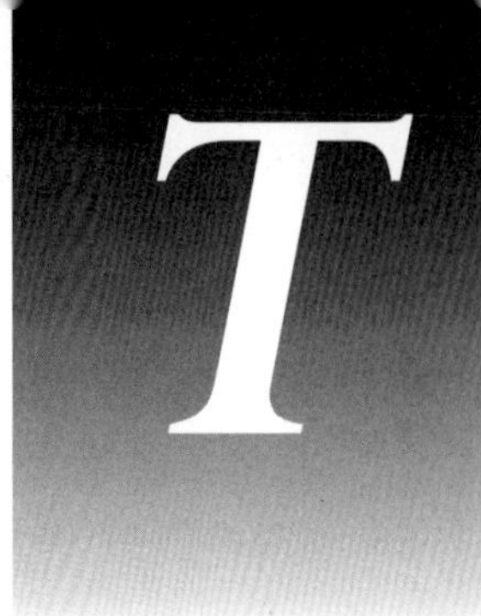

TALENT

Do I have to be talented to paint?

Talent, or facility, as it is defined in the dictionary, surely is beneficial to the quality of one's work, but I don't think that it's a definable ingredient in a painter because the quality of a painting, I feel, is a matter of opinion not fact. Some people who have seen Grandma Moses's paintings believed that she was talented; others didn't. The prime ingredients one has to have to paint is the desire to do so.

Our paintings determine whether we as artists are described as talented when, in actuality, our works look the way they do because of practice, study, sensitivity and dedication.

TECHNIQUES

What part of painting a picture takes you the most time?

I put the same amount of concern on every facet of the picture-making process. If I were to apportion time spent, I'd say that I devote more time on background than anywhere else. *(See Personal Painting Problems)*

What is meant by the statements "He thinks like an oil painter" or "He thinks like a watercolorist"?

In those two statements, the extremely different make-up of the two media is exposed.

A watercolorist renders his painting by applying his paint onto paper. He responds and deals with his paper, its texture and its whiteness.

An oil painter, on the other hand, uses his canvas as a support for his paint. His picture, therefore, is actually an independent layer of his material resting on and, he hopes, adhering to his surface. The watercolorist's picture *is* the surface.

You can see that this difference in both media demands different paint approaches. You can't paint in oil the way you would approach a watercolor painting, and vice versa.

To paint with watercolors, the color has to be applied transparently to make use of the whiteness of the paper to control the values of the colors. Oil colors must be mixed with white to establish the value of the color on the surface.

To sum up, it's safe to say that the differences are that a watercolorist makes his paper a painting; an oil painter makes his painting out of paint that's resting on a surface.

In starting a painting, be it a portrait, landscape or still life, where does one proceed with paint after the picture has been sketched in?

Many students think that when the shapes of the subject are sketched in with line, the painting process can begin. This is not advisable. Only when the allover pattern of the darks of the composition in relation to the light pattern has been established, can the actual lay-in of the paint begin. Then your starting place is mainly determined by the tone of the background:

1. If the subject is to have a light background, you can start with the subject.
2. If the subject is seen against a dark background the background tone must be painted first.
3. When working on a middle-toned canvas you can start almost any way you want to, but the focal point should be your priority.

In landscape painting, the basic rule of progression of application is: Paint that which is farthest from you and gradually work forward. This means — first the sky, then distance, then middle distance, then foreground.

In portraiture, after the pattern of the shape of the shadow has been established, the background should be painted in. Not that it doesn't have to be painted again, but its tone value should be established.

In flower painting, it's best to paint in a progression that preserves the delicacy of the colors of the flowers, which means painting the light, bright colors of the flowers first, then the greenery, then the more grayed or muted tones of the background. Just decide what's the most practical way to approach this. Surely, red roses on a white background dictates doing the white background first. Red roses on a dark background means that you should do the red roses first.

Is there a general, practical procedure for painting anything?

My procedure for painting almost anything is:

1. Establish a general tone and color of the object in the correct tonal relationship to its surroundings.
2. Then add the lighter tones that are seen where the planes of the object are directly in line with the light.
3. Then ease in the shadows on the shadowed side.

How can I translate texture into brushwork? My brushwork has been criticized as being flat and uninteresting.

There is a basic brushwork that can be used all the time. It is that of first painting in color in one direction and effecting it in opposite strokes. The two directions seem to suggest more dimension than strokes that are painted in one direction only.

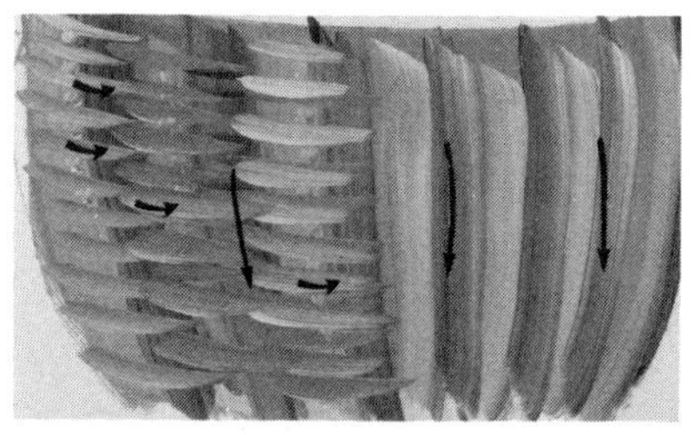

Basic brushwork that imparts interest as well as solidity:
1. *A basket. Down strokes to form; across ones to suggest the weave.*
2. *An apple. Opposing strokes to show the planes.*
3. *An onion. Using opposing strokes to achieve texture.*

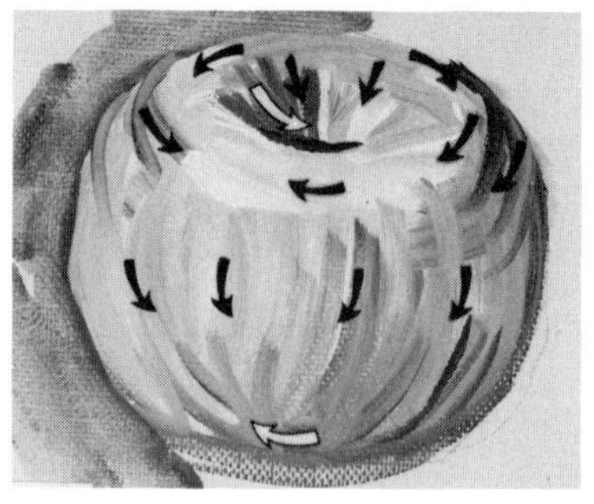

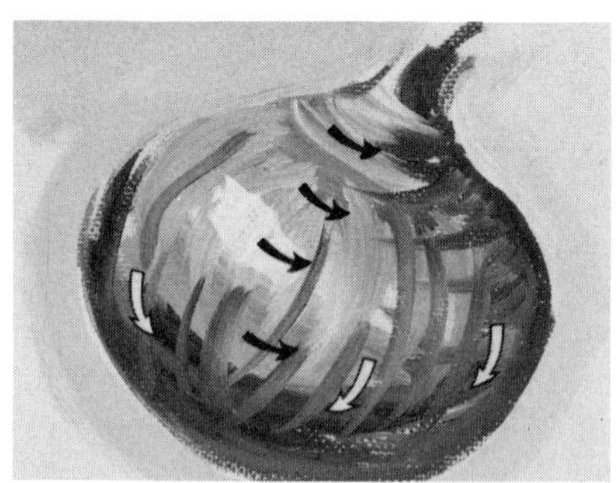

TEMPERA (see Painting Media)

TERRA ROSA (see Reds)

TEXTURES

How can I paint textures such as shiny things and dull things?

It may be easier for you to divide all textures into two major categories: Reflective and non-reflective (you may refer to them as shiny and dull) and approach these opposites in different ways. Reflective textures are painted by paying close attention to their highlights and reflections and painting them onto an overall mass tone. Non-reflective textures are ones painted by establishing the shape of the light on it, the body tone and the shape of the shadowed area (the body shadow). One last bit of advice — shines on any surface should be painted onto an established color.

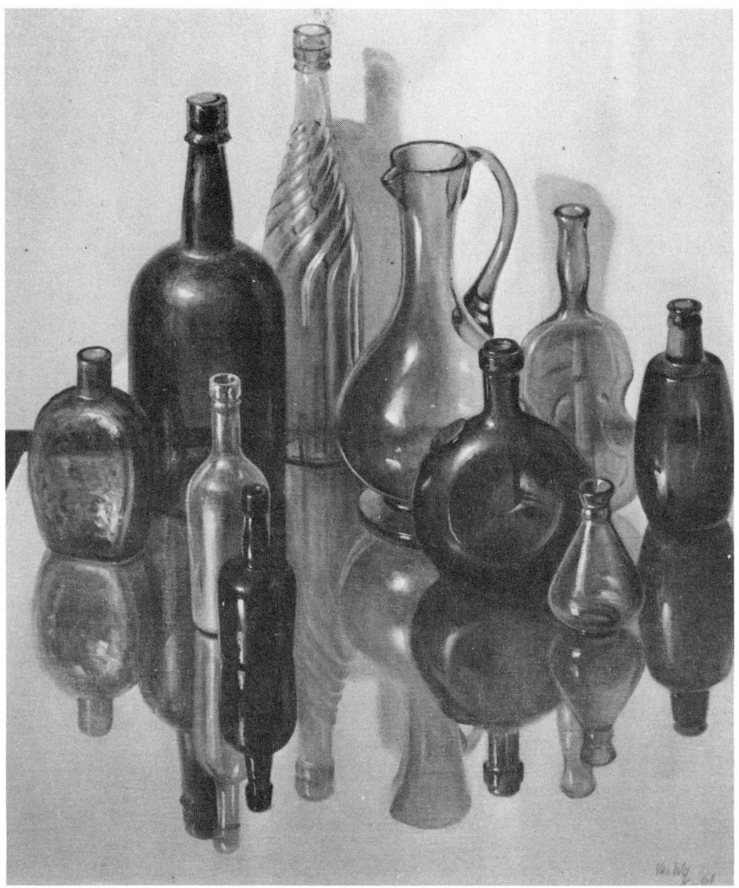

Each glass object was massed in a general, overall color. Their shine or reflective nature was recorded by adding highlights and reflections.

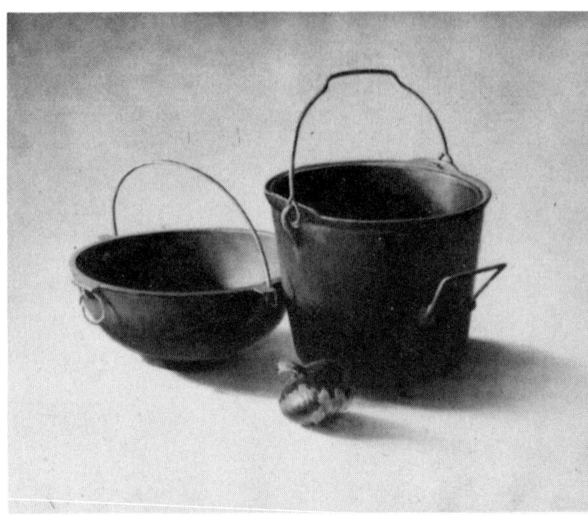

The non-reflective, or dull, black pots were initiated in two tones: The body tones and body shadows. These were then accented with more lights into the body tones and more darks into the body shadows.

THALO COLORS

I've been told that the Thalo colors are dyes. That's why I've been warned not to use them. Is this true?

No! There are no oil colors that are dyes. They are all pigments which, when mixed with a binder, linseed oil in the case of oil paints, form a paste-like substance. The pigments, therefore, are held in suspension by the binder, whereas dyes dissolve in their vehicles. The extreme brilliance of Phthalocyanine pigments (Thalo is Grumbacher's proprietary name for paints made with this pigment) and the staining characteristic of them have made many self-appointed experts suspect them as dyes and, unfortunately, will direct them to incorrectly caution painters away from their use. *(See Blues; Greens)*

THINNERS (See Painting Mediums; Turpentine)

TIGHT-AND-LOOSE PAINTING

What is the difference between tight-and-loose painting? How are the effects of loose painting achieved?

A painting that's described as tightly painted looks precise, neat and deliberately done. A loose painting looks more accidental. A tight painting doesn't usually have a record of brushstrokes; a loose one has obvious ones that record the planes, shapes and changes of color.

These different effects are not only a record of a personal approach but also a result of the artist's nature and personality. It can be compared to his handwriting in that he can't change or force his handwriting even if he tried. These styles are definitely the personal touch.

With experience, someone who paints tightly will loosen up. On the other hand, a person who has a natural loose approach usually has to learn some discipline to make his approach more accurate.

Often, these styles are a result of initial motivations for pictures. Artists see things in paint and then use and manipulate the paint to achieve that look. There is a factor that's an undeniable truth that influences a tight or loose look: *The time factor.* It takes time to paint a picture tightly; a loose painting is usually a record of a painter who has a limited time to work. He feels the pressure of time and simplifies his interpretation and approach, and is efficient about his procedure.

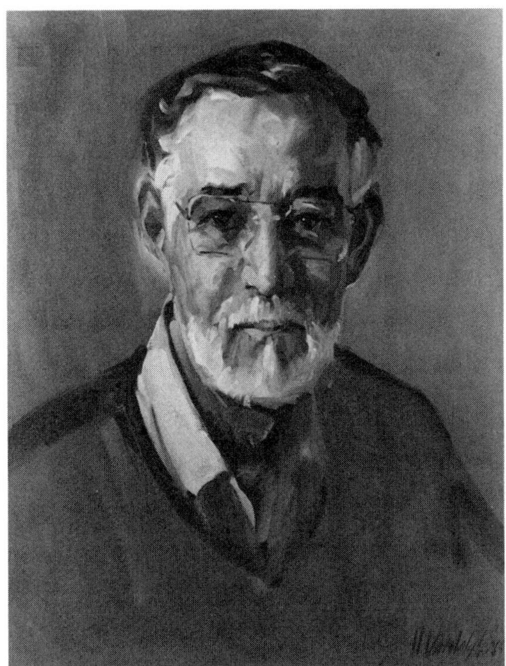

This loosely painted portrait sketch of Jim was done in one sitting. The unfinished foreground acts as contrast to the more carefully painted face and makes the face look more finished than it really is. This loose effect is mostly determined by the time you allot yourself to paint it.

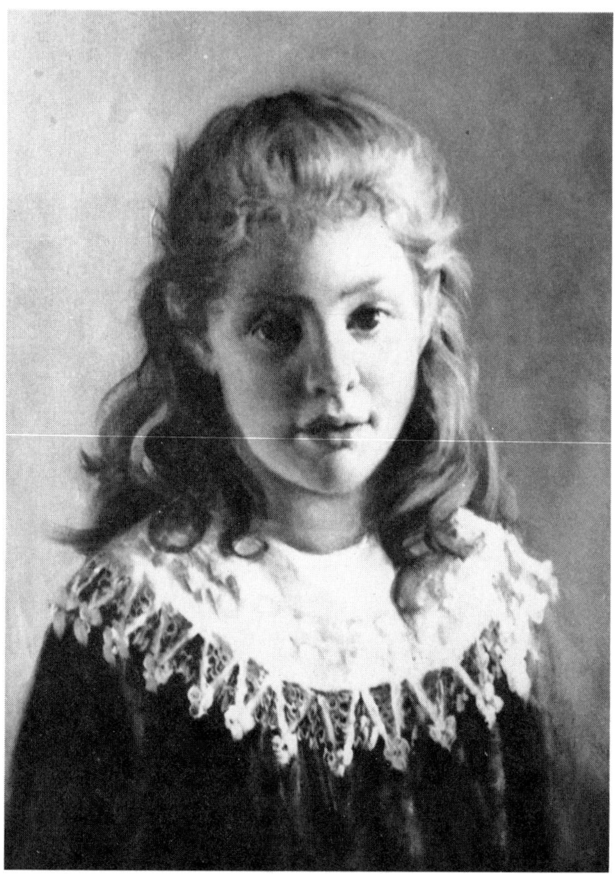

This more formal portrait of Melissa was done in about four sittings. The finished background and clothing put more of a demand on the artist to interpret the face and skin realistically. Again, painting time is an important factor.

A tightly painted picture puts a demand of accuracy from which loose painting is excused. One style is certainly not better than the other. People respond to them purely from a standpoint of personal preference.

An accomplished painter can paint both ways. Most paintings are started somewhat loosely. How much this loose beginning is tightened up is controlled by the painter's opinion of how he wants a particular painting to be. Style is an important characteristic of an artist's paintings. It shouldn't be forced and can't be changed or learned. It can only flavor the appreciation of the reliable components of pictorial expression.

TINT AND SHADE

Some of my colors have been criticized as raw looking. The suggestion was made that I tint my colors more or shade them more. What does this mean?

In oil painting, tint refers to a color that has some amount of white added to it. In contrast, shade refers to a color that either has a degree of black in it or contains the color's complement.

A color that's tinted looks more illuminated, a shaded color looks more shadowed, therefore, tints and shades make colors look more dimensional rather than flat and raw.

TINTING STRENGTH

What is meant by tinting strength?

Each pigment has its own capacity to influence another color in admixture. This can be determined by mixing it with white. So by tinting the color with white, you can find out how strong or weak a color it is. It is a good practice to mix each color you are going to use on your palette with degrees of white to acquaint yourself with its tinting strength before it surprises you at some strategic moment while painting a masterpiece.

The strongest tinting strength colors are the Thalos (and those labeled Phthalo and Phthalocyanine), Alizarin Crimson, Venetian Red, Indian Red, the Mars colors and the other opaque colors, such as Chromium Oxide Green. The one with the least tinting strength is Green Earth (Terra Verde). Other weak ones are many of the blues, such as Cobalt Blue and Cerulean Blue, all the violets and Viridian. You will find out for yourself, soon enough, how weak or strong various colors on your palette are. You will see that certain weak colors can't withstand large amounts of white, otherwise they will just die out. The strong colors, on the other hand, can stand an addition of a lot of white before they lose their intensity.

Since oil painting is so much a matter of adding colors into white, economy can be practiced by using the strong colors rather than the weak ones.
(See White)

TONE VALUE

What is the difference between value and tone?

This is a matter of semantics. Some artists like to refer to the lightness or darkness of a color as the *value* of the color; other artists use the word *tone* to describe the degree of light and dark. I prefer to use both words combined in one term: *"Tone Value."* Regardless of whether you use "tone" or "value," I can't stress enough the importance of recognizing the tonal value of colors. Seeing a color's tone value is the key to contrast, which is the key to design and the secret of making shapes appear.

Is the tone of an object more important than the color of the object?

Infinitely. Its tone value in contrast to its surrounding tones determines its shape. A red vase against a green background of the same tone would hardly be visible.

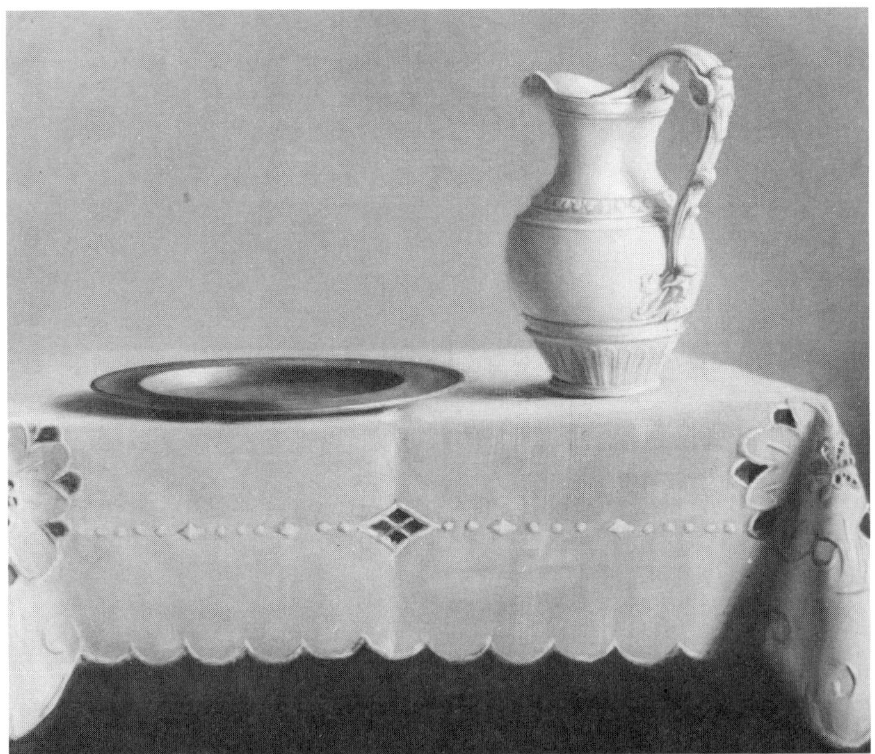

In this black-and-white photograph of the painting, "Cutwork Cloth," only the contrast of the tones of the painting are visible, as in all the other paintings that are reproduced in this book. We may miss the colors of these pictures, but we don't need them to recognize the subjects and the compositions.

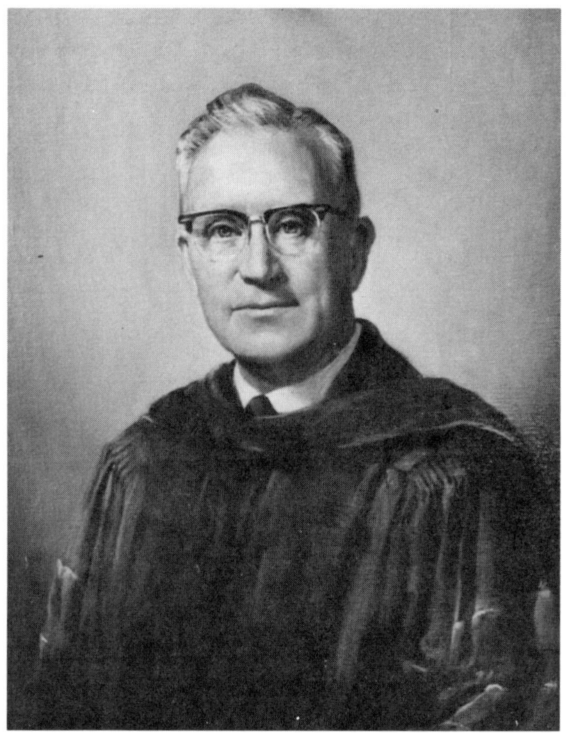

The body tone is the area wherever the model's facial planes are directly facing you. Body shadows are on all the receding planes toward the right.

What is a body shadow?

A body shadow is the darker tone seen on the area of an object that is shadowed because it is not in line with the light.

There are two parts to a body shadow: its edge, which is called the turning point, and its interior.

What is meant by body tone or mass tone?

Body tone is a term used to designate the tone and color of the area of an object that is illuminated by the light and, therefore, part of the light pattern of a composition. All subjects in a composition have a body tone. These body tones are all the same degree of lightness, depending on the manner of lighting. They can be accented or diminished for artistic interpretation.

Remember, to establish anything with paint on a canvas, you must determine its body tone. This tone is always evaluated by comparing it to its surroundings.

The body tone of a red rose on a black background is light; the body tone of the same red rose on a light background is dark. This is often referred to as mass tone because it describes the act of massing in an area to record the overall shape.

What is a cast shadow?

A cast shadow is an area that is darkened because something is standing in the way of the light, thereby stopping the light from shining on it. Cast shadows are darker than body shadows and are relatively complementary to the color they are on. The color of the cast shadow is not influenced by the color of what casts it. For example, the cast shadows on a brown table from a variety of colored objects will all be the same color — violet — the complement of brown, which is a dark yellow.

Cast shadows impose a dramatic effect on a composition as well as making any form seem to have weight and take up space on a flat surface.

I like to highlight the colors of my subjects but have been criticizeed for doing so. Please tell me when a highlight is acceptable.

Highlights are only acceptable if they are painted on planes that are directly opposite to one light source. Why only one light source? Because natural light is from one source, the sun. Artificial light should emulate this natural lighting. If you have many sources of light they will cause many highlights to appear.

Planes that are concavely or convexly in direct line and "stroked" by the light would more easily be recognized by you if I were to call them "bumps and dents."

Highlights contribute to the dimension of subjects as well as to show an object's texture.

To understand highlighting for dimension and texture, you must realize that a highlight appears wherever there is a definite shape change. The flat side of a barn, for example, can't be highlighted because it has no concave or convex planes. The barn's entire roof could be a massive highlight if it were in line with the light. Conversely, a colonial candlestick with many "in-and-out" shapes, will have several highlights, one on each change of shape.

Think of lighting as making direct hits that cause highlights. They are so shocked by the light that they are somewhat colorless in relation to the color they appear on.

SQUINT! SQUINT! SQUINT!

The best way to recognize the effect of light and the tone values it imposes is to squint at what you are looking at. Wide open eyes seem to make you only see a subject's function not its artistic situation.

How can I paint highlights to make them look real?

A highlight is one of the five values that imparts a three-dimensional effect to a two-dimensional surface.

Highlights vary in shape and character according to the *surface* they appear on, but one factor of a highlight remains constant: It is always a very light tone of the complementary color that it is applied on. For example — a highlight on a green bottle is red (white with a touch of red). A highlight on a lemon is violet (white with a touch of Alizarin Crimson). A highlight on a red apple is a very light green (Thalo Green and white).

The best way to apply a highlight is to first mix more of the color than you will need so you can scoop some of the mixture on the end of your brush and apply the highlight a little bigger than you see it. Then, with a clean brush, work around the highlight, cutting it down to size. This cutting-down process usually cuts the highlights down too much, so go back to the mixture, load the brush again and repaint the interior area of the highlight.

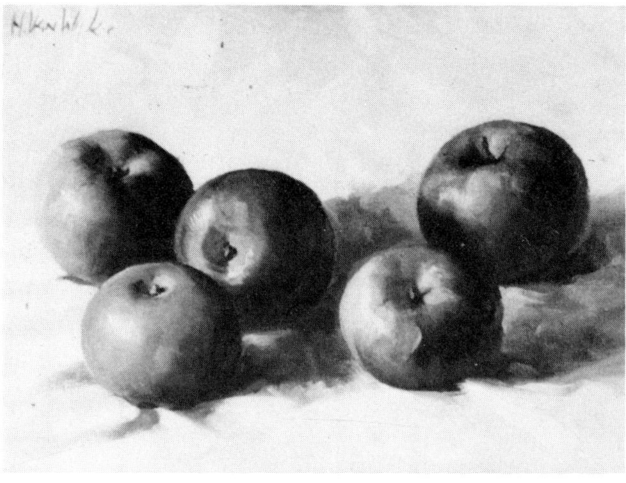

The lightest tones on the apples are the highlights. They are on the convex and concave planes of the apples' shapes that are directly illuminated by the light.

What is a reflection?

A reflection is a tone value imposed on a body shadow or body tone by its surroundings. For instance — a white shirt will reflect lightness into the shadowed chin area of a portrait. Snow will reflect lightness into the shadowed side of a barn. And a light background will reflect into the dark tone of a green bottle.

Always ask yourself: "What tone value am I seeing?" before you paint it. Identifying it will make it function.

TOOTH (see Canvas)

TOXIC

Do you feel that there are any health hazards in certain painting materials?

I'm not the least bit concerned about any hazards to my health because I use my materials in the age-old methods and never experiment with alien materials for unusual effects. The effects that I get in my painting come as a result of working within the confines of sound painting techniques. As far as there being any toxic materials that were manufactured by color makers in this country, all of them have been replaced by non-toxic pigments, except for Flake White, which contains lead. However, under normal studio use, Flake White should constitute no threat to the health of any painter.

TRANSPARENT COLOR

Why are transparent colors more luminous looking than opaque ones?

The word luminous suggests that light is shining. When light can shine through a clear color the color seems luminous. So when a transparent color is applied to a light area the lightness of that area can shine through the color. This is the very basis of the use of watercolor paints and the reason why a watercolor blue, for example, washed on a white paper will look more luminous than a blue color that has been mixed with white paint. The watercolorist controls his tones by using the white sheet as a tonal control, whereas the oil painter controls his tones by admixture with white. Luminous color is important to oil painting through the application of thin glazes of transparent color over opaquely painted areas. *(See Glazing; Opaque)*

TRIPOD EASEL (see Easel)

TROMPE L'OEIL

What does trompe l'oeil mean? What is a trompe l'oeil painting?

The term, *trompe l'oeil*, is from the French and means "deception of the eye." To accomplish the real trickery of *trompe l'oeil* you have to realize the extent of what is known as the picture plane, the surface of the canvas. On it, you can give a feeling of the depth dimension which would mean that all of the subjects in the composition sit in the space and behind the frame. A *trompe l'oeil* records subjects to look like they extend in front of the picture plane.

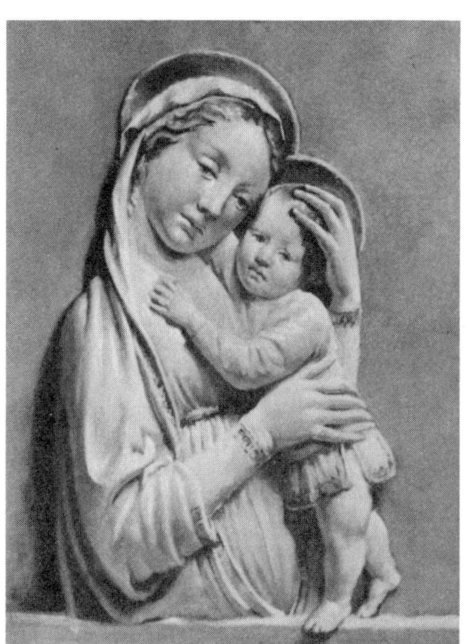

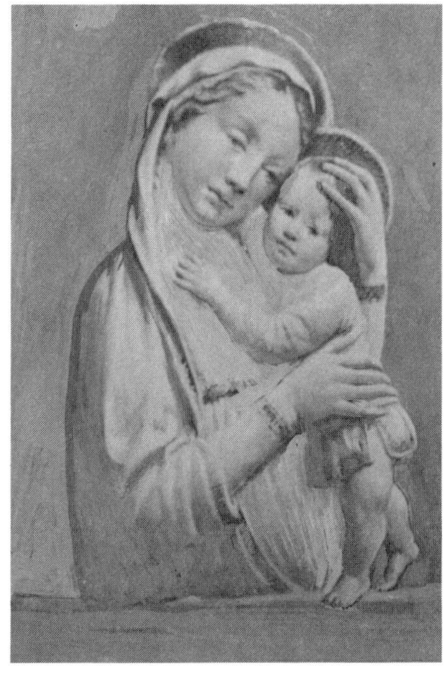

The five tone values all play important roles in giving us the look of dimension on a flat surface but it is the cast shadow that plays the starring role in a trompe l'oeil painting. The cast shadow is the tone value that makes things look like they have substance and take up space. On the left is a photo of my trompe l'oeil painting of a bas relief by sculptor Luca della Robbia (1400-1482). On the right is a photo of the same painting, with one exception: All the cast shadows have been removed. Compare the two and notice how the bas relief effect disappears without cast shadows.

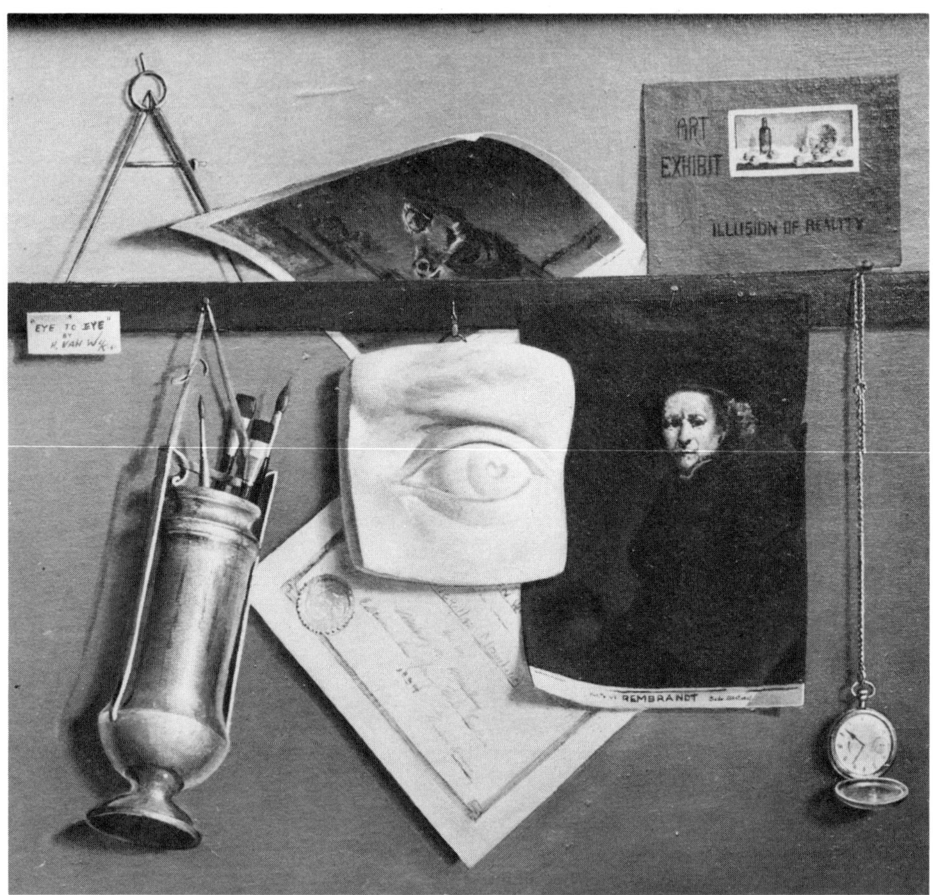

My trompe l'oeil painting, "Eye to Eye," is of things that suggest my involvement as a painter. I painted this symbolic picture in 1951, obviously when I was very young.

A good example of this is a picture of anything that hangs on a wall or of things that project off the edge of a table. The comment, "It looks so real that I feel I can pick it up," is associated with this type of illusion in painting. However, *trompe l'oeil* should not be confused with realistic painting. A realistic painting describes a specific composition that is realistically painted; in a *trompe l'oeil* painting, the objects seem to project from the picture plane.

TURNING EDGES

I've heard that turning edges makes things look round. What are they?

A turning edge is the shape of the body shadow as it meets the body tone. This is the area in painting that is the most difficult to do because it presents a blending manipulation as well as a respect for accurate shape. Turning edges also present a color problem because a color's complement must be used. To explain — many people can't imagine that the color violet has to be used to turn yellow into shadow. *(See Complementary Color; Shadows; Tone Value)*

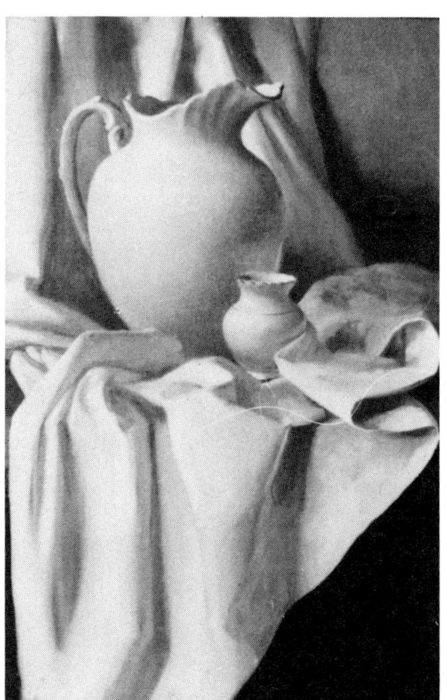

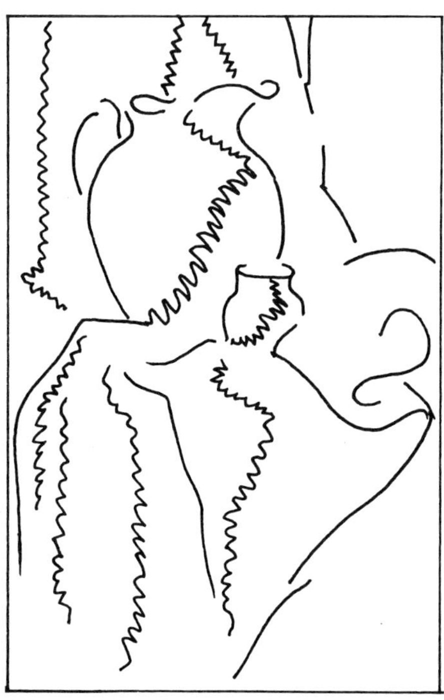

The painting on the left is of white things. To make white look real, you must use color. The diagram on the right shows — with wiggly lines — the turning edges: Where violet was used to blend with a yellowish white. The edges of the cast shadows, that are not diagrammed with wiggly lines, are also made with violet. The color of the shadow between the turning edge and the edge of the cast shadows is a darker, duller version of the object's body tone.

TURPENTINE

Can you give me a simple explanation of the use of a medium and the use of turpentine in oil painting?

Using oil paints is really quite simple. They can be thinned with turpentine to make a fluid application onto a surface. When more paint is painted onto oil paint, the paint can no longer be thinned with turpentine because it won't adhere and will be apt to flake off. In this case, a medium that has been fortified with linseed oil and varnish has to be used. The varnish in the medium imparts the necessary adhesion and the oil in the mixture helps the paint to film. A good general painting medium is equal parts of damar varnish, turpentine and linseed oil. Don't use mineral spirits in your medium; only the very best turpentine.

It's amazing that such beautiful effects can be made with such a simple make-up as oil paint is: Just pigment mixed with linseed oil. Many students ask and expect too much of mediums rather than realizing that effects come from observing, analyzing what they see and practicing. Constant experimentation for effects using the simple makeup that I describe is important to develop one's technique. Painting is a constant learning experience. You don't learn it and do it; you learn from doing it. *(See Painting Medium)*

In My Opinion:

RELATING TO THE CHARACTER OF OIL PAINT

An artist, working in any medium, has to contend with composition, drawing, tone and color to set down his artistic pictorial aspiration. A practical approach to a paint's capabilities is the clue to putting it to successful use. The oil painter's practical approach is a series of layers, one on top of another: Layer 1 — The composition; layer 2 — the drawing; layer 3 — the contrasts of light and dark; layer 4 — the colors of these contrasts; layer 5 — the refinement within these contrasts; layer 6 — and so on. Layer 7 — Don't start going backwards by "picking."

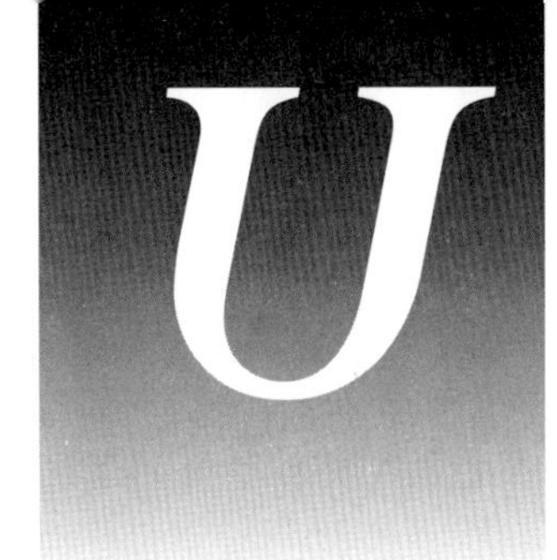

UNDERPAINTING

What is an underpainting?

A simple answer is that an underpainting is a preparation on the canvas that is meant to be covered with subsequent applications of color. However, this doesn't do justice to the value or worth of an underpainting to the procedure of oil painting. The way to truly appreciate the necessity of an underpainting is to first know some facts about the medium of oil paints and oil painting.

1. Oil paint is a medium that has a weak covering power. It is thick in consistency from the tube and has to be thinned with a medium to make it flow. This thinning further weakens the covering power, and not to thin it makes the application thick and difficult to work into. Just compare the covering power of oil paint with that of acrylics to realize the tender makeup of oil paints.

2. The pigment in oil paint is highly concentrated, therefore it's a waste of color to put oil paint on thickly just to make it cover a surface. We all know, of course, that a textural quality that brushwork makes with thick paint can add dramatically to a painting's impact. However, this is best done on a canvas that already has the composition of the dark and light pattern established.

3. Oil paintings that are painted in a series of thin layers will not yellow nor crack as readily as those that are painted thickly.

4. Painting with oil color is seen as easy in contrast to painting with watercolors only because mistakes can be wiped off or corrected by working into the painted area. But in reality, painting with oil colors is much more involved than painting with watercolors. I'm not comparing artistic content — that is the same — I'm only referring to the very nature of each medium. To sense what I mean, paint a wash of watercolor on a nice piece of watercolor paper. It really looks appealing just as it is: Luminous, colorful and as pleasant as the paper's texture allows. Now paint in an area of oil color with a mixture that matches, in tone and color, the watercolor wash you have already done. It necessitates much more involved use of color.

All of the factors I've just listed are what create a need for an underpainting. Let's first define an underpainting:

1. An underpainting adjusts the canvas for applications of oil so the oil paint will not be expected to do more than its capacity.

2. An underpainting adjusts the canvas so that painting on it in oil colors can be substantial in color and tone without having to be applied thickly.

3. By preparing an underpainting, a painter can focus his entire attention to the all important planning stage of his picture: The composition, the drawing and the basic tone values of his subject.

Now, what is an underpainting made of?

1. An underpainting is usually a monochromatic (one color) rendering of the composition either in detail or in a vague suggestion of the forms and contrasts. This can be done in washes of a color and turpentine; more color for dark passages and less color (more turpentine) for the light patterns. The color one should use for this underpainting should be one of the fast-drying earth colors. Don't use slow drying colors such as the cadmiums or Ivory Black. A gray made of Burnt Umber and Thalo Blue is a good one, as is Chromium Oxide Green and Venetian Red.

2. An underpainting can be painted with opaque colors (thinned with turpentine) to establish not only the tonal pattern but the color pattern as well. This type of underpainting is usually done for a subsequent painting with painting knife.

3. An underpainting can be painted in tones of gray made of mixtures of black and white acrylic. This application shouldn't be too thick. The acrylic should be thinned with water and a mixture of white with a colored acrylic: Violet (made of Thalo Green and Cadmium Red Deep) or a brown (made of Burnt Umber and some black) make ideal colors for underpaintings.

4. An underpainting shouldn't be done in tones made of charcoal unless the charcoal rendering is first varnished and isolated. *(See Grisaille)*

I want to underpaint in oils. What should I do?

Use fast-drying color and a fast-drying white. I recommend mixing Chromium Oxide Green into Venetian Red to make a neutral gray dark tone that can be mixed with degrees of white (Flake or Titanium) to record the values of the composition. Thin these mixtures with turpentine.

A

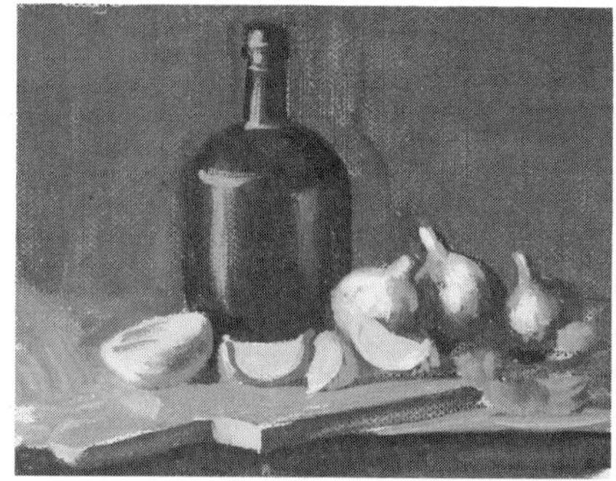
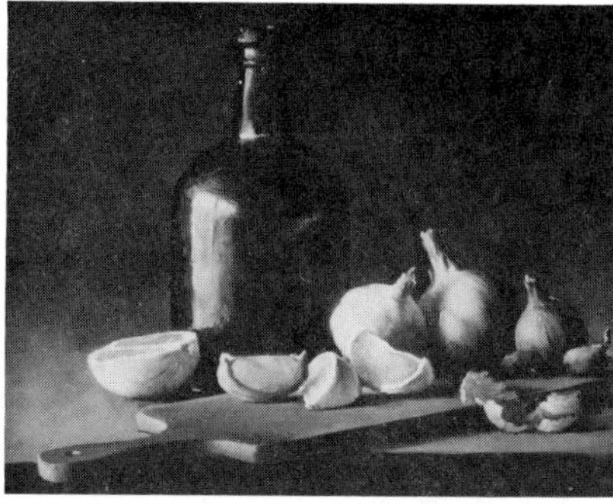

B

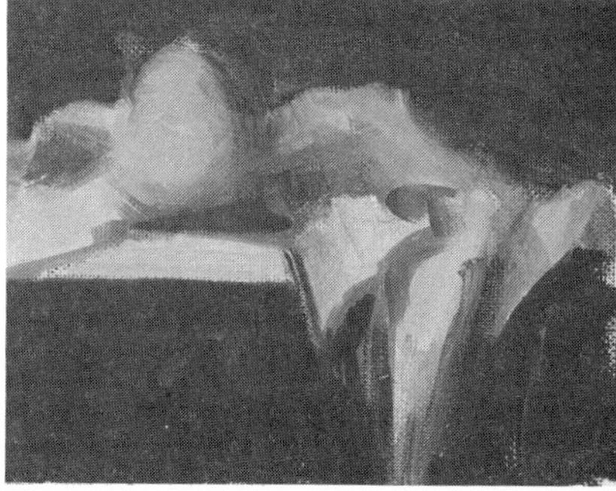
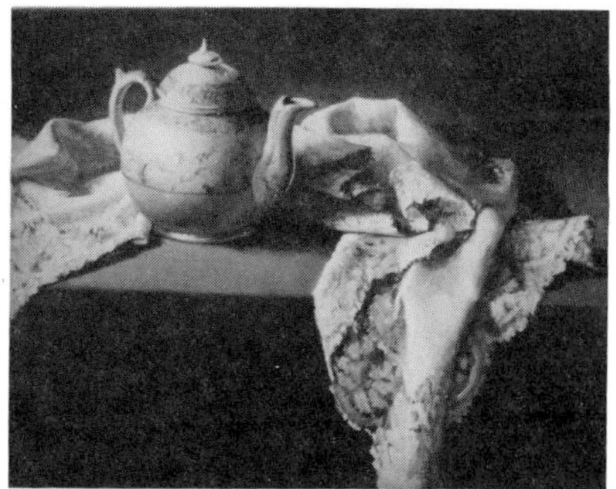

Underpaintings establish composition and become tonal assists to subsequent applications of color. They can clearly define the subject matter or just suggest patterns of light and dark. The first type (A) can be developed by glazing with just further definitions and refinement. The second type (B) can be painted in an alla prima technique.

You realize, of course, that before you even attempt to glaze over your oil painted underpainting that this underpainting has to be absolutely dry. *(See Glazing)*

UNITY (see Composition)

A ROOM HUNG WITH PICTURES
IS A ROOM HUNG WITH THOUGHTS.
— SIR JOSHUA REYNOLDS (1723–1792)

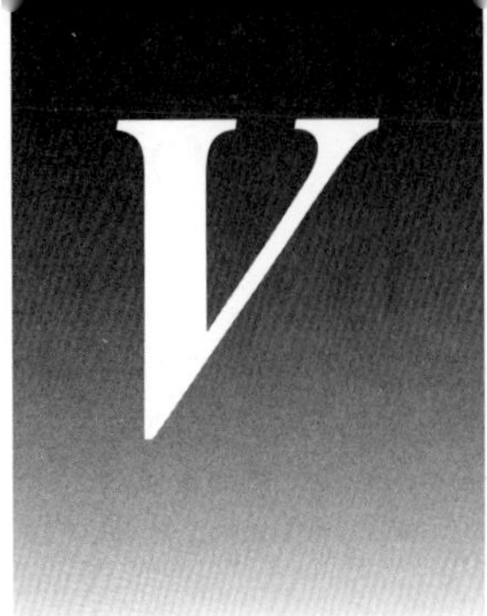

VALUE (see Tone Value)

VAN DYCK BROWN

Is Van Dyck Brown a permanent color?

Originally, Van Dyck Brown was a natural earth color but was not very permanent. Today, Van Dyck Brown is made by intermixing transparent colors that simulate the color of Van Dyck Brown and, what's more important, it is permanent.

The color of Van Dyck Brown is a very dull intensity of a yellow (brown) and its tone is almost as dark as black.

I use Van Dyck Brown now and then mostly as a glaze to impart a slightly warm darkening to an area which makes possible lighter passages to be added to improve and accent the subtle details.

I never use Van Dyck Brown in general painting, although it would probably make nice odd greens when mixed with cadmium yellows. Incidentally, some color manufacturers list this color as Van Dyke. Either one is correct.

VANISHING POINT

What is a vanishing point?

Vanishing points are where parallel lines of structures that diminish as they recede from your point of view actually converge at the end of your horizontal sight, which is called the horizon or eye level. Parallel lines that are below your eye level will recede and converge up to your eye level or the horizon; parallel lines that are above your eye level will recede and converge down to your eye level, or horizon. *(See Eye Level; Horizon)*

VARNISH

How can I get a high shine on my paintings?

You can get a high shine by applying about three coats of varnish, especially copal. You can also do this by mixing your colors with stand oil. I don't advise doing this, however, except for little pictures — no larger than 11" x 14". I find a high shine objectionable because it is so susceptible to reflecting the lighting in the room; the resulting glare obscures the painting. This glare may not happen as much on a small painting.

VARNISHES

Why are varnishes added to painting medium?

Varnishes add a degree of adhesiveness to a medium that's necessary for painting a layer of paint onto another layer. Since glazes are always painted over an already painted area, glazing mediums should always have varnish in them. *(See Painting Mediums)*

What are the differences between damar, copal and mastic varnishes?

The characteristics of damar varnish are:

1. It retains its colorless appearance longer than other varnishes.

2. Damar varnish will not yellow or darken as will copal and mastic.

3. Damar can be mixed with linseed oil in a painting medium whereas mastic shouldn't be. Damar is a pine resin from trees; copal is made by melting a resin and adding an oil medium.

Damar varnish can be compared to a light cooking oil; copal can be compared to cooking with olive oil. Using damar varnish in a medium, or as a final varnish, doesn't influence the paint's character as much as copal varnish would do.

Damar varnish is resin mixed with turpentine. Copal, because it dries very hard, is more apt to crack.

Copal is attractive to amateurs and beginners because it dries with a very high shine, which many non-professionals consider to be a decided advantage to the look of their paintings. But don't be beguiled — every reputable expert on the technique of oil painting decries the use of copal mediums and varnish as unreliable materials to put into, and onto, an oil painting.

VARNISHING

What is the best way for varnishing a painting?

The ideal way is to lay the canvas flat and apply the varnish with a lint-free cloth. Pour the varnish in a saucer and, dipping a wadded amount of cloth (turkish towel preferred) into the varnish, apply to the canvas with a circular motion. This method, I have found, is better than using a brush. First, because it is done more quickly this way, preventing the varnish from drying, thus avoiding overlapping which causes an uneven application. It's also better because applying the varnish with a cloth instead of a brush keeps you from applying a thick layer that is more apt to crack. Varnish in a spray can also does a good job because the varnish goes on in many tiny little dots which can't crack. But varnishing with spray can be tricky business. First, and most obvious, is that spraying varnish sprays your room as well as your painting. It's important, therefore, to spray outdoors where the fumes of the spray can be dissipated, keeping furniture, floors and your lungs free of the varnish being propelled. Naturally, you'll want to spray outdoors when there's no wind. Set your canvas on an easel that has been tilted back at quite a radical angle. Now, with the spray can directed slightly angled at the canvas, start by aiming not at the picture but in the air directly next to the canvas and start moving your aim across the canvas and not stopping until you have hit the air on the opposite side. This method stops you from applying too much in one place and ending up with just a dusting in other places.

The normal drying time before varnishing your painting should be three to six months (the former is minimum; the latter is ideal). However, when varnishing with a spray, you don't have to wait as long, although even in this area, a minimum of three months is much preferred.

I prefer to use damar varnish. It doesn't impart the painting with a high shine as copal varnish does and its film doesn't dry as hard, which becomes a surface than can easily crack. Restorers like the softer varnishes, like damar, because they can be easily removed. Copal, on the other hand, is difficult to remove and the process of doing so can endanger the actual paint layer.

You can use retouch spray varnish at any time during the painting process but it is not recommended for a final varnish.

VENETIAN RED (see Reds)

VENICE TURPENTINE (see Driers; Painting Mediums)

VERMILION

Is vermilion a better red to use than Cadmium Red?

No. Cadmium Red now is more available, less expensive and more reliable than Vermilion. Only the very best Vermilion does not have an erratic nature. Chinese Vermilion, being the best, is a beautiful red and is extremely expensive. Grumbacher Red is a satisfactory substitute in color, permanence and cost. *(See Reds)*

VIGNETTE

How can I incorporate vignetting into my painting technique?

Used as a verb, vignette means to soften away the edges of an image. A vignette is very helpful to the painter to focus more attention on the focal area of his picture.

I prefer a vignette to be subtle, which is not the easiest tonal manipulation to do. The best way to effect a successful vignette is to mass in a medium tone and then work the tones of the subject into that wet medium value. Images are more successfully vignetted into a darker tone than into a lighter one.

A certain degree of vignetting at the picture's outer edges is effective for pictorial impact and very helpful in portraiture.

It is important not to make your vignetted patterns too obvious. The vignetted area should look like it's seen by your peripheral vision instead of in sharp focus. *(Illustrations on page 188)*

VIOLET

What violets do you have on your palette?

I make most of my violets by mixing degrees of Alizarin Crimson into tones of black and white. I also have Manganese Violet on my palette and love its graying property when I mix it with yellows and yellow greens. There are many other violets available, but after trying them all out, I found them only helpful in painting violet-colored flowers.

VIRIDIAN (see Greens)

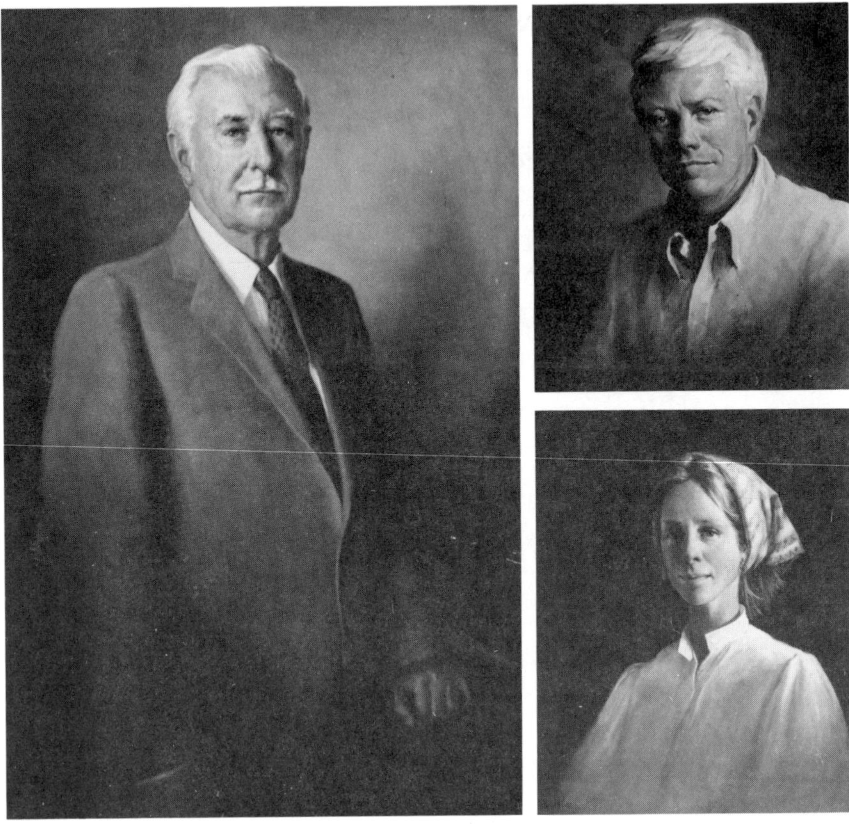

Notice in these three portraits how the bodies do not extend to the bottom of the canvas. This is called vignetting. It serves to keep your attention on the all important face.

My brushwork is quite unsystematic. I slam the paint on in all sorts of ways and leave each result to take care of itself.

—Vincent Van Gogh (1853–1890)

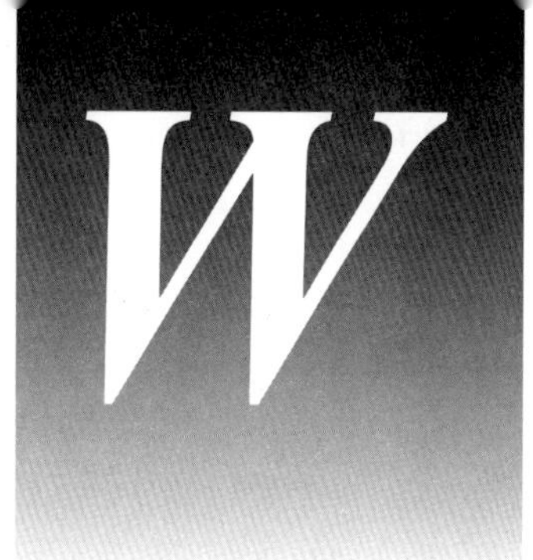

WALNUT OIL (see Painting Mediums)

WARM COLOR (see Cool Color)

WASH

What is the difference between a wash and a glaze?

Wash is a word that's used to describe paint that's greatly thinned with turpentine. A glaze is an application of transparent oil paint over a pre-painted area. A wash is a good way to set down the initial pattern of light and dark of a composition. It can be easily worked on with thicker applications. Glazes are used to develop an oil painting's appearance. *(See Glaze)*

WATERCOLOR (see Painting Media)

WET-IN-WET

Is there such a thing as a wet-in-wet technique?

Yes, there is. Working more tones of color into already painted wet areas to enhance and develop a picture is called wet-in-wet. I like to use the phrase wet-*on*-wet instead. Adding paint to an already painted area imparts more definition to an area. Painting into it seems to suggest correction rather than development; it also suggests that the paint is worked into the paint rather than just joining to it. Only the pressure of the brush makes the phrase wet-in-wet valid. *(See Alla Prima)*

WHITE SUBJECTS

What colors would I need to paint white subjects like snow and white clothing?

All seemingly white things cannot be painted with white alone because they are not really white; they are colored whites or off whites. All well and good, but what color is the "off" in off white? Let's examine this coloration: When the light shines on a white surface, such as sunlight on snow or artificial light on a vase, the white of these subjects becomes a warm color. White paint, then, mixed with any warm color (like Yellow Ochre, Cadmium Orange, Burnt Umber, and others) can be used to interpret that warm white. Now, instead of dealing with a white object, you are dealing with a colored one and you have to employ the complementary color theory to make the shadows and highlights. The shadows on these warm whites are darker cool tones, either violet, blue or green, greatly grayed with black and white. Reflected light will make the interior of the shadows warm again. So, add some warm color into the shadow mixture. The highlights on the light area (the body tone) are a cool white: Lots of white with just a light touch of a cool color.
(See Complementary Color)

Note of caution: Don't start painting white things so light that you can't add a highlight. The designation of "off" in white is color and a touch of black to darken the white enough to enable you to model into it with lighter off whites and finally be able to add a lighter tone for the highlight.

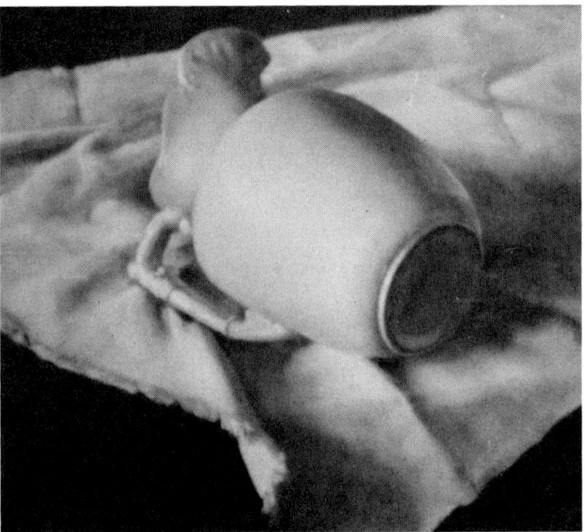

I'm particularly fascinated with painting white things, and have found many compositional opportunities to enjoy this intrigue.

WHITE (Tubed)

How can I choose the right white to use?

Since white is the artist's physical substitute for the illumination on a color, virtually every color seen in direct light has a white in its admixture, and any white will do. Listed below are the three major whites and their characteristics:

FLAKE WHITE. This is a lead type white, one of the oldest used, going back as far as the history of painting has been recorded. Flake White has many good characteristics, one being that it doesn't absorb much oil, thus preventing it from yellowing as much as the other white paints.

Flake White is also very opaque with strong covering power. Many people are afraid of Flake White because lead white has a toxic nature. Caution must be taken as with other lead-based pigments.

Flake White isn't the most popular white in use today because contemporary painting styles require a white that is more soupy than Flake White can be. Since the Masters of the past used Flake White we know how permanent it is, but we also have to respect the Masters' techniques in using it. These painting techniques are not the ones of today, the primary difference being that today we work more direct and with thicker paint while the Old Masters painted with thinner applications.

ZINC WHITE. The whitest of whites. Zinc White is an oxide white and is very slow drying. It is a cooler type of white color and has a delicate nature when compared to Flake White in that it is not as opaque. In *alla prima* painting, especially in portrait painting, the admixture of Zinc White with flesh color is very clean and lively. Because of its delicacy, Zinc White is not the white for use in landscape painting. Here, a white that saturates a color with lightness and can cover larger areas of light patterns is needed.

TITANIUM WHITE. The newest oil painting white, Titanium White is the best one for general painting. It has good covering power because it is the most opaque of them all and has the most powerful tinting strength. If Titanium White is used without knowledge of color theory in practice, this white is more apt to contribute to chalkiness than using Zinc White.

Generally speaking, all of the whites that are now available are reliable, and only when experience and practice develops a student's understanding can he become particular about the white he chooses to paint with. I have always preferred Zinc White but lately have tended toward preferring a more fluid consistency that I can't seem to find any more in the Zinc Whites that are commercially marketed today.

In My Opinion:

ON PAINTING WHITE

So many subjects are versions of white. A few examples: For the portrait painter gray hair, white colors and white clothing and accessories. The still life painter: White clothes, white pitcher and china and white flowers. The landscapist: White clouds, white houses, white breakers in the ocean. It's important to understand that white things are not pure white; they are off white — white with "off" in it. What is the "off"? White in light is usually a warm white (white with a touch of yellow). Whites in shadow are usually cool, darkened whites (white, black and a cool color).

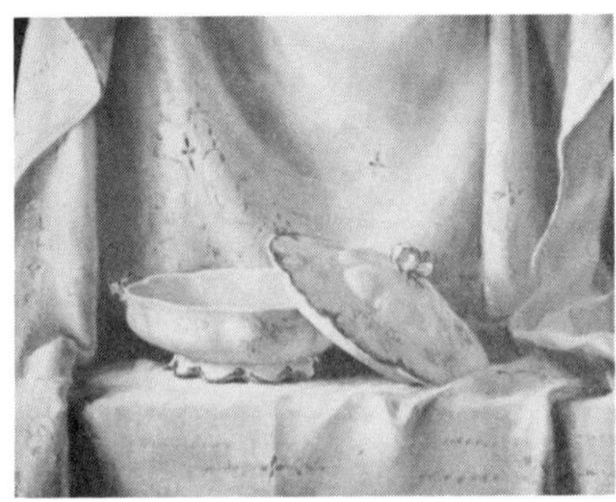

Two examples of the challenge of painting white. In still life (above), "Limoges Serving Dish," and in portrait (at right), "Meredith."

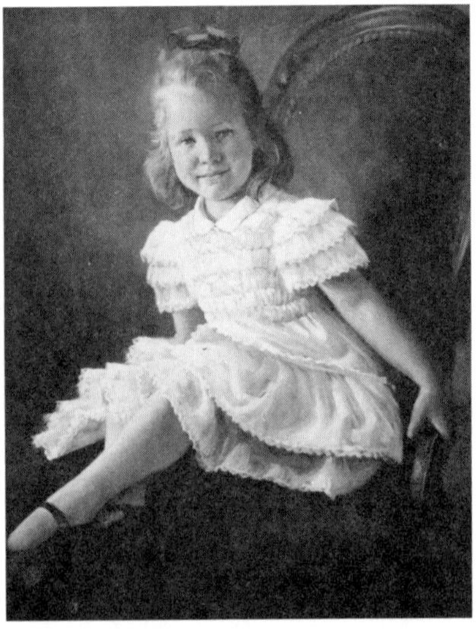

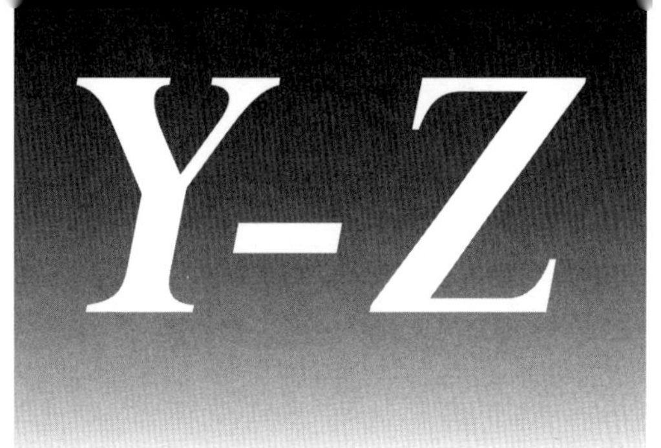

YELLOWING

What causes yellowing in oil painting?

Some oil paintings yellow or darken because of the linseed oil in the paint. When linseed oil films as it dries, it darkens ever so slightly. If the artist has used a lot of oil in his mixtures, or if the paint has been applied more thickly than recommended, the filming of the oil paint will be noticeably yellow, especially in the lighter passages of the painting.

Linseed oil in your paints, being lighter in weight than the pigment it's mixed with, will rise to the surface and will darken or yellow the light-toned areas of the painting, You can see this in a can of oil-based house paint which has been stored away for awhile. When opened, the paint is covered with a film of brown oil and has to be scooped away before getting down to any wet, colorful paint in the can.

If you have experienced any white that has yellowed in one of your paintings, you can remedy this, provided that the paint has been dried for some time. With a razor blade, carefully scrape away all the unwanted yellow that exists. You can avoid all of this, of course, by painting your pictures properly — not too thickly and with little or no addition of extra, unneeded linseed oil to your mixtures. *(See Linseed Oil)*

YELLOWS

What yellows are not permanent?

All the yellows are permanent but some are better to use than others.
The yellows are:

THE CADMIUM YELLOWS — Light, Pale and Medium. Very reliable.

ZINC YELLOW — has a toxic quality.

YELLOW OCHRE — very reliable.

RAW SIENNA — very reliable.

RAW UMBER — very reliable.

THALO YELLOW GREEN — an intermix of Hansa Yellow and Thalo Green.

HANSA YELLOW — a new pigment. More transparent than the cadmiums.

NAPLES YELLOW — possible toxic quality.

ZINC WHITE (see Whites)

ZINC YELLOW

How far from spectrum yellow is zinc yellow?

In the physics of light, primary (or spectrum) yellow is quite greenish, much like Zinc Yellow (also called lemon yellow in many lines of oil colors). To use it on a palette to generally represent bright yellow is limiting. Cadmium Yellow Light is a far better choice and it will offer the widest range of bright yellow mixtures seen in nature.

I BELIEVE IN MICHAEL ANGELO, VELASQUEZ, AND REMBRANDT, IN THE MIGHT OF DESIGN, THE MYSTERY OF COLOR, THE REDEMPTION OF ALL THINGS BY BEAUTY EVERLASTING, AND THE MESSAGE OF ART THAT HAS MADE THESE HANDS BLESSED . . .

— GEORGE BERNARD SHAW (1856–1950)

Index

Helen Van Wyk Teaches on Video

Helen Van Wyk has been immortalized on videocassette, which you'll want to own to study over and over again in your home. Each video teaches a phase of the painting process that is a tribute to the teaching mastery of Helen Van Wyk. In each video, you will learn the techniques and procedures that have made Helen a favorite among students and art connoisseurs.

While Helen tragically is no longer with us, her philosophy about art and painting instruction will live on forever. These videos present Helen in modes very much like those she exhibits in her nationally known television show, *Welcome to My Studio*, except in each video, she enjoys the luxury of extra time, and can embellish her instruction.

Oil Painting Techniques and Procedures

A two-hour demonstration of a still life, it starts with a monochromatic underpainting and is followed by glazing applications to end with direct *alla prima* touches. Finally, the technique of glazing is fully explained and illustrated. In this still life, you will see Helen paint every kind of texture which will help you with all the subject matter you may encounter in your still lifes. In the composition there is a non-reflective jug, a transparent green glass bottle, a copper pitcher, apples, lemons (cut and whole), grapes, white tablecloth and the all important background. It is safe to say that an entire painting course resides in this one video. ***Price: $49.95***

Painting Flowers Alla Prima

Alla prima is an Italian phrase that means "all at once." In this one-hour presentation, Helen demonstrates this direct application of paint to interpret a bouquet of daisies. Starting with four marks on the canvas, to indicate the outer reaches of her composition, she proceeds to build her painting, ending with the highlights. Throughout this video, you will learn how Helen gets her paint moist and juicy, a look that has entranced viewers of her TV show and live demonstrations. Helen Van Wyk is a fountain of information, never shying from dispensing it to all those interested in painting better. ***Price: $39.95***

A Portrait: Step-by-Step

One hour of painting a male model. In this video, Helen covers every facet of portrait painting, experience gained from fifty years of painting people. You will learn about mixing the right flesh color, getting the shadow to look just right, and that difficult "turning edge," the area between light and shadow. "Anyone can get a likeness," Helen says, "but the trick is to make the model look human." If portraits are your interest, you won't want to miss this sterling, informative video. Once in your possession, you'll find yourself watching it over and over. You will be amazed at how much it will help you with your portraits. ***Price: $39.95***